The Extreme Makeover of Hillary (Rodham) Clinton

The Extreme Makeover of Hillary (Rodham) Clinton

BAY BUCHANAN

Since 1947
**REGNERY
PUBLISHING, INC.**
An Eagle Publishing Company • Washington, DC

Cataloging-in-Publication data on file with the Library of Congress

ISBN 978-1-59698-507-0

Published in the United States by
Regnery Publishing, Inc.
One Massachusetts Avenue, NW
Washington, DC 20001
www.regnery.com

Distributed to the trade by
National Book Network
Lanham, MD 20706

Manufactured in the United States of America

10 9 8 7 6 5 4 3 2 1

Books are available in quantity for promotional or premium use. Write to Director of Special Sales, Regnery Publishing, Inc., One Massachusetts Avenue NW, Washington, DC 20001, for information on discounts and terms or call (202) 216-0600.

To my boys
BILLY, TOMMY, AND STUART
*Who have filled my life with laughs
and my heart with love*

Contents

Introduction

Shedding the Liberal Label

HILLARY RODHAM CLINTON has been many things through-out her life, but one thing she has always been is a dedi-cated, unapologetic liberal. In fact, with the possible exception of Ted Kennedy, she is the most identifiable member of the Democ-rats' left wing, a position she has earned through years of hard work. Since her days at Wellesley College, Hillary has been a pas-sionate advocate for every liberal cause known to man. And this ardent feminist, antiwar activist, and student radical did not leave her passion for all things liberal behind on the campuses of Wellesley and Yale. No, this passion, along with her insatiable desire for power, has been the driving force of her long and suc-cessful political career.

Now, after a lifetime as a liberal activist, Hillary, we are told, is no longer a liberal. Her philosophy has evolved. This philo-sophical change began in earnest after she assumed the title of U.S. senator. It was then that Hillary began to carefully put away the trappings of a liberal and wrap herself in a cloak of moderation. The national press has taken up her cause and spread the good news. Although it describes Hillary's base as liberal, the media is adamant she herself is not, and is committed to defending her image, chastening anyone (i.e., conservatives) who might suggest that Hillary is of the Kennedy school of left-wing thought. To make such a claim, they charge, is a mean-spirited caricature of the lady, part of the politics of personal destruction that the Right, they will tell you, so enjoys.

According to them, the former First Lady's political evolvement lies somewhere between having no discernible political persuasion to being a moderate, a centrist, or a "third way" politician like her husband. Her media friends don't really care where in the valley of political persuasions she might be taking up residency—only that she is not perceived as a liberal.

Hillary's transformation began in earnest when she was sworn in as the junior senator from the state of New York. For the first time since law school she was moving through life without Bill in the lead. As she dealt with the problems of the nation as a legislator and worked with others in the Senate, including Republicans, she evolved politically and matured personally, leaving behind her tough, arrogant, liberal image to emerge as someone different. It was then, in late 2004, that Hillary Rodham Clinton was reintroduced to America as a moderate-leaning, conservative member of the U.S. Senate. Or at least this is what Hillary & Friends would have us believe.

As reported by the *New York Times* in November 2004, Hillary's aides noted that "since arriving in the Senate, Mrs. Clinton has staked out moderate-to-conservative positions on a host of issues, from welfare to the war in Iraq, much to the chagrin of her liberal supporters and the satisfaction of some Republicans."[1]

Six months later, in a piece titled "The Evolution of Hillary Clinton," the *Times* again made the point: "Mrs. Clinton has defied simple ideological labeling since joining the Senate, ending up in the political center on issues like health care, welfare, abortion, morality and values, and national defense, to name just a few.... In many ways, her approach is reminiscent of what her husband once called 'the third way,' the path that exploited the political center."

The concept seems to have stuck—two years later in a *Time* magazine cover story titled "The Presidential Ambitions of Hillary Clinton," Karen Tumulty wrote, "Speculation swirls around a possible bid for the White House in 2008. [Hillary] may not have Bill's gift for campaigning, but her toughness and centrist vision could make her the Dem to beat."

Hillary: the lady with a centrist vision! Who would believe it?

If true, it is a remarkable conversion story. After forty years battling for every imaginable liberal cause on earth, Hillary Rodham Clinton goes to the Senate and becomes a right-of-center politician? Could this be? The darling of the Left, the Feminist in Chief, the architect of universal health care, the author of *It Takes a Village*, has abandoned the causes of a lifetime and turned to the Right? After years in the political trenches with the best the Left has to offer, Hillary Rodham Clinton has rejected the ideals for which she fought so hard?

Or could there be something else going on here?

The argument goes that Hillary's political philosophy began to evolve as she tackled the problems of the nation from her new perspective as a member of Congress. Equally important, we are told, the sincerity of her transformation is unquestionable.

New York Times reporter Raymond Hernandez explained in February 2005:

Conservatives have long caricatured Hillary Rodham Clinton, New York's junior senator, as a sort of Democrat whose positions on social issues are out of step with Americans deeply concerned about religion and moral values. But while Mrs. Clinton has been strongly identified with polarizing issues like abortion rights, the picture that conservative Republicans paint of her is at odds with a side of herself she has lately displayed as she enters a new phase of her public life.[2]

Is it possible Hillary is mellowing with age? It happens to the best of us, why not her?

Dan Balz, the *Washington Post*'s savvy political writer, is buying it, or at least selling it. In May 2006, under the headline "Clinton Is a Politician Not Easily Defined," he wrote that Hillary "defies easy characterization," and in spite of her vast experience in the various roles of lawyer, governor's wife, First Lady, and senator, "she is still trying to demonstrate whether these yielded a coherent governing philosophy. For now, she is defined by a combination of celebrity and caution."[3]

Wait a New York minute! Does Dan Balz really want us to believe that Hillary Rodham Clinton has been reduced to nothing but a "combination of celebrity and caution"—all in the course of a few years? Are we to forget about the eight years as co-president and decades as an outspoken advocate of most every left-wing cause and limit ourselves only to Hillary's six years in the Senate when assessing her political philosophy? We are to treat one of the most widely recognized women in the world as if she dropped out of the sky and onto the political scene just a few years back?

Okay, for the sake of argument, let's consider that Hillary does look at life differently now—that her years in Congress really have changed her. Then her Senate voting record will support the argument, right? Wrong again!

According to Donald Lambro of the *Washington Times*, as a senator Hillary has "led no great legislative offensives, proposed no major, original legislative reforms of her own, and seems bereft of any new ideas."[4] Liberal blogger Markos Moulitsas, writing for the *Washington Post*, made the same observation: "[Hillary] doesn't have a single memorable policy or legislative accomplishment to her name."[5]

Being a do-nothing senator doesn't give you a pass on a lifetime of liberal advocacy.

And her actual voting record belies any claim that Hillary has moved toward the middle. A *National Journal* analysis of her lifetime key votes puts Hillary as more liberal than 80 percent of her Senate colleagues. In addition, the left-wing crowd at Americans for Democratic Action gave Hillary a near-perfect "A" for her votes during her first four years in the office. (They stopped grading after 2004.)

So if it's not her voting record, what justification is there to suddenly call her a centrist? Amazingly, much of it comes from her willingness to reach out to Republicans. While First Lady, Hillary publicly paired with conservative congressman Tom DeLay on legislation that would remove barriers to adoption. The publicity was excellent and Hillary obviously didn't forget the advantages of this tactic. She took up the practice as a senator.[6]

In the Senate, Hillary has cosponsored legislation with Republican senator Trent Lott to move FEMA out of the Department of Homeland Security, joined Newt Gingrich to call for expanded health care, and befriended Senator Lindsey Graham, who was one of the House managers for the impeachment proceedings against her husband. One more thing—while traveling in Estonia with a congressional delegation, she had a drinking contest with John McCain.[7] (For what it's worth—she took him.)

Do you need any more evidence than that? Hillary not only works with Republicans—she drinks with them! Surely she must be a moderate! And in the event there is a cynic amongst us, Hillary added a drop or two of substance to this argument by voting for war, cosponsoring a bill to ban flag burning, and proposing a crackdown on violent video games. Then poof! Like magic,

Hillary the Left-Wing Ideologue is gone and in her place: Hillary the Common Sense Moderate.

The questions are: Is there discernible movement in her political leanings? Is there justification for the press to toss aside the liberal label that has accurately defined Hillary for the past forty years and replace it with a more moderate one? Has this new phase of her life truly brought about a fresh outlook on life—and politics? And, if so, is it a conversion of the heart?

Or are we witnessing a carefully planned and professionally orchestrated transformation of an unprincipled left-wing politician who will let nothing, not even her deepest-held beliefs, stand in the way of becoming the first woman elected president of the United States?

Consider the timing. Although her makeover began upon her Senate election in 2000, they went "public" in 2004. News stories about Hillary's newfound religion began appearing about the same time her colleague John Kerry, the liberal senator from Massachusetts, lost the 2004 presidential election. Within days of his defeat, her staff was making the case to the media that the liberal in Hillary was history.

Taking into consideration the 2004 election results, *New York Times* political reporter Adam Nagourney wrote of Hillary's potential candidacy in 2008: "Democrats and some Republicans said Mrs. Clinton was open to caricature by Republicans as the type of candidate that this election suggested was so damaging to the Democratic Party: a northeastern, secular liberal."[8]

Kerry's defeat was being blamed on his northeastern liberalism by Democrats and Republicans alike. The 2004 election must have sent a shock wave through the firm of Clinton & Clinton. And Kerry was a decorated veteran of the Vietnam War. How was Hillary to be a serious contender in 2008 if she had the same political profile without the medals?

Bill Clinton, no slouch when it comes to reading the public, assessed the problem in a private conversation with friends, telling them that while America may indeed be ready for a woman president, he believed that woman would most likely be a Republican in the mold of Margaret Thatcher. More precisely: America wasn't going to elect a left-wing, antiwar feminist president in a time of war.[9]

Los Angeles Times reporter Jonathan Chait summarized Hillary's problems perfectly:

> As a prospective national candidate, [Hillary] has two great vulnerabilities. First, many voters think she's too liberal. Second, many voters also see her as cold, calculating, and unlikable.... Her response to this was to position herself in the center, cozying up with her former GOP tormenters in the Senate, staking out hawkish positions and making an overture to cultural conservatives. The theory was that her centrist positions would endear her to moderates but that it wouldn't cost her on the Left, because years of conservative vilification caused liberals to bond with her emotionally.[10]

And so the makeover continued. The goal: to recreate Hillary Rodham Clinton into America's Margaret Thatcher by 2008.

The first thing that had to go: adjectives like "secular," "left-wing," and "liberal." Hillaryland let it be known these words no longer applied to the senator from New York. That it would be far more accurate to use terms like "centrist," "moderate," or "right-leaning." As for philosophy—nothing too specific—"evolving" or "developing" would be just fine. No telling what the voters would be looking for come 2008, so Hillary needed to be politically nimble. There would be plenty of time to define her once the presidential campaign began. In the meantime Hillaryland needed to rid themselves of troublesome suggestions that their candidate was anything like John Kerry: a northeastern, secular liberal.

According to the *Washington Post*, a close advisor explained why "undefined" is right where Hillary needed to be. In 2008 "[Hillary] will define herself, and we will have the money to do it. People have to get to know her, know that she was once a Republican, that she is a big Methodist."[11] (Not just any old churchgoing Methodist, but a "big" Methodist, whatever the blazes that is.)

Hillary Rodham Clinton—the prodigal daughter—was coming home to her conservative roots after forty years in the liberal wilderness. Now we have the theme, the core message of the 2008 Team Hillary $200 million advertising campaign. Hillary the God-fearing, values-loving war hawk will replace the Hillary of old. And don't be surprised if she dons a cross in those ads—just for the skeptics.

It could work. So what's the problem?

Hillary Rodham Clinton is going to run for president as someone she is not. This talk of an evolving Hillary is part of an extreme makeover to get the old Hillary remolded and repackaged into a marketable political force for 2008. It involves her looks, her voice, her rhetoric, her attitude, her religion, and her politics. By the time Team Hillary is finished, their product will be kinder, more thoughtful, a person of faith, a politician with beliefs and values that reflect those of Middle America, and a leader tough enough to be the nation's commander in chief in a time of war.

Gone from public view will be the entitled elitist, the angry feminist, the shrill accuser, the environmental extremist, and the "New Age" socialist. The new Hillary won't demean stay-at-home moms, demonize political opponents, or demand society be remolded. And the new persona will be dramatically more appealing and certainly more likable.

But will she be believable?

Will Americans forget all that Hillary has been, all that she has done, and all that she has stood for? Will they let her close the book on her past and look only at what she offers for the future? Will they allow her to run for president as someone new? And what would be the harm if they did?

After the election of 2006, as she looked at returning to Washington with both houses of Congress in the Democratic column, Hillary was quoted as saying, "We are ready to roll up our sleeves and work with our Republican counterparts. Our country works best when we govern from the vital dynamic center."[12] Can she be believed?

Or is this the opening round of the public relations campaign that is nothing more than a slick New York repackaging job? If so, we need to get to the bottom of it now. Who is this lady? What does she believe? How will she govern? In what direction will she lead this nation? We have a right to know the answers to these questions. And Hillary has a moral obligation to answer each candidly. Anything less is to deliberately deceive the nation to advance her personal career and agenda.

If this grand transformation of the former First Lady is nothing but an extreme makeover, if it is a massive deception using the press as coconspirators, then Hillary must be stopped, for two reasons.

First, there is only one reason a candidate would keep her true agenda under cover of darkness. It is because if this agenda were to be seen in the light of day, the candidate would be resoundingly rejected by the voters. Otherwise, why deceive the public? But it is this agenda, and not the one Hillary purports to hold, that Americans have a right to examine and consider before November 2008.

Second, if she is involved in a cynical plot to mislead and deceive voters, she cannot be entrusted with the most powerful office in the world. There's no telling the damage a person as deceitful and shameless as this could do to the nation.

As a senior Democratic official told me, "I think Hillary spends a great deal of her day and night...making sure that even if she votes one way, she's perceived another way. That's part of her 'gift.'" This official thinks this time around what Hillary is trying to do is "shape her image with the public, so that she's not seen as a polarizing figure—that she doesn't have any of the 'Clinton baggage.'" As a reminder of that baggage, this official said, "The reason that I never went over there [to the Clinton White House], was that I was afraid I would get snapped into something for which one day I would need a lawyer."

My friend Richard Viguerie underlined a related point:

Hillary Clinton terrifies conservatives. She seems to really believe that there is a vast right-wing conspiracy. Hence, conservatives are convinced that if elected, she will use the power of the presidency to silence her conservative opponents.

An overlooked aspect of her infamous statement regarding the vast right-wing conspiracy is that she invited—and even encouraged—the media to investigate the conservative movement, and by implication, expose their attacks on her and her husband using the power of the White House.

To achieve her agenda of moving America significantly to the left, she will try to silence her opponents. However, the rise of the new and alternative media makes that very difficult. Therefore you can expect the White House under a President Hillary Rodham Clinton to try and silence her opponents—including talk radio (by bringing back the Fairness Doctrine), the Internet, and direct mail (through crippling legislation).

After First Lady Hillary Clinton's attempt to have the government take over all health care in America had failed, she gave an interview to the journalist Adam Clymer that ran in the *New York Times* on October 3, 1994, where she said, "This battle was lost on paid media and paid direct mail." It's not likely she will make that mistake again and allow her opponents to communicate freely with the public. Therefore, watch her every move as calculated to suppress her critics.

So it is time to revisit Hillary Rodham Clinton, to look beneath all the trappings and see what we find. Has an honest transformation taken place, a heartfelt conversion? Or has one of the most famous women in the world undergone an extreme makeover? And is she so arrogant as to believe that it will work?

We will look at the many faces of Hillary Clinton—the woman, the wife, the lawyer, the feminist, the politician, the senator, and the aspiring president. We will scratch at the façade of this new version to see if the old Hillary still lurks beneath, or if parts of her have truly been replaced. We will examine her strengths and weaknesses, her fears and challenges, her beliefs and values, her passions and causes.

Who is the real Hillary Rodham Clinton? What is her political philosophy and where does she stand on the critical issues of the day? What are those things Hillary can't change, that can't be made over, only hidden from sight? Does she believe that government is the answer or, as Ronald Reagan used to say, the problem? And can she be trusted, her word believed? These are the questions we need to answer. Then, with this information in hand, readers can make their own judgments about whether Hillary is the right person at the right time in our history.

To establish whether we are witnessing a change of heart in Hillary or a cynical makeover, we must first establish a baseline. Since the reinventing began in earnest when Hillary took office as the junior senator from New York, we can use that moment in her life as our point of reference. We will establish who Hillary was when she entered the halls of Congress, her most prominent personality traits, and her character. These items define a person as much as her belief system and are as important when deciding whether a candidate deserves the privilege of your vote.

Then we will examine Hillary's policy positions as a senator—from the social issues to national defense—to determine what she believes. Of course everything doesn't always fit into tidy categories, so at times will we simply go where the story leads us. It should be noted as we examine the character and personality of this woman that the assessment relies almost entirely on, first, Hillary's own words, and next, on the words of her friends in the media. Information does come from other sources, but the case is predominantly established through Hillary and the liberal media.

In the end, however, we will have the answer to this question: who is Hillary Rodham Clinton, and for what does she stand? We will learn why it is so important to reveal this makeover—because should she become president, her cloak of moderation will be promptly shed.

Chapter One

The Personality

Insecurity, the underlying theme in Hillary's life

The Consummate Student

FEW ON CAPITOL HILL work harder than Hillary Rodham Clinton, and few are more determined to learn every minute detail about an issue. Hillary throws herself at each task, studying the issues until she has a command of all the facts and figures and can discuss them with anyone. Her goal is not to understand a problem or policy but to become an expert in the field.

This is a consistent trait throughout her life. Her academic accomplishments started early—in high school she was a National Merit Scholarship finalist and at Wellesley she became a Durant Scholar, the most prestigious academic award given by the school. Hillary excels at learning, has a curious mind, and, unlike most politicians, enjoys the details. No issue is too boring or complicated. Quite the contrary—she appears more in her element the more intricate or mundane the information gets. As Joshua Green wrote in *The Atlantic*, "Clinton shines in precisely the sort of situation where she is called upon to master a distinct body of knowledge."[1]

Health care reform was one such situation. Early in his first term, Bill Clinton named Hillary health care czar, giving her the responsibility of overseeing the development of the single most important aspect of his legislative agenda. After a few months on the job she was called to testify before Congress; her "dazzling performances"[2] wooed even her harshest critics. She had acquired an amazing command of the complexities of the nation's health care problems in only a few short months.

The pressure on Hillary had to be enormous. Not only was health care reform the president's principle policy initiative, but the issue itself was also daunting by any measure. Nonetheless Hillary thrived under it, according to her close confidant and former chief of staff Maggie Williams. "When I think of Hillary I have one enduring image," she is quoted as saying. "It's of her after a day of events and meetings in an elevator, her arms bursting with books and papers and briefings, all about heath care, on her way back to the residence. She looked extraordinarily happy."[3]

Hillary applied this same determination for excellence in learning to her Senate responsibilities.

When Hillary was first elected, General John Keane, then vice chief of staff of the U.S. Army, called her office to set up a meeting. With West Point and the 10th Mountain Division based in New York, it was his responsibility to brief New York's new senator on their priorities. Although he had to wait three months, the general had good things to say after they finally met:

> She committed immediately to West Point and the 10th Mountain Division with follow-up on-site visits. But it was her enormous depth of knowledge about the military and her sincerity about our people which surprised me.... She had an extraordi-

nary grasp of our military culture, our soldiers, our families, and what it was like for them.[4]

Hillary is always well informed; there is no question about this. However, as much as she may love the details, she also very much needs them. Hillary has no vision—so she compensates by knowing the facts. She is a learner, a plodder, a regurgitator, and a follower—never a visionary. She cannot create or even see past the information before her. Someone else has to take the information and turn it into action or policy or ideas for the future. So she falls back into the role in which she can compete with the best of them—the consummate student.

Being the most knowledgeable in the room gives Hillary some sense of security, making facts and the figures her lifeblood. In another profession—attorney, professor, or think tank guru—this intense interest in knowing every obscure detail would put Hillary in the top of her field. But as a politician, it makes her a bore.

And she knows it, making it all the more painful.

Communicating without Heart

Bill Clinton is also bright and knowledgeable. But his success in politics had more to do with his incredible talent to reach people when he spoke. In spite of his enormous personal shortcomings, no one can deny his ability to make millions of Americans feel he understood their problems, cared deeply about each of them, and had a vision of how their world could be better. They believed in Bill Clinton because they felt he believed in them.

He communicated with his heart, not his mind.

Hillary has no such gift, a point that is brutally made by the press time and again. The late Michael Kelly, an astute observer of politics, wrote, "While [Bill] Clinton is brilliant at performance politics, Gore is barely competent; Hillary is flatly incompetent."[5]

While being a policy wonk brings remarkable discipline and commitment to the office of senator, it leaves Hillary short when it comes time to speak. She impresses her audiences with her celebrity and her knowledge, but she doesn't connect with them. And, unfortunately for Hillary, this isn't something you can learn. Otherwise she would be an expert.

And so Hillary is perceived as cold, impersonal, and lacking the empathy her husband so exuded. Speaking before an audience and laying out the issues point by boring point is simply no contest to the warmth and passion that comes from the heart.

In her 2006 Senate campaign, Hillary not only put together one of the most impressive campaign organizations ever amassed, she also broke all fund-raising records, raising $49 million. Most pundits considered her nearly invincible for the 2008 Democratic nomination. So why, in October 2006, with Hillary as overpowering as ever, did Barack Obama's name get tossed into the ring? Why did he suddenly become the man to watch, the rising star, the one who could beat Hillary?

It certainly wasn't Obama's impressive résumé that propelled him onto the national scene. Two years earlier he was nothing but a state senator in Illinois who had won a seat in the U.S. Senate. Even in Washington he did little to get himself noticed other than write his second book, *The Audacity of Hope*, and get an appearance on *Oprah*. To his credit, he is an attractive, amiable, black American with an interesting personal story. Oh, one more thing—he gave a powerfully moving speech at the Democratic convention in 2004.

So the question becomes: would Democrats dump the frontrunner—a formidable politician who has dedicated a lifetime to the service of her party—for a fresh face with a speech? You bet they would. Obama's appeal comes from his ability to communicate, to touch and charm an audience, to move the voter—precisely the things Hillary so obviously lacks.

But winning the nomination of one's party is as much about money and organization as it is about message and delivery. Hillary will have the money, and as for organization—that is a learned skill. No one will match her.

Sending Messages with Your Hair

One of the few good things about middle age, especially for women, is that we have a "look" about us, one on which we are settled. After years of chasing constantly changing fashions, we have found one that fits our lives and in which we are comfortable. Oh sure, many of us are hoping to knock off a few pounds, drop a few sizes, but for the most part we have found a style of clothing, a level of make-up, and, yes, a hairstyle that suits us.

Admittedly we make occasional changes, especially if our lives take a dramatic change, such as with the birth of a child. But then we settle in for the long haul again, never varying much from what we've grown accustomed to. It is, after all, who we are.

Then there's Hillary. By age forty-five she had been a professor, an attorney, the First Lady of Arkansas, a mother, and was now the First Lady of the United States. What does she do? She starts changing her hairstyle, and keeps changing it for years. It was a most peculiar development for a woman in her position.

In her autobiography, *Living History*, Hillary confides that during the presidential campaign her friends convinced her she had to change her appearance. "What they understood, and I didn't, was that the First Lady's appearance matters. I was no longer representing only myself. I was asking the American people to let me represent them in a role that has conveyed everything from glamour to motherly comfort."[6] She really took this new role to heart. It was as if she were determined to represent all women, from "glamorous to motherly," in a period of a few years—using only her hairstyles!

The first few changes are completely understandable—Hillary was thrust onto the national stage and into a new, extraordinarily public role. But she didn't stop—she kept jumping from one style to the next, sometimes changing hairdos every few weeks. Watching her became embarrassing, more like voyeurism than curious fascination. The website "Hillary's Hair" made its debut,[7] and the late-night shows moved in for the kill, but not even these stopped Hillary. She just kept going—revealing more about herself than we wanted to know, and more than she cared to tell.

Hillary is intensely private. She holds her feelings and her thoughts close, sharing with few, if any, her deepest fears and concerns. Changing her look as often as she did revealed a deep sense of insecurity. Many viewed this strange behavior as a public manifestation of the turmoil Hillary felt about her new role.

In a lengthy profile in *The Atlantic*, Joshua Green writes, "Her famously changing styles during her husband's presidency...were an easy metaphor for her inability to find a comfortable role in his administration."[8]

Hillary doesn't believe her dozens of different hairstyles revealed any distress or discomfort, instead claiming she "was like a kid in the candy store, trying out every style I could. Long hair, short hair, bangs, flips, braids, and buns." She even goes so far as to suggest that everything about her, including her hairstyles, became a point of public debate because she "had turned into a symbol for women of my generation." (Hillary, a symbol for my generation of women? Surely she doesn't believe this stuff.)

At a bare minimum Hillary was feeling insecure, unable to settle on a new look for this new life of hers. Upon closer examination, however, we will see that the hairdos are just one of many indications that Hillary Rodham Clinton has had a lifelong battle with insecurity and that this struggle only intensified as she tried desperately to redefine the role of First Lady of the United States.

After leaving the White House and beginning life as a senator, Hillary joined the rest of her generation and settled on a hairstyle. For years now she has donned an easy, smart, and professional blonde look—one that suits her well. This was a key factor in the makeover. Voters may not like liberal, but had she become a presidential candidate with a 'do-a-day the liberal label would have been the least of her worries. If she couldn't decide on a hairstyle, they would surely think, imagine the difficulty she might have as the leader of the free world. Why, she could even make Jimmy Carter look good.

Preparing the Speech

In her senior year at Wellesley, Hillary was president of the college government. The school had never had a student speaker at graduation, but this year the seniors demanded they be represented by one of their own. Hillary was chosen for the honor.

As the day approached, Hillary met with classmates to solicit their advice and ideas. "I spent hours talking to people about what they wanted me to say and hours more making sense of the disparate and conflicting advice I received."[9] "I didn't have a clue about what I could say that could fit our tumultuous four years at Wellesley and be a proper send-off into our unknown future. I wondered how I could do justice to this time [my friends and I] shared."[10]

She had no clue? This was not some chemistry major yanked from the lab and told to report to graduation prepared to "make sense of our time and place."[11]

This was Hillary Rodham, the recipient of the highest scholastic honors Wellesley bestowed, who had spent two years on student government, one of which as president. She was a weekend volunteer for Eugene McCarthy's presidential campaign and a congressional intern in Washington (which led to an internship at the 1968 Republican convention).

This was the young woman who, after only a few months, had quit her position as president of the College Republicans her freshman year because "I realized that my political beliefs were no longer in sync with the Republican Party," especially with respect to "civil rights and the Vietnam War."[12] She abandoned that ship for the Democratic Party, where she emerged as an ardent feminist and antiwar activist. What's more, she was headed off to Yale Law School in just a few months.

And she wants us to believe she didn't have a clue what to say?

She had plenty to say, but instead of gathering ideas from friends and then barricading herself in her room until the speech was written, Hillary kept asking others what she should say. "[I] asked the class at our graduation rehearsal what they wanted me to say for them. . . ."[13] The night before graduation she still wasn't sure what to say, and stayed up all night "to piece a speech together from a communally written text."[14]

Why didn't Hillary just write the speech? She had been discussing ideas and debating the issues for the last four years with faculty and students alike. She comments in *Living History* that the summer after her junior year she didn't go on the family vacation, "which was just as well since I am sure I would have spent hours arguing with my father over Nixon and the Vietnam War." This is a knowledgeable, opinionated, accomplished feminist. Why all this uncertainty about what to say? Why didn't she just put a few of her own thoughts in writing?

Because she couldn't. It was literally beyond her abilities. She had no vision of the future—only the facts of the day. She was not, and is not, an original thinker, and she lacked the confidence to just give it a try. She was impressed with the thoughts, ideas, courage, and accomplishments of others, but saw no worth in her own.

Hillary devotes almost four pages of *Living History* to this graduation speech. Not once does she indicate that her own ideas were central to it, or were even a small part of the final product. Instead she talks of a "communally written text." Nowhere in her description of how this speech came to be does Hillary even so much as suggest that she interjected any of her own thoughts, or her own assessment of the times. Instead she describes herself as being nearly manic about asking others what she should say—up until the day before the speech—and then staying up all night to pull together the "disparate and conflicting advice" she had received.[15]

In all of Wellesley, Hillary was certainly one of the most informed, with a keen sense of what was happening on campus and in the nation. Yet she needed the words and ideas of others to communicate. Hillary's speech to her graduating class was nothing more than the thoughts, feelings, and ideas of others; all she did was pull them together. She takes no credit for the content—so insecure about her own feelings, she describes herself simply as the messenger.

Unfortunately for Hillary, this intense sense of insecurity was not the result of youth or inexperience. It was to be a lifelong battle. Hillary Rodham Clinton has been in constant need of validation throughout her life, which is the underlining force behind much of what she has done and much of what she has not done.

Graduation Day

In *Living History*, Hillary describes what she was trying to accomplish on that graduation day. "The speech was, as I admitted, an attempt to 'come to grasp with some of the inarticulate, maybe even inarticulable things that we're feeling' as we are 'exploring a world that none of us understands and attempting to create within that uncertainty.'"[16]

That being given, no human or divine form would have a clue what to say. But one thing is for certain: Hillary was as inarticulate as she was incoherent.

Consider a few of her pearls of wisdom:

"Our love of this place, this particular place, Wellesley College, coupled with our freedom from the burden of an inauthentic reality allowed us to question basic assumptions underlying our education."

"Words have a funny way of trapping our minds on the way to our tongues but there are necessary means even in this multimedia age for attempting to come to grasp with some of the inarticulate, maybe even inarticulable things that we're feeling."

"But there are some things we feel, feelings that our prevailing, acquisitive, and competitive corporate life, including tragically the universities, is not the way of life for us. We're searching for a more immediate, ecstatic and penetrating mode of life."

"Within the context of a society that we perceive—now we can talk about reality, and I would like to talk about reality sometime, authentic reality, inauthentic reality, and what we have come to accept of what we see—but our perception of it is that it hovers often between the possibility of disaster and the potentiality for imaginatively responding to men's needs."

What in heaven's name is this woman talking about?

Not only are the thoughts buried inside this speech incomprehensible, but Hillary doesn't even employ basic sentence structure. How is it that a woman graduating from Wellesley with honors, an incoming Yale Law student, failed so miserably to summarize the feelings of her day? The assignment wasn't all that difficult.

For Hillary, though, it was an impossible task. She had to analyze, assess, and then speak about feelings. There was no book to read, no notes to study. To succeed Hillary had to rely on her own perceptions and thoughts, and she had to use her heart as a guide.

This is the one thing Hillary could not do, not then, not now—so she muddled through asking others for guidance. She couldn't produce a coherent result and rambled on about who knows what. (For entire text see Appendix A.)

According to Hillary her speech received an "enthusiastic standing ovation."[17]

Drugs must have been in heavy use that day.

Hillary and Her Health Care Guru

Within weeks of taking office, President Clinton named Hillary chair of the newly formed President's Task Force on National Health Care Reform. Ira Magaziner, a friend of Bill's from his days at Oxford, would handle the day-to-day operations. Health care reform was to be the centerpiece of Clinton's agenda, and Hillary was in charge. In her own words, she was responsible for producing "the Social Security Act of this generation and the defining legislation for generations to come."[18]

Hillary was thrilled. She had a significant and challenging role in the administration, one befitting a co-president. She was to remold 14 percent of the nation's economy—and give quality, affordable health care to all Americans.[19] And she answered to no one—not the cabinet, not the vice president, and, surprisingly, not even the president.

Hillary had redefined the role of First Lady into one suitable for her intelligence and talents. Life didn't get better than this.

True to character, she threw herself into the project. Initially unaware of the complexities of the nation's health care system, she met with the experts, studied volumes of documents, and became as knowledgeable as anyone in Washington on the intricacies behind the spiraling costs of medical care and prescription drugs, the layers of bureaucratic paperwork required by insurance carriers, and, most important, the compelling stories of the uninsured.

Hillary was indisputably an expert—she understood the problem. And she believed universal health care was the solution. But how do you get there? Her strength was not in solving problems, and this one was particularly difficult. Solutions to the health care crisis varied widely according to, among other things, your philosophy of the role of government in a free society. Personal judgment was to be a critical element in the process of developing the needed legislation.

But again, this is where Hillary comes up short—she can learn but she can't create. She lacks confidence in her own judgment, just as she did when called upon to give the Wellesley graduation address. But she has learned to compensate—she surrounds herself with smart people who share her liberal philosophy and relies on them to guide her.

The health care mission was like none other—the eyes of the nation were on her. Hillary overcompensated. All she needed was a couple of sharp health care policy wonks, a few experts from the various medical fields, and a few of the fellows in the White House's legislative office. Instead she built an army of advisors six hundred strong. Then she demanded everything be done in secret. It had political disaster written all over it.

But the underlying flaw of the entire fiasco was Hillary's desperate need to rely completely on the judgment of others. She had to trust someone to do it for her—an ideologue like her, someone who saw the world as she did. Ira Magaziner was the perfect fit.

"Ira, with his brilliant and creative mind, had a knack for coming up with inventive ways of looking at issues," Hillary writes in her autobiography. "I believed that access to quality affordable health care was a right American citizens should be guaranteed. I knew that Ira felt the same way."[20]

How could she go wrong? Ira was "brilliant and creative" and had already written widely on the subject. Hillary was assured they were philosophical soul mates on the obligation government had to its people. What's more, Bill respected him. And so Hillary became the pupil and Ira the teacher. He instructed and she followed.

In his book *Rewriting History* Dick Morris asks, "How did Hillary let herself be brainwashed?"[21]

In one sense Morris makes a point. Hillary was an experienced politician, Ira was not. She should have been able to see the warning signs. But by then Ira and friends had reinforced the glorious concept already swimming around in Hillary's mind that this was a moment in history—they were going to succeed where Presidents Roosevelt and Truman had failed. What she was about was grander than politics—she was remolding society, putting government to use for the good of all citizens.

They were a team—Hillary, Ira, and their six hundred advisors—the best and the brightest, in her mind. The legislation they proposed was theirs, and no one was going to change it. What's more, she was co-president and had the power to see this through to the end. All that was necessary was for her to remain focused and vigilant, and the dream of health care for all would be realized. And so she took up her position as advocate and defender of the plan, the public face of universal health care. It was to be a glorious mission.

Morris continues, "Not only did the liberals around Hillary hijack the [health care] cost-cutting initiative and transform it into a campaign for universal health coverage; they also persuaded Hillary that the incremental change was impossible. Either the entire system would be fixed, or nothing at all would be accomplished."[22]

Morris seems to think that somewhere along the line Hillary should have stepped in, overruled Ira, and moved on to a plan B— or some variation of plan A. A reasonable suggestion, if it weren't Hillary, but impossible for her. It would have required her to critically analyze Ira's work. But he was the one with the brilliant and creative mind, not her. She was just the student.

Ira and the army of advisors had told Hillary this was the most important piece of legislation for generations. Who was she to refute such great thinkers? What's more, who would have developed plan B for her?

In an editorial years later, Morris nailed it: "[Hillary] fell under the spell of Ira Magaziner, the utopian guru."[23]

Ira was not Hillary's first guru, and he would not be her last.

Hillary's Other Gurus

Don Jones, Minister of the Social Gospel

Mentors can play an invaluable role, especially in the lives of young people. So when I first read about the influence Methodist youth minister Don Jones had on young Hillary, I thought nothing of it. In fact I was pleased for her—as a young teenager she had the good fortune to have someone other than her parents take an interest in her. Don Jones was like no one she had ever met before, introducing her to art, literature, and the world beyond the security of her hometown. In her own words, Jones threw her into "liberalizing" experiences.[24]

Don Jones was, as my friend the late Barbara Olson pointed out, "a radical leftist preacher of the 'social gospel,'" and within a few years Minister Jones was sent packing by the Rodhams' Methodist church. They had had enough of his Marxist approach to religion.

But he was around long enough to have a profound impact on Hillary. He raised questions in her mind. He told Hillary and her friends that the greatest crisis they faced was the crisis of meaning and alienation, whatever that was. Forty years later, Hillary was still talking about it.[25]

There is no question that as a teenager Hillary was particularly impressionable. Her ninth grade history teacher encouraged her to read Barry Goldwater's *The Conscience of a Conservative*, and she emerged from those pages as a Goldwater gal and a Republican, just like her dad. Then along comes Don Jones, who introduces her to the civil rights movement, the plight of the migrant workers, and a new kind of Christianity. Hillary's heart bleeds, she moves left, and throws away a solid Christian foundation for one with a Marxist spin.

She quotes Don Jones in *Living History* as saying he and her history teacher were "locked in a battle for my heart and soul."[26] Hillary undoubtedly enjoyed the attention and possessed an inquisitive mind that was open to new ideas. And young people are often impressionable.

But Hillary never grew out of her "impressionable" phase. She falls under the spell of others almost as often as she changed hairdos. And unfortunately for Hillary her gurus are right out of central casting. She can't find the answers on her own, so she seeks out the confident and self-assured, and she takes to them like a fish to water—hook, line, and sinker.

Saul Alinsky, Left-Wing Radical Activist

In high school, Hillary had Dad at home to give some balance to the liberal teachings of Minister Jones. At Wellesley all that came to an end. The school was drenched in left-wing ideology, and it wasn't long before Hillary dropped all pretense of conservative thought. She embraced feminism, threw herself into the antiwar movement, and found herself a new mentor: Saul Alinsky.

Alinsky, a left-wing radical from Chicago, was a legend when it came to left-wing protests. "[A] portly balding man with a wizened face," Alinsky was a master agitator and organizer, and when he put his formidable skills to use in Chicago on behalf of the poor, the *Chicago Tribune* referred to him as a "public enemy of law and order, a radical's radical."[27]

Hillary was completely enamored with the little radical, and he became a significant guru in her life. She studied his works, delved into his ideas and tactics, and wrote her senior thesis on him. Then she applied all she learned to her own life. A few years after Hillary graduated, Alinsky's final book was published: *Rules for Radicals*. It reads like the gospel according to Hillary.

Consider a few of his precepts:

"Ethical standards must be elastic to stretch with the times."[28] Hillary mastered that little rule right along with her husband.

"Pick a target, freeze it, personalize it, and polarize it."[29] Ask Bill's girlfriends if Hillary nailed this one (or the vast right wing, for that matter).

Then there are these two little charmers: "power is the very essence, the dynamo of life" and "let nothing get you off your target."[30] What a student she was; Alinsky would be so proud.

Hillary's gurus had captured her heart and soul—she graduated from Wellesley a deeply committed left-wing ideologue, having absorbed the socialist theology of Don Jones, the liberal philosophy of Wellesley, and the political "ethics" of Saul Alinsky.

Bill Clinton, Prince Charming

At Yale she met Bill. This time she married her guru. He was everything she wanted—smooth-talking, smart, self-assured, and knowledgeable about so many different things. And he had a plan: he was going to be president of the United States. It didn't get better than this. She would follow him anywhere. Bill was her ticket to power and she would let nothing get her off her target—no matter what he did. Saul Alinsky would expect no less.

Michael Lerner, Devoted Leftist, New Age Rabbi

About the time the President's Task Force on National Health Care Reform was hitting the skids, Hillary turned herself over to a New Age guru by the name of Michael Lerner. A Berkeley radical in the '60s, Michael Lerner had become a New Age rabbi with a far-left agenda. Much of his writing is psychobabble, but what must have caught Hillary's attention was the phrase "the politics of meaning," which Lerner had coined in his magazine, *Tikkun*.

True to the counterculture of the university days, Lerner had his wedding cake inscribed with the words "Smash Monogamy," a slogan used by the Weathermen terrorist group in the late '60s. His book *The Politics of Meaning*, written after his relationship with Hillary had ended, has chapter titles that include "The Tyranny of Couples" and "Overcoming Patriarchy as Family Support." He's divorced.

According to R. Emmett Tyrrell, Jr., "[Hillary] would sweep into interviews and public meetings announcing, 'As Michael Lerner and I discussed, we have to first create a language that would better communicate what we are trying to say, and the policies would flow from that language.'"[31]

Likewise, Barbara Olson wrote that Lerner would often use the phrase "Hillary and I believe...."[32] Hillary had the power to make things happen and Lerner was the provider of ideas. Hillary swallowed them whole. Hillary's 1993 speech to students at the University of Texas at Austin was an attempt to put into words Lerner's "politics of meaning." At age forty-five, Hillary was still trying to find the meaning of it all and was failing miserably. Consider a few of her comments to the students:

> We are, I think, in a crisis of meaning. What do our governmental institutions mean? What does it mean to be educated? What does it mean to be a journalist? What does it mean in today's world to pursue not only vocations, to be part of institutions, but to be human?
>
> ...the answer is "all of us," because remolding society does not depend on just changing government, on just reinventing our institutions to be more in tune with present realities. It

requires each of us to play our part in redefining what our lives are and what they should be.

We need a new politics of meaning. We need a new ethos of individual responsibility and caring. We need a new definition of civil society which answers the unanswerable questions posed by both the market forces and the governmental ones, as to how we can have a society that fills us up again and makes us feel that we are part of something bigger than ourselves.

It's a frightening flashback to that strange compilation of words Hillary delivered to her college graduating class in 1969—"come to grasps with some of the inarticulate, maybe even inarticulable things that we're feeling" and "talk about reality sometime, authentic reality, inauthentic reality, and what we have come to accept of what we see."

Thirty-four years later and Hillary is not only as inarticulate and incomprehensible as ever, she is still desperately looking for meaning in life. Now a wife, a mother, a successful attorney, an advocate of causes, and the First Lady of the United States, and she asks, "What does it mean in today's world...to be human?" I have no clue what this woman is trying to say, but I do know she lacked grounding in her life. She calls for remolding society— which, she explains, includes changing government, reinventing institutions, and redefining ourselves.

Hillary, as First Lady and co-president, was as much a far left-wing ideologue as she was in college, with Michael Lerner sitting in for Saul Alinsky as philosopher-king. But Lerner was a devoted leftist and became disillusioned when President Clinton chose to replace political philosophy with political expediency when the former sent his administration into a political tailspin.

Hillary was in turmoil. Her New Age speech was criticized by the liberal media as "didactic moralizing" and "intellectual incoherence,"[33] her health care package was on its way to the dumpster, there were no more "Michael Lerner and I" discussions to guide her to the meaning of life, and her number one guru, Bill, was abandoning the cause. Where was Hillary to turn?

Jean Houston, New Age Altered-State Expert

By late 1994, the pressure of the job really must've been taking its toll on Hillary: she went psychic.

After she had botched her attempt to make national policy and Republicans had run roughshod over Democrats in the off-year elections of 1994, Hillary was understandably low. Her co-presidency was in shambles, and she was getting much of the blame for the shellacking her husband took at the polls.

To make sense of it all she turned to Jean Houston, co-director of the Foundation for Mind Research, a group that studies the psychic experience and altered and expanded consciousness. According to the *New York Times*, Houston was a "sacred psychologist and global midwife."[34] (Now, that clarifies things.)

During the 1960s, Houston and her husband studied the influence of the drug LSD on human subjects. They concluded that the drug-induced altered states of consciousness "were most effective in conveying psychic truth to the participant," and "that authentic religious and mystical experiences occur among the drug subjects."[35]

Houston's subsequent work was based on these ideas as well as in the New Age notion of "imminent planetwide transformation of the human race,"[36] a reaching of a "critical mass in consciousness (enough people with the New Age worldview, all thinking and feeling the right way), inaugurating a quantum leap into utopia."[37]

A quotation or two from Houston's books offer greater insight into her thinking:

Presently we are living at a time of extraordinary insight into both the microphase and macrophase of the phenomenal world.[38]

> There really may be an underlying unity of all kinds of life
> [Monism/Pantheism], a pool of consciousness in which every
> being is affected by whatever may happen to another being, even
> plants, are able in some sense and to some degree to share the
> conscious experience with all other living things.[39]

This should give you some idea of what we are dealing with—
a certifiable nutcase. Hillary, on the other hand, was mesmerized
by the woman.

Jean Houston became a close advisor of Hillary's, and on
numerous occasions she stayed at the White House for days at a
time. She worked with Hillary through therapy sessions designed
to help the First Lady reach her full human potential. Part of the
therapy, often called "channeling," included guiding Hillary in
conversations with the dead—Eleanor Roosevelt and Mahatma
Gandhi to be precise.[40]

Houston understood firsthand the value of this exercise. In a
1989 conference she told a crowd of 6,000 she had contacted the
Hindu goddess Sarasvati while meditating on the Ganges River in
India.

In his book *The Choice*, Bob Woodward writes that one day,
after finishing up a discussion with Eleanor, "Houston asked
Hillary to carry on a conversation with Mahatma Gandhi, the
Hindu leader, a powerful symbol of stoic denial. Talk to him,
Houston said. What would you say and what would you ask?"
And Hillary did. "It was a strong personal outpouring," Wood-
ward reported.[41] Gandhi's response went unreported.

While Woodward refers to Houston as Hillary's "spiritual advisor," the First Lady refutes it in her book, instead calling Houston
a dynamic, witty, and knowledgeable woman who was great medicine for "anyone in need of a good laugh." Hillary has a point
here. Tell me to talk to the dead and I'd fall over laughing.

But that's not what Hillary did. No, this smart and successful professional woman from a middle-class Methodist family started to talk to the dead, continuing the dialogues through many sessions, with her New Age psychic Jean Houston.

It must be a terrible thing to be as deeply insecure as Hillary. It has made her so incredibly susceptible to the ideas of those she believes to be wise and insightful, so needy for the validation of people she deems deep or brilliant thinkers. She should feel great confidence in her own intellect and abilities. Instead she goes through life attaching herself to people whom she views as having figured it all out—the meaning of life or some significant insight—then she follows them anywhere.

As she traveled through life, Hillary's gurus moved further and further from acceptable liberal philosophy until she found herself at its outermost edges. In her formative years, she indulged in the social gospel of Don Jones and the radical ideology of Saul Alinsky, and moved left to the New Age psychobabble of Michael Lerner and the psychic world of Jean Houston in midlife.

Hillary doesn't always employ full-fledged gurus. She also relies on little ones all along the way.

Influenced by Random People, Particularly Famous Ones

Hillary's judgment is so lacking, her understanding of life so dependent on the thoughts of others, that even the smallest, most basic decisions of her life are made at the encouragement of others. Just as with the graduation speech, Hillary has others tell her what to do, from her clothes and hairstyles to where to vacation. They aren't her ideas, they are someone else's—and usually the "someone else" is a famous person. Consider these clips from *Living History*:

On changing her name to Clinton: Vernon Jordan "urged me to do the right thing: start using Bill's last name."[42]

On why she had no makeover when she first became First Lady: "I asked [Jackie Onassis] if I should just turn myself over to a team of famous consultants as some in the media had recommended; she looked horrified. 'You have to be you,' she said. 'You'll end up wearing someone else's idea of who you are and how you should look'.... Her words were a relief."[43] She needed Jackie O to tell her it was okay to be herself?

On hair color: In *Rewriting History,* Dick Morris reports that Hillary told him she went blonde because "she read that Margaret Thatcher said that 'at a certain age' every woman should."[44]

On clothes: "Some of my friends began a mission to spruce up my appearance."[45]

On hairstyles: "My good friend Linda Bloodsworth-Thomason suggested that a friend of hers in Los Angeles, the hairstylist Christophe Schatteman, cut my hair. She was convinced it would improve my appearance."[46] Oops, Jackie O's advice just went out the window!

On vacationing at Martha's Vineyard: "It was Ann and Vernon Jordan who persuaded us to come to the Vineyard, where they had been vacationing for years."

On how she came to find herself standing on a platform forty feet above the water: "Chelsea said, 'Come on, Mom, try it!' Of course, Ted [Kennedy] and Bill started yelling, 'Yeah, give it a try, give it a try!' For reasons that escape me today, I said okay."

On whether to jump off this platform into the water below: "Then I heard Jackie's voice rising above the rest: 'Don't do it, Hillary! Don't let them talk you into it. Don't do it!'... She knew exactly what was going through my mind, and she came to my rescue." She needed someone else to make it okay not to jump!

On whether to run for the Senate: "Sofia Totti, the captain of the girl's basketball team, introduced me. As I went to shake her hand, she leaned toward me and whispered in my ear. 'Dare to compete, Mrs. Clinton,' she said. 'Dare to compete.'"[47]

On raising Chelsea in the White House: "[Jackie Onassis] confirmed my instincts that even though security was necessary, it was important to stress to Chelsea . . . that she owed respect to the agents sworn to protect her."[48] Chelsea, now age twelve, had lived in a governor's mansion most of her life; surely Hillary had already taught her to respect the security personnel—and everyone else around her, for that matter!

More Jackie O advice on Chelsea: "'You've got to protect Chelsea at all costs,' Jackie said. 'Surround her with friends and family, but don't spoil her.'"[49] Hillary found this advice valuable? She had been Chelsea's mom for twelve years already.

On changing the White House menu: "[Julia] Child had written Bill and me at the end of 1992, urging us to showcase American culinary arts."[50]

On choice of White House chef: "[Alice] Waters wrote to encourage us to appoint an American chef."[51]

On her outfit for Bill's second swearing-in ceremony: "In a break with tradition, and with Oscar's strong advice, I ditched the hat."[52] That would be Oscar de la Renta, of course.

There are two issues here—the first is that Hillary has a need to justify so much of what she does as a response to the advice of others. From her days as a teenager through her life in the White House, Hillary has had a compelling need to be instructed and guided in almost every area of her life, however personal or insignificant. "Who cares if you wear a stupid hat to the Inaugural?" I want to yell. "Do what you want, do what makes you feel comfortable!"

The second point is Hillary's insatiable desire to impress her reader with how many famous people she knows. *Living History* should be subtitled *My Life with the Rich and Famous*, as it is replete with references such as the ones above. Hillary may be one of the most famous women in the world, certainly in America, yet she feels compelled to drop on her reader the name of nearly every famous person she has ever known, most of whom, she wants us to believe, became close and trusted friends almost immediately upon meeting her.

She writes of having "a small, informal dinner in the second-floor dining room of the residence to celebrate our friend Mary Steenburgen's fortieth birthday. Mary, a fellow Arkansan, had done well in Hollywood, winning an Academy Award for acting." Hillary goes on to say that Mary was "among our closest friends."[53]

In Ireland "we were thrilled to meet Seamus Heaney, Nobel Prize–winning poet, and his wife Marie."[54]

"The most eloquent messenger of this viewpoint was Elie Wiesel . . . a Nazi death camp survivor and winner of the Nobel Peace Prize . . . and since that day, he and his wife Marion have been friends."[55]

"Although there was little time to talk during this visit, I came to know and like [Princess Diana]."[56]

"[The late Admiral Zumwalt] will be remembered by his country as one of the great patriots and humanitarians of his generation, and by me and my family as a true and steadfast friend."[57]

Hillary writes about how after Bill's affair with Monica became public she was comforted, encouraged, and inspired by Nelson Mandela, Stevie Wonder, Walter Cronkite, Katharine Graham, Maurice Templeton, and the Dalai Lama, among others.

But nothing relays this need of Hillary's like this prizewinning snippet: While vacationing in Martha's Vineyard with Ann and Vernon Jordan, where they stayed in a "small, secluded house that belonged to Robert McNamara, the Secretary of Defense under Kennedy and Johnson," they celebrated Bill's birthday with

"Jackie Kennedy Onassis and her longtime companion, Maurice Templeton" and "the always gracious Katharine Graham, publisher of the *Washington Post*, came, as did Bill and Rose Styron, who became trusted friends. Styron...had recently published *Darkness Visible: A Memior of Madness*." And "Jackie and Maurice invited us to go sailing on Maurice's yacht with Caroline Kennedy Schlossberg and her husband, Ed Schlossberg, Ted and Vicky Kennedy and Ann and Vernon Jordan."[58]

It is painful to read so much name-dropping in one book—and she does it for the same reason that other people drop names. She is insecure about who she is, and so she builds herself up reflectively. Success isn't enough for her—she needs to be something more, something grander, something that will satisfy those constantly churning feelings of insecurity. So she seeks out gurus who shower her with praise and encourage her to reach for new levels of greatness. And she surrounds herself with famous people, because their acceptance of her as an equal helps subdue the insecurity gnawing away at her heart.

Hillary has been First Lady of Arkansas, First Lady of the United States, and a United States senator. She has traveled worldwide and is recognized as an international leader in feminist circles. Yet she is still heartbreakingly insecure.

Compensating

But Hillary has learned to compensate remarkably well. She conquers issues, letting no fact escape her grasp, and, in the words of Dick Morris, she has become an "advice addict."[59] Her compulsion for information and her inability to turn data into a coherent policy has driven Hillary to build a huge campaign staff, with a cadre of consultants to guide and direct her. According to Larry Sabato, a University of Virginia political scientist, it's the "biggest, best campaign machine ever built."[60] Its job: to remake Hillary into a confident leader who understands the problems Americans face and who has a vision for a better tomorrow.

But it is all store-bought. Hillary can never be a confident leader. Confident people don't rely on famous people to tell them where to vacation, or whether to wear a hat to some ceremony.

She does nothing by chance. In her Senate campaigns, she doesn't just win—she overwhelms. She amasses a staff that is presidential in size and quality, raises more money than a Senate candidate could possibly need, and then spends twice the money necessary for a solid victory. She takes no chances, polling everything from image to ideas. Then she becomes the winning image, remaking herself into exactly what the voters want. It is a virtual no-risk strategy, allowing nothing to chance—and so far, it has worked flawlessly.

One wonders what ever happened to the Hillary who fought so long to keep her own name after she married, the one who remained true to her bohemian appearance and liberal ideas for years after moving to Arkansas and becoming First Lady of the state. She was a tough, passionate advocate for so many causes. She was largely her own person in those days—a left-wing liberal to be sure, but one with spunk and determination, ready to take a stand and let her opinions be known. I kinda miss the old gal. She was a formidable opponent worthy of respect.

But Hillary lost her way, giving in to her insecurity by conforming. She couldn't keep faith with who she was; she didn't have the confidence to follow Jackie O's advice: "You have to be you." There is very little of her left, except that which is lurking deep down below the surface, far away from public view.

Returning home from junior high one day proudly carrying a straight-A report card, young Hillary showed her dad at the first possible moment. His only comment was, "Well, Hillary, that must be an easy school you go to."[61] Hillary never forgot those words, recalling them some thirty-five years later. Standing alone they were mean-spirited and cutting. But for young Hillary, so desperately looking for validation, for praise from her distant dad, for some recognition of her accomplishments, it had to be particularly painful. And it is safe to assume that this was not an isolated incident.

While we can't be certain that Hillary's father was one of the underlying causes of her insecurity, there can be no question that he played a significant role.

It is also safe to assume that her choice of husbands did not help the situation. While Bill has certainly supported Hillary in her professional life, his habitual and reckless adultery throughout their married life has unquestionably undermined her self-respect and sense of worth as nothing else he could ever have done.

The Blame Game

Hillary admits no weaknesses, takes no responsibility for failure, and sees the devil in anyone who accuses her of either. Her carefully scripted image can't handle flaws or mistakes.

In *Rewriting History*, Dick Morris recounts a personal story that took place early in Hillary's White House days. Polls indicated that the public thought Hillary "presented too perfect an image to be believable." He suggested to the First Lady that she "let people know about some imperfection—put a story out there. Eleanor Roosevelt let people know she was insecure about her appearance and felt awkward about public speaking. It made her more believable. More human." "'I'll think about it,' she promised." "A few days later, I asked her about it again," Morris writes. "I really can't think of anything," she told him.[62]

Here you have Hillary working overtime to disguise an overwhelming sense of insecurity—that at the time was becoming nearly unmanageable—and along comes Morris suggesting she let some fault or two out of the bag. She must have thought him out of his mind.

The reader, I am certain, recalls Hillary's accusation on the *Today* show when Matt Lauer asked her about the nature of Bill's relationship with Monica Lewinsky: "Look at the very people who are involved in this. They have popped up in other settings. This is—the great story here for anybody willing to find it and write about it and explain it, is this vast right-wing conspiracy that has been conspiring against my husband since the day he announced for president."[63] The very people involved? Let's see now. That might be Bill and Monica.

Five years later—with all facts known—Hillary writes: "New facts were emerging daily about the mechanics of what was essentially a sting operation to entrap the president."[64] Then again, "in my view, the prosecutors [Starr & Co.] were undermining the office of the presidency by using and abusing their authority in an effort to win back the political power they lost at the ballot box."[65]

She excuses her husband's serial adultery to early childhood conflict between his mother and grandmother. According to Barbara Olson, Hillary told a reporter in August 1999 that Bill's infidelities were rooted in personal tragedy. "There was terrible conflict between his mother and grandmother," Hillary said. "A psychologist once told me that for a boy, being in the middle of a conflict between two women is the worst of possible situations. There is always the desire to please each one."[66]

Hillary is an enabler—one who allowed her husband to repeatedly abuse her (and their daughter) emotionally. Yet she refuses to hold Bill responsible, blaming his selfish, outrageous, and often criminal behavior on his grandmother, mother, prosecutors, and the vast right-wing conspiracy. She does no less for herself.

With respect to the health care debacle, Hillary accepts little responsibility. The former First Lady has revised history and now is ready and willing to point the finger at the real culprits: "At the time we went forward, the Democratic leadership told us how they wanted us to do it. It turned out they were wrong."[67]

But why, then, was she blamed? "The fact that I was doing it was such a shock to the Washington system. I don't think I ever recovered from that. That was the real challenge: 'He put his wife in charge!'. . . I think it was very convenient to hang this all on the First Lady."[68] Convenient? Does she not understand that when you are "in charge" you are also responsible? Or is that just a man thing?

In *Living History* Hillary accepts a tiny part of the blame, but only to get to the important part about her difficult role in history. "I knew I had contributed to our failure, both because of my missteps and because I underestimated the resistance I would meet as First Lady with a policy mission."[69] This debacle had nothing to do with Hillary being First Lady—that's just a transparent excuse because Hillary can't accept her blatant failure at making policy.

She suggests maybe, possibly, a few "missteps" of hers may have played some minor role in the outcome. That's hardly an accurate portrayal of her contribution to the health care disaster. She pushed for universal health care, demanded every living soul be covered, and then produced a 1,342-page plan that would have cut the number of doctors in the country by 25 percent and the number of specialists in half. Democrat Daniel Patrick Moynihan called her plan the "deliberate dumbing down of medicine."[70]

In addition, Hillary demanded that everything—from the list of the task force members to the proceedings themselves—be kept secret. Bad call, Hillary. Turned out it was illegal to keep the public out of the meetings, and the subsequent legal challenge dashed all hope for success. Hillary had indeed "made a ham-fisted mess of her one formal attempt to craft national policy"[71] and—while she may spin it differently now—at the time, she knew it.

She is reported to have commented to an aide, "Remind me, have I ever done anything right in my life?"[72] She was devastated— that's to be expected. But why would one failure, no matter how massive it may have appeared to be, put into doubt all that Hillary had accomplished throughout her long, successful life? Only the frailest sense of self-worth would have been so easily destroyed.

Hillary's strength is her intellectual power, and combined with her unmatched determination and near total focus, she is a formidable individual. But Hillary is also needy and painfully insecure—traits she despises about herself. But she will not let them thwart her progress; instead she turns to others to validate who she is and direct what she should do.

Mystic Jean Houston told Hillary the human race was at a five-thousand-year turning point, that women were at the brink of finally achieving equal partnership with men, and that she, Hillary, was to be a stand-in for all womankind at the moment of equality. Houston explained that if she could do this, Hillary would be the most consequential woman in human history.[73] Hillary takes it all in—firmly believing she was, after all, born to be great.

Whether this is the case or not, I cannot judge—my experience tends to be a bit more mundane than Jean's. The only dead person I speak to is my mother, and so far she hasn't talked back. And if she does, I won't be telling anyone.

But even rationally speaking, Hillary is a fascinating person, full of extreme contrasts—intellectual without insight, formidable without confidence, powerful without class. Unfortunately for Hillary, the driving force behind so much of what she has become is her deep underlying sense of insecurity.

As I studied Hillary from her early years through her days as First Lady, it became more and more evident that extreme insecurity is a dominant personality trait. Not being a medical professional, I decided to look more deeply into the condition. After days of research, I was led to a fascinating field of study involving narcissistic personality style. The symptoms of the related disorder were intriguing. I have included them in an endnote.[74] I pass no judgment as to whether this shoe fits the Lady Hillary.

Deep insecurity and its related symptoms, in and of itself, in no way precludes Hillary from consideration for the presidency or any other position of responsibility. It is not the insecurity that is the problem. For example, John Adams had difficulty with this condition and others and surely proved himself to be a remarkable leader.[75]

So, you might ask, why raise it in the case of Hillary? Because she has allowed a chronic lack of confidence and self-esteem to define her—rather than rise above the challenge, Hillary has been consumed by it. One simply cannot study Hillary without understanding how debilitating this trait has been to her development as a human being. That being said, it is no excuse for her behavior, rather it is an explanation.

Whether it is a pathology that makes Hillary do what she does or just good ol' God-given free will, matters little. What is important, however, is how her pattern of behavior offers a window to her heart. This is what should be on the minds of Americans should Hillary be on the ballot in November 2008.

Chapter Two

The Character

WE ARE EACH BORN with strengths and weaknesses, and with them we face our own unique path as we travel through life. How we use what God has given us—and how we deal with our challenges—defines our character. It is the most important part of who we are.

Not long ago, character was central to a candidate's appeal. The logic was simple: if a person couldn't be trusted, what did his experience, skills, or vision matter? Put another way— if the scoundrel lies to his family and friends, he'll not hesitate to lie to the rest of us. So you couldn't believe a word he said. That mattered to the voter (unless, of course, you were from Louisiana).

In recent years, however, character has been downgraded as a campaign issue. While this is unfortunate for the nation, it's a really good thing for Hillary.

Without dwelling on the many scandals that have plagued her over the years, we must nevertheless touch upon them. How she became the target of so many investigations and how she dealt with them reveal a great deal about Hillary the person.

Character is a work in progress, developed and reinforced as one passes through life. While Hillary may want to leave some of her past behind as she looks forward to becoming the first woman president of the United States, she can't. Her history defines who she is and gives insight into who she will become.

The specific challenges that Hillary faced aren't what's important—it is the manner in which she handled them. And it is on this point that she has been extraordinarily consistent over the years, having created a steady pattern of behavior from her days in Arkansas right through her years as First Lady. Observing this pattern develop as she responds to her many crises brings her character into clear focus. Hillary can't leave this behind her. It is the character she has spent a lifetime developing.

Hillary's extreme makeover has done much to cause the public to forget the old Hillary—changing her looks, her rhetoric, her politics, and placing her into settings that make her appear thoughtful and bipartisan. But character transplants don't happen, at least not in this business—unless, of course, there is a religious conversion. But that requires a great many mea culpas, and I haven't seen a one.

So who is Hillary? What kind of person lies beneath the façade?

First, as has been noted, Hillary was gifted with a strong, focused, and curious intellect. She used this gift to become an attorney—but not just any attorney. Hillary went to Yale, one of the most respected law schools in the nation. Considering this degree, along with her interest in detail and her dedication, one has to believe she was capable of being an extraordinarily competent attorney. How is it, then, that she managed to get caught up in so many murky, legally questionable, and in some cases blatantly illegal activities?

Arkansas Shenanigans

Cattle Futures

In 1979 Hillary played the cattle futures, turning a $1,000 investment into $100,000 in ten short months. She used a fellow by the name of "Red" Bone to handle the deal for her. Red had lost his license to trade a year earlier, having been accused of allocating trades to investors after the market had determined the winners and losers.[1] It was a sure deal if he liked you. And he liked Hillary... or maybe he liked the fact she was married to the governor. Whatever the case, Hillary hit the jackpot.

Hillary kept news of her good fortune private—even from the IRS.[2] But as luck would have it, a dozen years later, when she was living in the White House, the news broke. Hillary was asked to explain how she took $1,000 and turned it into $100,000 in less than a year.

Her initial stab at an answer was to explain that she studied the commodities market by reading the *Wall Street Journal*. That proved to be a hilarious lie. She finally settled on the "I was just lucky" version. Then she paid back taxes on her previously undisclosed $99,000 profit from cattle futures.[3]

You have to wonder, if she was "just lucky," why not shout it from the rooftops—or at least report it to the tax man? And, when asked how she got so lucky, why not tell the press she had an unbelievable broker who advised her? There is no crime in making money in the market.

But Hillary couldn't tell the truth, any more than she could have shouted the good news from the rooftops back in 1979. As one Chicago-based investment advisor explained it, "The average retail customer has about as much chance of that kind of success as I have of driving to Hawaii."[4]

Insider trading and/or manipulation of client accounts are the most likely explanations for Hillary's impressive success in her introductory course in commodities, and both are criminal in nature. It may explain why Hillary wasn't interested in advertising her good fortune or giving much detail to the press years later.

The statute of limitations had run its course by the time her little foray into the commodities market became public, so no formal investigation was convened. The broker and the brokerage firm that had assisted her, however, were not so fortunate. After she had taken her winnings and moved on, they were prosecuted for conduct similar to that which they had so kindly provided Hillary.[5]

She lucked out. But what is a smart attorney like Hillary doing counting on luck to keep her a step or two ahead of the long arm of the law?

Whitewater

In 1978 she and Bill entered into a land deal, the Whitewater Estates, with Jim McDougal. They put up no money but co-signed a mortgage note for up to $200,000. The deal went south.

It happens to the best of us.

But what McDougal did next was where the trouble began. He bought himself a rural Savings and Loan, called it Madison Guaranty, and milked it—possibly in part to keep Whitewater properties afloat. By the mid-1980s Jim McDougal had federal regulators on his back, Whitewater was sunk, and Bill Clinton was governor.

McDougal understood the mess he was in, and more important, the embarrassing spot he had put the Clintons in. He offered to assume all financial responsibilities if Bill and Hillary signed over their holdings in Whitewater to him. They would be out from under a bad investment that was now tied to a failing S&L, and

McDougal would take the hit for the Madison fiasco. Bill was more than ready—Hillary adamantly refused.[6]

According to several reports, Hillary had specific plans for their share of the Whitewater profits and wasn't about to turn them over to McDougal. She simply wouldn't accept the evidence that her Whitewater investment was belly-up. So rather than cutting her losses and distancing herself from the murky waters of Madison Guaranty, Hillary rejected the deal McDougal offered and instead plunged herself into the legal morass that was swallowing him up.[7]

With Madison's survival a critical part of keeping her dreams for Whitewater alive, Hillary agreed to become the legal representative, through the Rose Law Firm, of McDougal's Madison Guaranty before the state securities and exchange commission. She immediately contacted the state's newly appointed commissioner, Beverly Bassett.

Bassett, an attorney friend and supporter of Bill's, had done legal work for Madison Guaranty before her appointment to the commission. Her appointment was no accident; Bill had appointed her in January. Hillary became McDougal's legal representative in April. Bassett approved McDougal's recapitalization scheme in May.[8]

McDougal, Hillary, family, and friends all won—their favorite S&L was back in business. But the taxpayer lost—to the tune of $65 million—when Madison finally failed.[9]

It was cronyism at its finest. It was also unquestionably unethical. According to the Arkansas Rules of Professional Conduct for attorneys, Hillary had an "obligation to avoid even the appearance of impropriety." But on a personal level she had an investment to protect—one she was bound and determined to make work.

The truly amazing aspect of all this is that this bright, competent, Yale-educated attorney managed to take something as innocent as a bad real estate investment and turn it into an uncontrollable scandal that demanded the appointment of a special prosecutor and plagued her for years. Whether it was greed or pride that drove her, or just very poor judgment, matters little. What matters is that as the years passed Hillary kept repeating the pattern, never learning, never maturing, and never caring.

In Arkansas, Hillary was undeniably foolhardy in her business deals, at times even reckless—but let's for the moment give her the benefit of the doubt. She was the breadwinner of the family—her husband, the governor of the state, had a salary of only $35,000 a year. While a mansion and expenses came along with that, it is reasonable to assume that Hillary felt a pressing need to begin "building up a nest egg." She knew full well that "politics is an inherently unstable profession,"[10] and she also knew it was the one on which her husband would focus all his attentions. The pressure was on her to make money, and Hillary was intent on doing so.

What's more, which of us hasn't made a bad decision or two in life, paid the price, and been grateful to get a chance to move on?

But Hillary doesn't seem to get it, and in fact seems almost empowered by her good fortune at playing loose with the law and getting away with it. She headed to the White House with just that frame of mind.

Hillary: No Respecter of the Truth or the Law

Hillary was the First Lady less than a year before the media began to hound her with questions about Whitewater. No amount of stonewalling worked—the president was forced to call for a special prosecutor. That, in turn, led to questions about Madison Guaranty and Castle Grande—another failed land development in which Hillary was entwined, this one fraudulent from the get-go. Soon Hillary found herself entangled in a web of lies, some uttered under oath.

Her refusal to deal honestly with the press led to the appointment of a special prosecutor. Then she refused to deal openly and honestly with the prosecutors. The question everyone was asking was: if all she had done in Arkansas was make a few bad business deals, what in the world was she hiding? So the press kept looking.

They soon caught wind of her profitable little activity with Red Bone and the cattle futures. While the land deals were too complicated for the average Joe to fully grasp, the public had no trouble understanding this little arrangement. Hillary had turned $1,000 into $100,000 in less than a year—in cattle futures, no less. *Sleazy* and *corrupt* were words that quickly came to mind, especially when her versions of what transpired lost all credibility.

No matter what the questions were about—Whitewater, Madison Guaranty, Jim McDougal, cattle futures, Red Bone, Castle Grande, or Rose Law Firm records—Hillary never gave a straight answer. She bobbed and weaved her way through every inquiry, whether the questions came from the press or from the investigators, whether it was a casual conversation, or whether she was under oath. Her explanations of what had occurred changed constantly to keep up with facts that slowly found their way into the public arena.

In the words of Joyce Milton: "When she was asked [about Castle Grande] she decided not to take the risk of telling the whole truth. Like her husband . . . she seemed to see testimony under oath as a kind of word game, in which she gave answers that might be technically compliant, but that appeared to be lies to people who did not have the benefit of Ivy League law degrees."[11]

Because she refused to level with the public, Hillary was under siege with questions about Arkansas for years. She remained defiant but her reputation paid an enormous price. Her credibility was nearly nonexistent.

Then, to make matters worse, the First Lady made a colossal mistake. The White House had been under subpoena for years to provide prosecutors with Hillary's itemized legal work for Madison Guaranty. The White House had repeatedly denied knowledge of their existence, and Hillary had specifically told investigators she had ordered those records shredded years earlier. Turns out the Rose Law Firm billing records were resting comfortably on the third floor of the White House in Hillary's private book room.[12]

Hillary must have had cause to review the records, and she foolishly left them out, with her fingerprints all over them. Her secretary inadvertently picked them up and took them with her. Weeks later, when Carolyn Huber realized what she had, she called Hillary's attorney, and then in a moment of sheer brilliance called her own attorney as well.[13]

America had had it with Hillary. The miraculously recovered records proved beyond a shadow of a doubt that Hillary had lied about her involvement with both Madison Guaranty and the corrupt real estate deal, Castle Grande. In the words of *New York Times* columnist William Safire, "Americans of all political persuasions are coming to the sad realization that our First Lady—a woman of undoubted talents who was a role model for many in her generation—is a congenital liar."[14]

These records categorically proved she lied under oath. Hillary became the only First Lady ever called to testify before a grand jury inquiry.

This was January 1996, and Hillary had been in the White House for three years. In her first two years she had managed to fail miserably as co-president. After three years she had managed to fail miserably as First Lady. National polls showed her to be the most unpopular First Lady in history. Fifty-two percent of Americans believed she was a liar; 68 percent believed she had done something wrong or illegal.[15]

Hillary's problems were not about her Arkansas past catching up with her. Having the light of day focused on the shenanigans of her early life gave the nation a sense of concern. But America is always ready to move on, to give someone a pass for mistakes of yesterday. Hillary, though, was unable to admit to a few dumb mistakes, most of which were too complicated and boring to sustain much public interest. She choose instead to dig herself in deeper with one lie after another.

Once Hillary was firmly in power, she did not become the historical figure she dreamed she would be. There were no moments of gracious reflection, no thoughts of the near sacred nature of the place she now called home, and certainly no respect for the great traditions all around her. It was all about her: her power and how she could use it—or, if necessary, abuse it—for the benefit of herself, her family, and her friends. Her attitude: America be damned. She was now co-president.

While Hillary did make history as First Lady, it was not as co-president. It was for her ability to introduce more scandal into a White House than any other First Lady ever—cattle futures, Whitewater, Madison Guaranty, Castle Grande, Rose Law Firm records, Travelgate, and Filegate. And what other First Lady can claim to have escaped the consequences of so much perjury and obstruction of justice as Hillary successfully did? Bill had nothing on this woman.

The Clinton administration was scandal-packed, with Bill providing the most memorable moments with intern Monica. But Hillary provided the largest number of scandals. While Bill was reckless in his pursuit of a skirt, Hillary was no less reckless in her absolute disregard for the law and the truth.

But equally alarming was that as the nation's First Lady, Hillary ruthlessly exercised her authority over the most innocent and harmless people, exposing herself to be so flawed a human being that one wonders how she got out of bed in the morning.

Treats the Humblest around Her with Contempt and Disdain

Wonderful, nonpolitical people work at the White House. They go about their daily chores virtually unnoticed, performing their jobs with dignity and skill. They have little to no expectation of promotion or raise, but they take great pride in their work, considering it an honor to play a small role in keeping the home of their president running smoothly.

Many of these folks had been faithfully working at the White House for years when Hillary arrived. They were excited and a little anxious about the new administration. But as in the past when a new president was sworn in, they would prove themselves to be both dedicated and reliable. They manned phones, prepared meals, answered mail, landscaped the grounds, secured the facilities, and ran the travel office. They were nonpartisan civil servants with no axes to grind.

Little did they know that the second most powerful person in the world was out to get them.

Hillary entered the White House with a vengeance. First, she had to prove she was the boss, the co-president. Taking charge of the hiring and firing would make that point perfectly clear. And she would exercise this power over the presidential appointments as well as the civil servants. It was all part of her domain. Second, Hillary was paranoid. She trusted no one who might have some allegiance to anyone other than Bill and herself, which in her mind included everyone who had worked for previous administrations.

But former presidents and First Ladies, as well as their staffs, had, as one would expect, developed respectful relationships with those who worked to make their lives comfortable. Therefore all the White House's nonpartisan civil servants were suspect.

Take poor Chris Emery. One of four White House ushers, Chris took a phone call from former First Lady Barbara Bush. Mrs. Bush was having trouble with her computer and as Chris had programmed it for her she thought he could help. That call cost Chris his job—Hillary had him fired.[16]

Chefs, assistant chefs, a dishwasher, switchboard operators, and the ladies keeping the generic correspondence were fired, their livelihoods callously taken from them. Even the barber, Milton Pitts, found that his services weren't required. He had cut the hair of four different presidents—no telling what information Hillary thought he could reveal to the outside world.[17]

Hillary even tried to replace the Secret Service with private security or FBI agents. Why? The national press reported that Hillary had thrown a lamp at Bill during one of their spirited exchanges. Hillary assumed the leak had come from the agents on duty. She had a right to be upset—but all she needed to do was tell the agent in charge. He would have handled it immediately and transferred anyone found guilty of violating the president and First Lady's trust.

The Secret Service is one of the most professional agencies in government. Having personally worked with them, I know these men and women to be some of the finest, most dedicated people you will ever meet. What's more, they're ready to throw their bodies in the path of a moving bullet to protect the president. Surely that counts for something. Not for Hillary—she wanted them out, every last one of them. She was thwarted only by statute, which places the protection of the president in the hands of the Service.

In Hillary's world, all threats of disloyalty, real or imaginary, had to be removed. The consequences of her paranoia were irrelevant. The lives of the dedicated, hardworking Americans who loved their jobs at the White House mattered not at all to her. They were insignificant and therefore disposable. She exercised her power over them and rid herself of them.

But sometimes simply eliminating the threat wasn't enough. Hillary had to destroy it.

Destroys the Reputations of Innocent People

Even before Hillary arrived in Washington she had the White House Travel Office in her crosshairs. It wasn't just the seven travel office jobs she wanted for her trusted aides. It was the lucrative business that would flow to her friends the Thomasons. Harry Thomason had an interest in an air charter company and was intent on adding the White House to its client list. Hillary could have just fired the travel staff, but at the recommendation of the politically deaf Thomason decided instead on a more elaborate plan.

First they sent a Clinton loyalist to work in the office alongside those who were to be replaced. This gal was to learn the ropes and report back to headquarters—a mini spy operation. She performed her responsibilities well and reported what she found to David Watkins, the White House director of administration.

It appeared that Billy Dale, a thirty-two-year veteran of the travel office, ran a bit of a sloppy shop when it came to record keeping. This, however, was to be expected. As someone experienced in the field of accounting, I can personally attest that if you put the same person in a small office without supervision for a few dozen years, that person will inevitably find and use his or her own unique accounting system—one that works for that particular person.

Harry Thomason learned from Watkins that money management wasn't Dale's strength. He then convinced Hillary that she should fire the travel staff under the guise that the Clintons were cleaning up the corruption left behind by the Republicans. She followed his advice and Billy Dale and his colleagues lost their jobs as well as their reputations. (Billy Dale was indicted, only to be later found innocent of all charges.)

But Hillary, this smart and powerful co-president, had foolishly overlooked a small detail. The travel office had friends in high places—the press. Part of the job of the White House travel office was to book travel arrangements for the traveling party, including the traveling press, which Billy Dale had been doing for three decades. He and his staff probably had more friends among the press corps than any other office in the White House.

When the press heard about the firing of their friends they were stunned. For years the civil servants of the White House travel office had taken good care of the press. Now it was their turn to take care of the travel staff. And that they did. As the White House should have expected, the press sought out a firsthand account of what had happened and got it immediately from Billy Dale and his coworkers. Once again Hillary found herself in the middle of a firestorm.

The press demanded answers; in particular, they wanted to know who had ordered the firings. True to character, Hillary claimed to know nothing. The White House, hoping to cut its losses, hired back five of the fired staffers, the ones who never handled the money. But it didn't work. Hillary had triggered another investigation, and rather than just tell the truth she chose to lie her way out of it.

This scandal was called Travelgate, and was an early indication that Hillary had left no part of her Arkansas life back home. She was not turning over a new leaf, or rising to the level of her newfound prestige. When the investigation began Hillary did what she always did. She lied, denying any involvement in the firings.

But the paper trail led right to her. In a memo "for the file," purportedly written to chief of staff Mack McLarty but never actually sent, David Watkins reviewed the events leading up to the firings, exposing Hillary as the instigator. Barbara Olson explained that Watkins's memo was the kind in which the author intends "to get a set of facts on record in the event of an investigation or indictment."[18]

In his final report, special prosecutor Robert Ray cited "substantial evidence" that "directly contradicts [Hillary]'s long-standing denials that she had nothing to do with the controversial turnover" in the travel office. According to NBC's Peter Jennings, "The independent counsel said...that Mrs. Clinton gave false testimony about her role in the firings of White House travel workers."[19]

FOX News reporter David Shuster gave a more detailed analysis:

> Under oath, Mrs. Clinton flatly denied any role... but later a memo surfaced from administration chief David Watkins suggesting Mrs. Clinton wanted the travel staff fired. Watkins said there would be hell to pay if swift action was not taken in conformity with the First Lady's wishes.... Independent counsel Robert Ray cited eight separate conversations between the First Lady and senior staff and concluded: Mrs. Clinton's input into the process was significant, if not the significant factor influencing the pace of events in the Travel Office firings and the ultimate decision to fire the employees.

Shuster then asked George Washington University law professor Jonathan Turley for his assessment, which was: "[The Ray Report] essentially says that [Hillary] satisfies all of the components of an indictment and is ultimately safe from trial simply by the discretion of the prosecutor. That's pretty damning."[20]

Again, evidence overwhelmingly suggested Hillary had lied under oath. As in Arkansas she was playing the odds with the law, but her luck had followed her to Washington. She escaped prosecution. However, she wasn't so lucky when it came to the public. They found her guilty.

Americans have a tradition of loving and respecting First Ladies just for being themselves. So it was particularly unsettling to have one who spent her days skirting the law.

Equally troubling was that this First Lady used her power to destroy the livelihoods and reputations of innocent people. Seven months after they fired him, the White House requested Billy Dale's FBI file. Hadn't they done enough to damage this man? Billy Dale spent his life savings defending charges leveled at him by a woman looking for a "good story."

But this outrageous violation of privacy wasn't limited to a few minor figures—nine hundred former Reagan and Bush staffers were abused in this manner.

Uses Her Power to Illegally Collect and Misuse the Private FBI Records of Her Perceived Enemies

Craig Livingston was a barroom bouncer, a Democratic operative, and an employee of the Clinton Inaugural Committee before he went to work as the White House director of security. He landed this impressive position while under suspicion as the person in charge of over $150,000 worth of inaugural equipment, which had either been lost or stolen.[21]

So, you might ask, how in the world did someone with a résumé like this get one of the most sensitive jobs in the administration? Because he was made to order—with Livingston in charge Hillary would have her own lowlife at her beck and call. Livingston was a political sleaze who had done time in presidential campaigns digging up personal dirt on candidates (euphemistically called "opposition research").

There was a time when opposition research was a respectable living. It involved researching every written or spoken word your opponent had ever uttered. If you were dealing with an elected official you also studied every vote the person had ever cast. The purpose was to find some juicy morsel or two that could be blown out of proportion to throw your opponent on the defensive.

But that was child's play for the Clintons. When it came to opposition research, they borrowed a page from J. Edgar Hoover's playbook. Hillary investigated the public and private lives of anyone and everyone who could ever present a threat to Bill, and therefore to herself. She left no stone unturned, using detectives to delve into the secret corners of an individual's life in hopes of uncovering some little tidbit that could be exploited to potentially humiliate, and therefore quiet, the source of her concern. Nothing was too low or too personal if it could be used to keep the Clintons on their path to power.

Hillary even hired detectives to learn the identities and addresses of a threat's family members, roommates, boyfriends, and anyone else who could be used to effectively deliver a message to the intended target.

Craig Livingston was an ideal candidate for Hillary's director of security. He had experience with just this kind of research, and proved to be without scruples or conscience about it. It was a perfect match for a First Lady who was accustomed to getting regular reports on the private lives of opponents and potential enemies from paid private detectives.

As one would expect, the FBI raised a concern about Livingston when they learned he was being seriously considered for the security job. FBI agent Gary Aldrich, who was familiar with the ongoing investigation of the missing equipment from the inaugural committee, spoke directly to William Kennedy, White House counsel and former Rose Law Firm associate of Hillary's, about Livingston. He suggested that the position of director of security should go to someone "squeaky clean." Kennedy understood his point but quickly added, "It's a done deal," explaining to Aldrich that "Hillary wants him."[22]

None of this was particularly interesting until it was learned that Livingston had taken opposition research to a new level, one that would have impressed old man Hoover. He had the FBI send to his office the private personnel records of those who had worked for the previous Republican administration—over nine hundred files! Livingston was collecting them! It was a landmine of sensitive personal information—an illegal one.

The FBI was aghast at what had happened, claiming it had been "victimized" by the administration. Law enforcement agents had acted as virtual accomplices to the scheme—having responded to requests from Livingston's office and forwarded the files. Then director of the FBI Louis Freeh explained how it had happened: "The prior system of providing files to the White House relied on good faith and honor." The FBI had made the mistake of believing it could do the same with Hillary and her handpicked security man.

When the press got wind of this story it became another scandal, and there was no way to defend it. To procure, examine, and store the private FBI records of nine hundred Republicans was unethical, illegal, and in violation of every imaginable principle of decency.

The White House did the only thing it could—admitted a "bureaucratic snafu," and blamed the little mess on a communication mix-up with Livingston, the FBI, and the Secret Service.[23] Livingston and his assistant Anthony Marceca testified before Congress that they had requested the files to update old security files for those who needed clearances.

According to Ronald Kessler, a former reporter with the *Washington Post* and the *Wall Street Journal* and the author of several investigative books on government agencies, "the sole legitimate purpose of looking at these files is to grant clearances for people who actually work in the White House. These people knew who worked in the White House and who didn't. They knew that these Republicans were not working in the White House, but still kept their files."[24] Kessler utterly dismissed as inconceivable the explanation given—that these files were gathered in error. Livingston had worked on three Democratic presidential campaigns and knew well that prominent Republicans such as James Baker, Marlin Fitzwater, and Brent Scowcroft were not working in the Clinton White House.

Even the Clinton-friendly press was having a tough time buying this one: "[I]t remains hard to believe that these Democratic operatives accidentally stumbled onto" the FBI background documents.[25]

So the question became: How did the beefy bar bouncer become director of security? Who hired Craig Livingston?

As director of security, Livingston had to have been hired by someone in the counsel's office. His position was part of their operation. But amazingly, when the press asked White House Counsel Bernard Nussbaum and his associate William Kennedy who hired Livingston, both said they knew nothing about it.

And of course Hillary was all denials—she not only didn't hire Livingston, but she also claimed she didn't even know him. But that begged the question: if it wasn't Hillary who hired him, why not just tell the world how this joker got the job? Instead the public was expected to believe that the former bouncer just showed up one day and took over as director of security, working directly for the White House counsel.

Hillary did, of course, know Livingston, according to her former mentor Bernie Nussbaum. While conducting the congressional investigation into the matter, Congressman William Clinger of Pennsylvania learned that in 1993, during the FBI background check on Livingston, one of the agents interviewed Bernard Nussbaum, who volunteered "that [Livingston] had come highly recommended to him by Hillary Clinton, who has known his mother for a longer period of time."[26] In addition a White House intern testified under oath that he saw Hillary "warmly greet Livingston" in the hallway of the White House.[27]

It takes enormous audacity to order up the FBI files on your political enemies. It is unfathomable that Craig Livingston was openly carrying out this illegal operation on his own. But suppose for a moment he was. Then why not say that—why not admit Hillary had done a favor for an old friend by asking Nussbaum to hire her friend's son and then fire Livingston for his indefensible violation of the privacy rights of nine hundred American citizens?

Instead Nussbaum lied under oath, Hillary lied to the public, and Livingston remained on payroll for over three weeks before the public outcry demanded his resignation. Then a month after this story broke, the White House—in a move that ranks up there with the tackiest of the tacky—attempted to blame the hiring of Livingston on Vince Foster, who having committed suicide three years earlier couldn't very well defend himself.

There can be only one explanation for all these lies—someone higher up than Livingston had authorized this cloak and dagger operation, and there was reason to believe Livingston, if left out to dry, might rat out his handler.

So the First Lady and two White House counsels lied, and Nussbaum gave conflicting accounts of what he knew under oath.[28]

Just another day at the Clinton White House.

Allows Investigators to Intimidate, Harass, and, if Necessary, Destroy the Reputation of Women Who Speak Out against the Man They Say Sexually Abused Them

Exactly when Hillary came to realize what a rogue Bill was is anyone's guess, but there can be no denying that she knew of his philandering ways before she married him and was constantly reminded of them after they wed. For whatever reason, she learned to accept his foul behavior and refused to see him held accountable for it.

In November 1974, about a year before they were married, Hillary was informed by Mary Fray, the wife of Bill's campaign manager, that Bill had "special friends." Bill had just lost a close congressional campaign and Mary believed that all the deceit related to his sneaking around played a role in the outcome. She chose to share these feelings with Bill and Hillary.[29]

In 1981 Hillary hired Ivan Duda, an Arkansas detective, to produce a list of Bill's infidelities because she "wanted to be prepared for any charges that might come up in the course of the [gubernatorial] campaign."[30]

In 1987, with Hillary's encouragement, Bill considered getting into the presidential race when Gary Hart was forced to drop his bid because of an adulterous relationship. Betsey Wright, Bill's tough and competent chief of staff, threw a bucket of frigidly cold water on that idea. She had been trying to keep his affairs out of public view for years and told him flat out he couldn't run. There can be no doubt that Hillary knew why Bill wasn't running for president. Bill even admitted to the editor of the *Arkansas Democrat-Gazette* that he had a potential "Gary Hart problem."[31]

Then in 1992, according to Clinton strategist Dick Morris, Hillary was deeply involved in the hiring of detectives during the presidential campaign "to find information to discredit the women who posed potential problems, and to use that information to 'convince' them to remain silent."[32]

During that same campaign, Hillary spoke at an American Bar Association luncheon in honor of Anita Hill. She had nothing but the highest praise for the attorney who, on the eve of his confirmation hearings for his appointment to the Supreme Court, accused Judge Clarence Thomas of sexual harassment. Anita Hill "transformed consciousness and changed history with her courageous testimony," Hillary said. "As women and as lawyers, we must never again shy from raising our voices against sexual harassment."

"As women and as lawyers, we must never again shy from raising our voices against sexual harassment." Interesting choice of words for a woman who had recently engaged detectives to rummage through the lives of women who might one day find the courage to speak out against her husband.

"*Courageous testimony.*" I suspect these words were particularly heartfelt by Hillary. She wholeheartedly believed every word Ms. Hill uttered against the judge. At the time it was a popularly held feminist belief—having the status of doctrine in many circles—that women don't lie about being harassed, abused, or raped. The violation itself is so personally devastating and going public is highly risky and enormously painful. Hillary understood this well, and knew the level of courage required—far more than she herself had.

She had allowed Bill to emotionally abuse her for years, and she had enabled him to keep it up; first, by not holding him personally responsible and second, by going to extreme measures to make certain he was not held politically accountable either.

Bill used, abused, and discarded woman for decades. With all the input from her hired guns, Hillary knew plenty. She couldn't stop him and she couldn't leave him, so she put up with him. Nothing particularly courageous or honorable in that; it was just life. But she also protected him at all costs—he was her ticket, her ride to power. She had her career to consider.

Paula Jones, young state employee

When Paula Jones accused the president of sexual harassment, Hillary must have known she was telling the truth. She was doing exactly what Hillary had called on other women to do—she was "raising her voice against sexual harassment." And if Hillary believed it courageous for a law professor with job security to speak up against a Supreme Court nominee, did she not consider for a moment the enormous courage of this young, uneducated, low-level state employee to speak out against the president of the United States?

Whether or not she appreciated Paula's courage, Hillary knew her story had truth written all over it. Not only did her feminist psyche tell her so, but the situation also fit Bill's pattern exactly.

And Paula's charges against Bill were, according to one reporter, "so graphic, and so impressively corroborated, that they would dwarf Whitewater in the public mind."[33]

Yet all Paula wanted was a statement from the president that she had done nothing wrong when they met in his room at the Excelsior Hotel. Paula Jones didn't want money and didn't want any admission by the president that he had acted inappropriately toward her. She wanted her reputation intact and instead the Clintons sent out the dogs to destroy it.

Hillary was the one who refused to give Paula her due. Instead the powerful co-president, the feminist in chief, decided a better way to handle this courageous twenty-seven-year-old woman was to send in the goon squad to dig deep into her life and reveal its most intimate details. The destruction of Paula began immediately—a Clinton operative went on national television and suggested Paula was nothing but "trailer trash." It went down from there as the most powerful couple in the world tried to crush this woman's courage and spirit with heavy-handed, despicable tactics.

"We expected this story to die like the other phony scandals," Hillary wrote in *Living History* of Paula's accusations, with an air of superiority. But Paula proved herself to be a most worthy opponent, and she won the day. Her lawsuit went forward, which led to the deposition of the president, during which the president was asked about his relationship to another woman, Monica Lewinsky. The president chose to lie under oath, which led to his impeachment, temporary suspension of his law license, and an $850,000 payment to Paula.[34]

Kathleen Willey, Clinton supporter and volunteer

Kathleen Willey, an enthusiastic campaign supporter, accused him of unwelcome sexual advances during an appointment she had with him in the Oval Office. Kathleen's husband was in serious financial trouble and she was desperate for a job, so she went to see the president for help. Then, according to her, he assaulted her. Kathleen left the office disheveled and in tears. That evening she learned her husband had committed suicide.

Willey decided not to go public with any accusation against the president. "It was the choice I made," she told CBS's Ed Bradley after being forced to testify. "It was the choice I thought was the best one. I was embarrassed for the president's behavior, and saw no benefit whatsoever in filing a complaint."[35]

When the investigation of sexual misconduct and cover-up came around to her, she engaged an attorney to quash a subpoena that required her to testify before the grand jury. The effort failed and only then did Willey tell her story.

Kathleen Willey had no political ax to grind—she was a White House volunteer. There was no reason for her to make up such an accusation. And it would have been completely counterproductive for a woman in such need to falsely accuse her most powerful ally of anything. What's more, Willey went beyond the call of duty fighting the subpoena.

The lawyer in Hillary knows facts don't lie—and with the facts in this case as they were, she must have been able to see from afar that this one could be a slam dunk.

But even the potential threat of an accusation against the president had consequences—for friend or foe. The Clinton dogs were called in to intimidate and terrorize Kathleen Willey in the hopes of quieting the new menace. The goons swooped into her neighborhood, puncturing her tires, stealing her cat, and then sending a stranger to frighten her even further—mentioning the names of each of her children before asking if she had gotten the message yet. They failed—Kathleen testified truthfully before the grand jury.[36]

When Ed Bradley asked Willey why she was now speaking out publicly, apart from her testimony, she responded, "I think that too many lies are being told, too many lives are being ruined. And I think it's time for the truth to come out."[37]

I often ask myself what Hillary expected these women to do. She knew enough about Bill and enough about human nature to know that all these stories weren't fabricated. So what did she expect the women to do? Should they have just let this man mistreat them and say nothing? And if so, why? Did she believe these women should just excuse Bill his abusive treatment of them, as she had done for so many years? Why should these women not expect Bill to be held accountable for his crude and vulgar behavior? What gave him a pass? Why was he somehow different than other men? Why did the rules not apply to Bill Clinton? Or was it Hillary for whom the rules didn't apply?

Juanita Broaddrick

For years there had been rumors of a rape in Bill's past. But it was not until twenty-one years after the alleged attack that the victim gave a powerful, detailed, public account of what she claimed had occurred decades earlier. In an interview with NBC's Lisa Meyers, Juanita Broaddrick painfully recounted the day that, according to her, then attorney general of Arkansas Bill Clinton viciously raped her. You could not escape her sincerity. She just broke your heart. You cried with her and you cried for the nation—to think that the president of the United States was being accused of rape by a woman who appeared so credible.

According to Juanita, Hillary was well aware something untoward had happened. Several weeks after the rape, Hillary and Bill were picked up at an airport by an individual who happened to be a friend of Juanita's, and driven to an event at which Juanita was expected to attend. This friend told her that the conversation between the Clintons during the drive was all about her. Then when the Clintons entered the event, Juanita saw them speak to a few guests who then pointed her way.

Juanita half expected Bill to approach her and say something, but it was Hillary who approached Juanita, took her hand, and told her how much they appreciated all she did for Bill. Juanita turned to leave when, according to Juanita, Hillary kept holding her hand and added coolly, "Do you understand everything that you do?"[38]

During the NBC interview Juanita explained that she did not come forward earlier because she lacked the courage. "I was afraid I would be destroyed like so many other women had been."

This much is certain. Hillary was an enabler. She allowed Bill to treat their marriage with utter contempt—betraying and humiliating her constantly and causing enormous emotional upheaval in her life. He was a bum and Hillary paid the price, again and again and again.

Hillary was insecure about many things when she married Bill, but he was her knight in shining armor, her anchor in life, and she loved him dearly. The damage he did to her fragile sense of self is unimaginable.

But none of this gave Hillary the right to pry into the private lives of Bill's girlfriends. It is understandable that she didn't think much of the women who had consensual sexual relationships with her husband. And Hillary was also plenty smart to fully appreciate the threat they posed to Bill's future, and to her own. But nothing can justify her use of detectives to investigate, intimidate, and blackmail these women to prevent them from speaking out about their personal relationships with her husband. This was a new low in politics.

Hillary's response to Bill's affairs was inexcusable. But what she allowed to happen to the women publicly accusing her husband of sexual crimes was as callous and repugnant as anything I have ever seen in politics.

It is one thing to sign up for a life of politics. You have to expect the brutal rough and tumble that comes with it. But Paula Jones, Kathleen Willey, and Juanita Broaddrick didn't sign up for that.

They were most likely victims of Bill's deviant ways, and Hillary knew that that was possible. They deserved the same benefit of the doubt, the same respect Hillary showered on Anita Hill. Her charges against Judge Thomas were far less serious than those of Paula Jones—and not even in the same criminal class as those of Kathleen Willey and Juanita Broaddrick.

Hillary had become so hardened by her husband's treatment of her, and so committed to obtaining power, that she stopped caring about other people. Uneducated, unprofessional women weren't going to stop her climb to the top. Not them and not anyone else, for that matter. Hillary would stop at nothing to keep Bill and herself on track.

Hillary should have been excommunicated from the feminist movement for her contemptible treatment of these women and for her indefensible role in protecting Bill from ever being held accountable. Instead her sisters were shamefully silent, for the most part. One rare exception was radical feminist Andrea Dworkin. "What Hillary is doing is appalling," she is quoted as saying. "Being a feminist has to mean you don't use your intellect and your creativity to protect a man's exploitation of women."[39]

Hillary, Stoically Suffering in the Name of All Women

Hillary has any number of explanations for the accusations, investigations, and charges of obstruction and perjury that plagued her throughout her days as our First Lady. But never does she take any responsibility for what happened.

Dick Morris cleverly calls Hillary's response to criticism the "class action" defense. In *Rewriting History* he writes, "The attacks are never about her; there is no need to take them personally, because there is nothing wrong with her. They're criticisms of all women, or working women, or women in politics, or women in particular professions, or women in public life, or Democrats, or liberals, or supporters of the Clinton administration in general. They're never critiques of Hillary Rodham Clinton in particular. And, because all criticism is about her class, not her, she neither listens to it nor learns from it."

After Hillary had left the White House, and long after America had learned the ugly truth about the level of duplicity and moral corruption of this First Couple, Hillary received $8 million to write her autobiography. In it she portrays herself as a courageous trailblazer who willingly took upon her broad shoulders all the criticism that goes with forging change. It verges on the delusional.

In 1992 a reporter asked Hillary if she couldn't have done more to avoid the appearance of a conflict of interest when her husband was governor of Arkansas. (Think Madison Guaranty.) "I wish that were true," she replied, "You know, I suppose I could have stayed home and baked cookies and had teas, but what I decided to do was fulfill my profession."

It was political dynamite tossed into the middle of a presidential campaign. But in *Living History* she takes no responsibility for this foolish remark, blaming instead Republicans and society as a whole. She writes:

> Some of the attacks, whether demonizing me as a woman, mother and wife or distorting my words and positions on issues, were politically motivated and designed to rein me in. Others may have reflected the extent to which our society was still adjusting to the changing roles of women.[40]

What is she talking about? It was 1992 and 40 percent of the students graduating from law schools were women, and every one of them understood that the code of conduct for their chosen profession required absolute diligence in avoiding the appearance of conflict.

The way Hillary practiced law in Arkansas gave rise to legitimate questions regarding her ethics. When the press confronted her she lost her cool—a major faux pas for a candidate's wife—and ended up giving the reporter a pithy little quotation that revealed her utter disdain for stay-at-home moms. The Republicans picked up the fumbled ball and ran with it. It was as simple as that.

Again in reference to questions raised regarding conflict of interest charges, Hillary writes:

> I had made an awkward attempt to explain my situation and to suggest that many women who juggle careers and lives are penalized for the choices they make.[41]

This is a remarkable statement. Hillary doesn't believe women should be held accountable for their decisions. Grown women make the choice to have a family and a career and if it doesn't work out perfectly they are "victims"? She acknowledges no responsibility for individual choice.

And exactly how was Hillary penalized? Does she actually believe it was so "pathetic" for the media to ask her why she hadn't upheld the professional code of conduct that dictates acceptable behavior for all attorneys? And for that matter, why shouldn't the public expect Hillary to live by the same rules the rest of us do? Because she was juggling a career and life? So are many of the rest of us and yet the rules still apply to us.

The following is a sampling of explanations for why, in Hillary's mind, there were so many investigations during her days in the White House:

> "The purpose of the investigations was to discredit the president and the administration and slow down its momentum."[42]
>
> "It didn't matter that we had done nothing wrong; it only mattered that the public was given the impression that we

had.... It only mattered that our lives and the work of the president were disrupted over and over again."[43]

Monicagate "was essentially a sting operation to entrap the president."[44] (My favorite.)

"In my view, the prosecutors were undermining the office of the presidency by using and abusing their authority in an effort to win back the political power they had lost at the ballot box."[45]

"It is this vast right-wing conspiracy that has been conspiring against my husband since the day he announced for president."[46] (This has to be the most creative explanation for an extramarital affair ever proposed.)

Dick Morris tells a story about a time when Bill, Hillary, and he were discussing several of the accusations being made against members of their inner circle when Hillary volunteered, "Do you know why these reporters keep attacking us? Keep investigating us?" she asked angrily. "Because they're jealous. We are the same age they are. They're all boomers. They don't have to get jealous of Bush or Reagan. They're too old. But we are the same age as they are and they can't get over the fact that we're here [in the White House] and they're not."[47]

No investigation was legitimate—not a one. She and Bill were victims—just good people trying to do good for their nation and bad people were using every means possible to stop them. In addition, Hillary had spent a life forging ahead where few had gone before—breaking down barriers to the advancement of women. In her mind, these challenges were just part and parcel of the life of a crusader. But no burden was too great, not for Hillary—she would soldier on.

After ten years and a landfill's worth of evidence to the contrary, Hillary still believes she can sell this fairy tale. Responsibility isn't about to be part of her life—not then, not now. But then why should it be? She never required Bill to live up to any standards—why should she? It wouldn't be Clinton-like.

Miscellaneous Lies and the Classics

Interestingly, it isn't only under threat of prosecution that Hillary resorts to the make-believe. She often does it spontaneously.

Take her trip to Nepal back in 1995. Hillary met briefly with Sir Edmund Hillary, the first man to reach the summit of Mount Everest. Hillary was thrilled to meet the famous mountain climber, especially since, she was quick to inform the traveling press, he was her namesake. While she was pregnant, Hillary's mother had read about Sir Edmund's feat and was so moved that she decided to name her child after him, hence the two l's in Hillary.

Charming personal anecdote—but pure fabrication. Hillary was six when Edmund made it up that mountain. Prior to that, her "namesake" was a quiet beekeeper living in New Zealand. Not likely her mom named her after a beekeeper.

The story has never been so much as mentioned in the press prior to this encounter, and no biographer had ever heard it. Now what are the chances that Hillary overlooked mentioning this interesting tie she had with Sir Edmund for all these years? Hillary met Sir Edmund and made this story up on the spot—she couldn't resist another close association with someone famous.

In spite of being literally impossible, a fact widely covered on the Internet, Hillary didn't correct it until she was ready to run for president. In October 2006 her campaign spokesman admitted the story was a hoax, or in her words, a "sweet family story her mother shared to inspire greatness in her daughter." What's worse—lying or blaming your mother?

As a United States senator, Hillary dropped another fictitious family story on the press. On NBC's *Dateline*, Senator Hillary

Clinton reported that Chelsea was near danger the morning of September 11:

> "She had gone on what she thought would be a great jog," Hillary explained. "She was going down to Battery Park, she was going to go around the Towers. She was going to get a cup of coffee and that's when the plane hit. . . . She did hear it. She did."
>
> "At that moment, she was not just a senator, but a concerned parent," the *Today* show's Katie Couric told viewers.

A few weeks later, an article appeared in *Talk* magazine in which Chelsea described where she was the morning of September 11. It was nowhere near the Towers, and bore no resemblance to what Hillary reported earlier on NBC. Chelsea was alone at a friend's apartment when the friend called to tell her what had happened. She then "stared senselessly at the television."[48]

Senator Hillary had lied to make herself more relevant to the day's news—much the same as she had in Nepal after she met Sir Edmund. Unfortunately, who Hillary really is doesn't seem to be good enough for her. So she lies to make it appear she is something more.

There are a few all-time classics that only Hillary could have provided.

In December 2000 Hillary was the First Lady, a senator-elect, and was putting the final touches on her $8 million book deal. Her immediate attention, however, was furnishing the two multi-million-dollar homes she now owned with Bill.

She was moving out of the White House in January and in a few weeks she would be restricted by Senate rules from taking gifts of more than $100—chump change. She came up with a two-part scheme.

First, she registered with several high-end stores and requested friends and supporters to buy her gifts. This is an accepted practice for brides-to-be, but is unconscionable for anyone else. With eight million dollars coming her way, surely she could afford to buy her own tables and chairs.

Hillary called in a few friends to help, and they in turn put out the word to all the rich and famous that Hillary would love for them to shower her with gifts before the third of January. To make it easy, the rich friends were told, Hillary had graciously listed the items she wanted at a few of her favorite shopping spots.

Hillary received china, silverware, couches, chairs, tables, lamps, sculptures, wall hangings, a television set, and a DVD player. The total value was estimated at $190,000.[49]

To further heighten the crassness of this act, Hillary requested gifts of sweaters, pantsuits, and a leather jacket. And she got them, thousands of dollars worth. It is unimaginable for a woman in her position and with her income to ask random people to buy her pantsuits.[50] Most women would prefer death.

But gifts were only going to take her so far. Those homes of hers were big and needed a lot of furniture. What's more, she had her eye on some great stuff that would be perfect in her new home in Chappaqua. Problem was, it wasn't for sale.

So she stole it.

In January 2001, Hillary began moving White House furniture to her home in New York. When the White House usher expressed concern, explaining that the items she was removing were government property, Hillary sent her personal aide, and then a lawyer from the counsel's office, to tell him otherwise. The furniture they were taking, he was told, was "the Clintons'" personal property. The intimidation worked. The usher hesitated just long enough to see the furniture head out the door and into the moving truck.

Hillary got away with $360,000 worth of White House property, including art objects, books, furniture, china, and more clothes for herself.[51]

The public outcry was deafening, and the Clintons were forced to return some of the spoils. It is anyone's guess how much they got away with. In addition, to quiet the storm created by the tacky gift scheme, they agreed to pay back $86,000 for the $190,000 worth of gifts.[52]

Hillary, of course, denied any wrongdoing. In *Living History* she writes: "The culture of investigation followed us out the door of the White House when clerical errors in the recording of gifts mushroomed into a full-blown flap, generating hundreds of news stories over several months."[53]

A few clerical errors and Hillary winds up with a fully furnished house. Dang, that's good—she is getting better every day. Imagine what she can accomplish as president . . . better not. You might not sleep.

Some suggest life has been difficult for Hillary. But, for the most part, she has brought it upon herself. Somewhere along the way Hillary decided she was different, that the rules didn't apply to her. She has developed a keen and powerful sense of entitlement, defining "hers" to be all that she wants. And from that she takes liberally.

Virtues that most of us are constantly striving to perfect in ourselves—honesty and integrity, decency and graciousness, humility and kindness—have no place in Hillary's life. Even the most basic standards of behavior—responsibility, accountability, and respect for the law—are dismissed by this woman who aspires to be our president.

Hillary worships at the altar of the elite, where the gods are education and intelligence, money and fame, power and prestige. The important people in her life, those she treats with deference or respect, belong to this class. She needs them to like her—to have them feel she is one of them.

The rest of mankind she treats like pawns on a chessboard. Their lives have no intrinsic value; she will use them, abuse them, discard them, or destroy them—whatever best suits her needs. Her cause is nothing higher than herself and she does whatever is necessary to advance it, no matter the consequences to those who get in her way.

But the most revealing aspects of Hillary's character is her casual relationship with the truth. It is as no more than a menu item—she may order it today or she may not be in the mood. Hillary lies, changes lies, denies lies, justifies lies, and lies about lies. She lies to anyone and to everyone, under pressure, under oath, or casually, for any reason or for no reason. Lying has become central to her ability to communicate.

In 1999, *New York Times* columnist Maureen Dowd wrote: "[Americans] have lost all hope of getting any shred of authenticity from either Bill or Hillary—unless it's the authenticity of the deluded. They have chosen tactics over truth with such consistency that it's impossible to accept anything they say."

Hillary's character is not a pretty sight. In stride she can lie, cheat, steal, commit perjury, obstruct justice, malign reputations, and destroy the lives of innocent people. Driven by ambition, arrogance, greed, elitism, power, and entitlement, Hillary's road to the top has been a bloody one. Reputations and lives of real people have been left in the dirt along the way. But it has worked for Hillary. She made it to the top—and may do so again.

Chapter Three

The Woman Who Would Be President

The permanent temptation of life is to confuse dreams with reality. The permanent defeat of life comes when dreams are surrendered to reality.

—James Michener

THE FIRST HALF OF OUR TASK is complete. We have answered the questions: "Who is the real Hilary Rodham Clinton?" and "Can she be trusted, her word be believed?" The picture is not a pretty one but it is one that she painted all by herself. On the bright side, Hillary is a competent, ambitious, hardworking woman with a quick and curious mind. But she is also a calculating, controlling, power-driven, insecure personality not limited by principles, ideals, or values. In short, she will do anything, say anything, and be anything to attain the goals to which she has set her mind.

Hillary was once a passionate liberal, a left-wing devotee, a radical feminist, and an antiwar activist. Now, forty years later, the idealism that once had a proud claim on her heart seems all but gone. The same is true of the many causes that once defined her. They have been replaced, for the most part, by a single, all-important one: herself.

Ideals, anchored by principles, create within you a passion for something good, something better, and drive you to be part of a cause bigger than yourself. This is the very essence of an activist. As nothing else can, your ideals define who you are, give you a reason to get up early in the morning and the energy to work long into the night. Hillary's early aspirations offered even more—a place of great comfort, a sense of belonging, and the thrill of a movement. What's more, she was a natural. She had found her home. Few are so fortunate.

But some years back, in a Faustian bargain, Hillary bartered it all away—sold the very contents of her heart—for a pint of power.

In November 2006, Joshua Green, senior editor of *The Atlantic*, observed: "However flawed Clinton's health care plan was in execution, it was undergirded by an element of sincere idealism that is all but absent from her Senate record. . . . Today Clinton offers no big ideas, no crusading causes—by her own tacit admission, no evidence of bravery in the service of a larger ideal. . . . Her main accomplishment in the Senate has been to rehabilitate the image and political career of Hillary Rodham Clinton." Green concludes that, "Senator Clinton has plenty to talk about, but she doesn't have much to say."[1]

I often wonder if Hillary has regrets as she looks back at the wide-eyed liberal and remembers all that passion that flowed though her veins, all the excitement of the cause. I wonder if she regrets trading it all in for fame and power. And as I wonder, I also hope that somewhere in her heart she has a place that's full of joy. It is too heartbreaking to think that after having given up so much and come so far she might not have picked up a bit of peace along the way.

"Back to Her Old Habits"

We have proved beyond a reasonable doubt, and described in great detail, the character of the woman who became the junior senator from New York in January 2001. But the question is: Has she changed? Is the lady running for president this same person? In many ways it doesn't seem so. But let me assure you, it is. While the old gal has been out of sight, our memories have faded, and the extreme makeover has been doing its job—putting a far more pleasant woman in our line of vision. Nonetheless the old gal is there.

The evidence is ample—Hillary is the same today as she was yesterday. It's not from lack of trying—the makeover team has been working overtime to sweeten and soften her—but they haven't laid a glove on her true nature.

In her first Senate campaign Hillary assumed a kinder, more caring persona—one befitting a candidate doing a statewide "listening tour." The press raved that the First Lady had come into her own. But within weeks of the election the old Hillary was back, soliciting $190,000 worth of gifts from her rich friends and making off with the White House furniture.

After traveling for months on the campaign trail, Michael Tomasky of *New York* magazine commented, "I watched [Hillary] go from a lousy politician to a pretty good one. But then she went back to her old habits."[2]

The old gal is always there, because that's who she really is. Her handlers can dress her up and take her out—but they can't take the Hillary out of Hillary.

In *Living History* Senator Hillary writes, "[Pakistan's prime minister Benazir] Bhutto acknowledged the difficulties faced by women who were breaking with tradition and taking leading roles in public life. She deftly managed to refer both to the challenges I had encountered during my White House tenure and to her own situation. 'Women who take on tough issues and stake out new territory are often on the receiving end of ignorance.'"[3]

There she is again—in all her arrogance. Even after deep reflection, which is often associated with writing one's memoirs, Hillary doesn't budge an inch. It's still the same angry feminist taking no responsibility for her scandal-scarred life. All the fault lies with the insidious investigators, the agenda-driven prosecutors, and, of course, the vast right wing. She was a victim, yada, yada, yada, paying the price for offering a nation bold female leadership—just an American-born Joan of Arc.

But it is fitting that Hillary chose Bhutto to be her soul mate in this common struggle. After Mrs. Bhutto's government was dismissed for corruption and her husband jailed for the same, she was convicted of laundering millions of dollars that had found their way into her personal Swiss account. When caught red-handed Benazir denied all wrongdoing. Two peas in a pod.[4]

On to another one of her personality traits: her compulsion to lie. You might ask, is there any chance that once she was out from under the pressure of the White House, and had a prestigious seat at the table of one hundred, that she would try to break this addiction? Answer: nope, none.

It was as a sitting U.S. senator from New York that Hillary went on national news and made up the story about her daughter's near-death experience on September 11. Okay, maybe this was just a momentary lapse—recovery is a long, hard road, you might suggest, setbacks are to be expected.

But then she writes *Living History* and crushes that theory with one whopper after another. Most glaring was her inane insistence that Bill never lied to her before the Monica incident. She writes that she believed him when he told her Monica was just "an intern he had befriended . . . that she had asked him for some job-hunting help." She then drops: "This was completely in character for Bill." So was something else, Hillary, something a whole lot more interesting from Bill's perspective. Her position is so ridiculously far-fetched, it is difficult to comprehend why she would even suggest it.

As if this weren't enough, she adds that she believed her husband "when he told me there was no truth to the charges [about Monica],"[5] and that she had no idea of Bill's true relationship with

Monica until seven months *after* it broke on national news.[6] We know she isn't such a fool as to have believed him—does she take us for such fools as to believe her? She does—and she will every time she lies.

In fairness, Hillary has cleaned up her act on at least one front since becoming senator. There have been only two scandals since she left the White House, and only one is not resolved. The first, in which Hillary hauled the White House furniture out with the family photos, was covered in the previous chapter.

The other dates back to her first Senate campaign but is still making its way through the courts. It concerns Peter Paul, a wealthy Hollywood supporter.

Paul claims that in 2000 the Clintons asked him to help Hillary raise money for her Senate campaign. He agreed on one condition—that Bill become a sort of "goodwill ambassador" for his media company when Bill left office, for which the former president would be handsomely compensated.[7]

According to Paul, the Clintons directed him to bankroll a lavish Hollywood gala designed to benefit Hillary's Senate effort and the Democratic Party. It failed miserably as a fund-raiser. Had her campaign paid its share of the cost, as is legally required, the press would have written "Hillary goes to Hollywood and gets soaked." But the Clintons couldn't have that. So Paul picked up the tab—estimated at upwards of a million dollars—to give the event the appearance of success, which constituted a substantial illegal contribution to her campaign. Paul kept his part of the deal—Bill reneged on his. In January 2007, a civil lawsuit was filed by Paul alleging Hillary engaged in criminal misconduct; specifically, that she knowingly accepted his incredibly generous illegal contribution.[8]

It should be noted that Peter Paul is "a thrice convicted felon who pleaded guilty in March [of 2005] to securities fraud charges."[9] In addition Hillary claims to have no memory of any agreement with Paul, and she denies any prior knowledge of the illegal transaction.

You can almost see the old Hillary lurking in the shadows of this fiasco. It has all the markings of her Arkansas deals—a shady partner, a shadier financial deal, denial, and no recall. It is a formula that has never failed her.

But if Paul isn't telling the truth, what are we to believe? That a Hollywood con man illegally dropped a million dollars on Hillary's campaign because he believes in good government?

Either way, the FEC fined Hillary's New York Senate 2000 organization $35,000 for improperly reporting the money spent on the fund-raiser.

One more familiar detail: Paul has been relentless in exposing Hillary's role in the deal, naming her in two civil lawsuits and ratting her out to authorities. He even launched a website called "Hold Hillary Accountable." Good luck, pal.

Madam President, Who's in Charge Today?

Hillary has a history of dependence on gurus, one loonier than the next. While this has been a terrific source of entertainment, the laughing stops if and when Hillary is sworn in as president of the United States. She will have gurus—this much is certain. She can't function without them. The critical question is, of course, who they will be. They could have tremendous influence over the direction of the nation, far more than the usual array of presidential advisors. Americans need to know who these people will be before they cast their votes—but how can America know when Hillary doesn't?

Come January 2009, however, if Hillary is successful they'll all be lining up for auditions—every one of them claiming they can help Hillary find the true meaning of life. And there'll be policy gurus as well—each with a bright new way for government to step in and remold our lives. And then there will be Bill. I wonder if he'll be asked to audition. Or will he be the master guru?

Bottom line: can Americans risk putting our future in the hands of someone who agreed to converse with the dead at the suggestion of a friendly psychic?

Unfit to Serve

If Joshua Green, senior editor of *The Atlantic*, is correct, and I believe he is, the primary purpose of Hillary's stint in the U.S. Senate was to rehabilitate her image for a presidential run in 2008. While not necessarily in the interest of good government, it is not all that unusual. Politics breeds opportunists, and for the most part these philosophically unconnected human beings can consume their polls and adjust accordingly, virtually without notice.

But Hillary is not just any politician—she is a superstar. The expectations that followed her into the Senate chambers were unrealistically high, which in turn made her subsistence-level performance all the more evident. Her self-proclaimed "school of smaller steps"[10] impressed no one, disappointed many, and led to an embarrassingly shallow legislative record. Hillary as a senator did little more than fill the seat.

Then came the war. Initially it worked perfectly into Hillary's grand plan, providing her with a quick and easy means of gaining the coveted national security credentials she needed. But Hillary's two-step between supporting the war and then repudiating President Bush's conduct of it in an effort to appease her left-wing anti-war base has been clumsy at best.

The critical question is: can Hillary handle the enormous responsibility that falls squarely and entirely on the shoulders of the commander in chief? And to anyone who answers "yes" to this question—give me one time when Hillary has accepted full responsibility for anything she has ever done. And if she can't accept responsibility, how can Americans place the lives of our young men and women in her hands? This point goes to character, not policy.

Returning again to Joshua Green's interview with the senator four years after she voted for war, we find his words: "I asked whether Bush's decision to go to war was really something she didn't expect at that time. 'Well, I've said that he "misused" the authority granted to him.'" Green continues: "Most people correctly foresaw the vote as authorization for Bush to invade Iraq. Did she really mean to suggest she had not been among them? 'Well, I think that's correct.'"[11]

But here are the facts. A heated national debate preceded the vote, with the antiwar voices from the Left and the Right, demanding the president seek congressional authority before proceeding. He did so. He took his case to Congress and they gave him the authority he needed. The measure was entitled, "A Joint Resolution to Authorize the Use of United States Armed Forces Against Iraq." Nothing ambiguous about it—and Hillary voted for it.

Now Hillary claims she didn't believe that she was voting for war—that is a lie. She doesn't have the courage to defend her vote or the courage to call it a mistake—she wants to blame it on someone else. He "misled" me—it's all his fault.

But the bravery and sacrifice of our soldiers—over three thousand of whom gave their lives—demands more from our leaders, especially those who would be president. Whether President Bush's decision was right or wrong, wise or foolish, he has always accepted full responsibility for it. For this much, he must be commended.

Hillary, on the other hand, accepts no responsibility. She is, therefore, not fit to serve, unqualified to command, and not worthy to be the commander in chief of our fine young men and women. It's about character.

Chapter Four

The Rebirth of Princess Peacenik

Now that we have a firm fix on who Hillary really is, it is time to turn our attention to what it is she really believes. The next four chapters are dedicated to just that.

Like many of her generation, Hillary Clinton started her political life as a peace advocate. During the Vietnam War era, her opposition to U.S. intervention in that country was a marked part of her political identity. In her memoirs, she writes, "It's hard to explain to young Americans today, especially with an all-volunteer military, how obsessed many in my generation were with the Vietnam War."[1]

This obsession, however, was not rooted in moral outrage, or high principle of any sort, according to her own analysis. On the contrary, it was inextricably tied to the draft—not the idea of conscription per se, but the likelihood of being called up. "We had long conversations about what we would do if we were men," Hillary recounts, "knowing full well we didn't have to face the same choices. It was agonizing for everyone." They didn't call it the Me Generation for nothing: it wasn't the fate of South Vietnam, or the millions slaughtered in the killing fields of Southeast Asia, or principled opposition to interventionism as a policy, but naked self-interest that governed the passions of Hillary and her fellow antiwar activists.[2]

It wasn't about foreign policy, it was all about them—Hillary and her generational cohorts. She complains that "some contemporary writers have tried to dismiss the anguish of those years as an embodiment of 1960s self-indulgence." Yet her own words are a convincing testimony that those fellows were on to something.[3]

Yes, she's right that "Vietnam mattered, and it changed the country forever," but the question is: Why did it matter? Was it because of the millions killed and thousands jailed after the Communist takeover of South Vietnam, Laos, and Cambodia? The tragic loss of tens of thousands of American soldiers and uncounted Vietnamese? Or is it just because the nonexistent moral choices faced by Hillary and the gals at Wellesley were so "agonizing"?

This approach to foreign affairs—and political questions in general—becomes apparent in Hillary's chameleon-like opportunism. A classic example is her complete flip on the Palestinian question.

Speaking to a youth summit of the Seeds of Peace group in May 1998, Hillary laid out her vision for the future of the Middle East: "It would be in the long-term interests of peace in the Middle East for there to be a state of Palestine...a functioning modern state that is on the same footing as other states." The White House raced to clarify the remarks as Hillary's own, not the administration's position—she had moved across the line and they weren't ready to follow.[4]

It was a bold step for the First Lady and she wasn't backing down, at least not yet. Several months later while attending a meeting of the Palestinian National Council, Hillary praised

■ The case of Billy Dale and the White House travel office showed how Hillary was willing to destroy the lives of innocents to get her way.

■ Spiritual guru Jean Houston, the New Age psychic who helped Hillary communicate with the dead.

▪ Bill and Hillary: Love at first sight?

▪ Keep an eye on your back, Obama...

© REUTERS/CORBIS

■ a) "I'm serious."   b) "I'm nice."   c) "I'm Lady Di."   d) "I'm smart."

© THIERRY ORBAN/CORBIS SYGMA

■ e) "I'm French."

■ Hillary graduates from Wellesley College after delivering the first of many incoherent speeches.

■ Hillary unveils her plan for socializing American medicine.

- Hillary claimed she was named after Sir Edmund Hillary. Only problem was Sir Edmund Hillary was only a beekeeper when Hillary was born. He didn't climb Mount Everest until Hillary was six years old.

- While she was still "for" the war, Hillary visited American troops in Iraq to beef up her presidential credentials.

■ "The kiss carried 'round the world." Hillary kissing Suha Arafat after Suha claimed Israel was poisoning Palestinian children.

■ Hillary plots her changing course on Iraq.

■ Hillary has faced many scandals. Here, the investigators were closing in—her lies were catching up with her during Whitewater, 1996.

To Michael Lerner with appreciation for your commitment to meaningful political change ~ Hillary Rodham Clinton

■ Hillary and guru Michael Lerner "creating a new language" together.

Hillary Rodham Clinton

■ Even on her signature issue, health care, Hillary remains the perpetual student, parroting the lines of others.

Yasser Arafat's leadership and again called for the establishment of an independent Palestinian state.[5]

As one would expect, the Palestinian Authority was thrilled to have her support. Their minister of health, Dr. Riad Zanoun, found an occasion to publicly praise Hillary for her courageous remarks to the youth group: "Mrs. Clinton, our first lady, a great lady," he said, "I would like to remind you of the words you have spoken and that have entered into the hearts of every Palestinian."[6] But this love affair could last only so long. Hillary had her eye on a U.S. Senate seat opening up in New York, a state where 12 percent of the voters are Jewish. It took a kiss carried around the world to teach Hillary the error of her ways.

In November 1999 while traveling in the Middle East, Hillary had a joint appearance with Yasser Arafat's wife, Suha. With Hillary sitting next to her on the stage, Mrs. Arafat took the occasion to accuse Israel of poisoning her people. "Our [Palestinian] people have been submitted to the daily intensive use of poisonous gas by the Israeli forces," she said, "which have led to an increase in cancer cases among women and children."[7] It was an outlandish accusation, but it didn't stop Hillary from giving Suha a hug and a kiss when she finished talking.

The New York press was on the story before nightfall. Hillary's press secretary, Marsha Berry, initially dismissed Suha's comments as "a local issue" and doubted the First Lady would be responding further. It was local all right—New York local. Jewish leaders back home were furious, forcing Hillary to issue a delayed statement that was remarkably lame: "I do not believe any kind of inflammatory rhetoric or baseless charges are good for the peace process."[8]

Roll forward eight short months. Hillary, now a candidate for the U.S. Senate, called for moving the U.S. embassy in Israel from Tel Aviv to Jerusalem, "the eternal and indivisible capital of Israel," adding it should be done by year's end.[9] When the Camp

David peace talks collapsed, she released this statement: "It must be clear that any unilateral declaration of Palestinian statehood would be entirely unacceptable and should be met with a cutoff of United States assistance."[10] It was an impressive reversal for its speed and thoroughness, if nothing else. Hillary now belonged to another—"Israel's cause is our cause," she is quoted as saying.[11]

Some, however, were not convinced her change of heart was entirely sincere. "I would believe what she said before," said Najat Arafat Khelil, national president of the Palestinian American Congress. "Now she is pandering and she's looking for votes."[12] Bull's-eye.

From Peacenik to Warrior Princess

Hillary's most significant political asset may indeed be her endless capacity for adaptation. When antiwar protests were all the rage, there she was in the front ranks. But when the political atmosphere underwent a sea change, she turned with the rest of them, eventually striking a pose as a virtual Amazon in the realm of foreign policy. This is the politics of self-regard. Hers is a credo to fit the times: if she ever establishes her own political party, its symbol will be a weathervane.

"You don't need a weatherman to know which way the wind blows," went the old Weatherman Underground Organization slogan, ripping off lyrics from Bob Dylan's "Subterranean Homesick Blues," and yet Hillary developed this ability in a far different manner than her New Left radical counterparts in the student movement of the 1960s. Most of the "revolutionary" wing of the New Left eventually either blew themselves up in a bombing mishap in a Greenwich Village townhouse or degenerated into a criminal gang. The more respectable ones of this leftist movement, Hillary being one, geared up for a long march through the institutions. In her memoirs, she is insistent that her basic disagreement with New Left radicals was that she believed it was possible to work within the system, while Saul Alinsky, the professional left-wing agitator—and the subject of her senior thesis—preached change must come from the outside.[13]

That didn't stop Hillary from vicariously enjoying the "revolution" from the sidelines though, as when she and a friend went to gawk at the 1968 Chicago riots. She recounts in her memoir that a thrown rock barely missed her head, and yet a few paragraphs later she testifies at being "shocked" by "police brutality" she saw that day.[14] Doubt it was a policeman who nearly beaned her with that rock.

As a congressional intern, Hillary went to Capitol Hill a budding McGovernite Democrat, though she was assigned to Republican minority leader Gerald Ford. During this time she had the opportunity to discuss the Vietnam War with Congressman Melvin Laird. "In the meeting with interns," she recalls, "he justified American involvement and advocated vigorously for greater military force. When he stopped for questions, I echoed President Eisenhower's caution about American involvement in land wars in Asia and asked him why he thought this strategy could ever succeed."[15]

It was not long after Hillary memorialized this "heated exchange"[16] with the congressman that she was doing the same as he had done—voting for war in a faraway land and vigorously defending it against a chorus of criticism from the Left. Unlike Laird though, when that chorus became increasingly louder, Hillary joined it.

Her quest for insider status has taken Hillary on a journey from one extreme to another when it comes to foreign policy. More precisely, she has shifted from an explicitly anti-interventionist position to one that could be called neoconservative—especially when it comes to the vital question of war and peace in the Middle East.

This reversal of perspective is starkly dramatized in her memoirs when she expresses her horror at the death of four students gunned down by National Guardsmen at Kent State. The famous photo of a woman holding the body of one of the young victims had a profound effect on Hillary: it "represented all that I and many others feared and hated about what was happening to our country."[17]

No doubt. Yet one might then wonder how she felt about the equally infamous photos of Waco set afire as a result of orders from her husband's attorney general. It was a slightly different take. Concerning that fiery massacre that took some eighty lives, including those of nearly two dozen children, she wrote of the "regret we all felt over the violence and death caused by a perversion of religion."[18] Perversion of religion didn't kill those kids! And Hillary knows it—but she wasn't about to hold the Clinton administration responsible, not even in the slightest way. Most would argue that however justified the government's fifty-one-day siege of the Branch Davidian compound might have been, some terrible miscalculation was made that allowed it to end so tragically. Hillary is open to no such consideration and, of course, makes no mention of the several pyrotechnic tear gas canisters tossed into the compound by the FBI before they bulldozed it with tanks.[19] Does indeed suggest a hardening of the heart, and spirit, of the former flower child.

Hillary out of power was one thing; Hillary in power was quite another. Gone were the moral compunctions of the peace activist who heckled her elders for fighting Communism in Vietnam. In fact, the only remnant of the passionate antiwar activist is a tone of self-righteousness that tolerates no hesitancies or subtleties. In her new incarnation as Warrior Goddess, there are no shades of gray—a dangerous outlook.

Hillary had Bill's ear during his presidency, perhaps much to his chagrin, and her aggressiveness in manner was matched by her policy prescriptions. As Gail Sheehy reported:

On March 21, 1999, Hillary expressed her views by phone to the president: "I urged him to bomb." The Clintons argued the issue over the next few days. [The president expressed] what-ifs: What if bombing promoted more executions? What if it took apart the NATO alliance? Hillary responded, "You cannot let this go on at the end of a century that has seen the major holocaust of our time. What do we have NATO for if not to defend our way of life?" The next day the president declared that force was necessary.[20]

The former peacenik who quailed when Richard Nixon bombed Hanoi was reborn, on account of her ascension to power, as a left-wing Amazon. She deserted the antiwar crowd right away. In order to justify the war, its advocates utilized hyperbole as their primary weapon, exaggerating the extent of the "ethnic cleansing" undertaken by Serbs and overlooking similar "cleansings" undertaken by the Croats and the Bosnian Muslims, our allies in the region. Hillary went so far as to liken what was happening in the former Yugoslavia to the Holocaust—an outrageous assertion that minimizes the scale and the unique evil of Hitler's horrible crime.[21]

It was necessary to bomb Serbian cities, Hillary explained in a 1999 speech delivered in Marrakech, Morocco, because of an alleged "campaign of massive and systematic destruction" being carried out by Belgrade. After the war, however, there was no sign of massive "genocide." The reality was that the number killed in the former Yugoslavia's civil war totaled less than ten thousand, including Serbs, Croats, and Gypsies as well as Kosovars.[22] This glorious "victory," so often cited by Hillary as the exemplar of her brand of "humanitarian" interventionism, succeeded in driving out the few remaining Serbs and setting up a gangster state in the heart of Europe, where weapons of any sort are readily available and where radical Islamists have established a foothold.[23] In 2006, James Bisset, the former Canadian ambassador to Yugoslavia, described the situation in Kosovo this way: "[it is] the main hub on the continent for heroin and human trafficking into Western

Europe, living standards are comparable to those of Haiti, abductions and murders of non-Albanians citizens happen on a daily basis, and civil society is practically non-existent."[24] An interesting success story, wouldn't you say?

As troubling as the Kosovo postwar findings were, Hillary's bombing campaign wasn't followed by a vigorous debate over faulty prewar information or the possibility of having been misled and having rushed to judgment. Hillary reserves that kind of criticism for another president, as we will see later in this chapter. But those seventy-eight days of dropping bombs from high above Kosovo had a lasting effect on Hillary—she felt the power of the military and she loved it.

In an interview with CNN's Wolf Blitzer, she proclaimed that Democrats do war better than Republicans, boasting "we didn't lose a single American military person" during the Kosovo war. "I resent it when Republicans say that they're better on national defense," she told Blitzer. "It was Democratic presidents who prosecuted the wars that were successful in this past century."[25]

But does America want a president who boasts that her party is better at war? What kind of recommendation is that?

Hillary's entire approach to the realm of foreign affairs has no doubt been colored by her presidential ambitions—and by her sex. There is an underlying concern among voters that a woman might not function well as commander in chief of our armed forces. Hillary was determined to convince them otherwise—at least in her case. It has, perhaps, caused her to err on the side of military activism. This in turn has led to a bit of trouble with her left-wing base, when back in October 2002, she said regarding Iraq:

In the four years since the inspectors left, intelligence reports show that Saddam Hussein has worked to rebuild his chemical and biological weapons stock, his missile delivery capability, and his nuclear program. He has also given aid, comfort, and sanctuary to terrorists, including al Qaeda members.... Left unchecked, Saddam Hussein will continue to increase his capacity to wage biological and chemical warfare, and will keep trying to develop nuclear weapons.[26]

She then voted for war.

When questions about the presence of Iraqi WMDs surfaced, Hillary stated, "[Saddam Hussein] was seeking weapons of mass destruction, whether or not it ever turns out he actually had them."[27] She stood her ground. As she explained to Larry King in 2004, the information about the weapons of mass destruction, indeed, about the overall threat Saddam Hussein posed "was the same, from the Clinton administration to the Bush administration. It was the same intelligence belief that all our allies and friends around the world shared."[28]

After two years of war Hillary was still bullish. In February 2005 she visited Iraq with a five-member congressional delegation, where the war-torn country was experiencing some of the deadliest suicide bombings to date. Again, she didn't hesitate. The attacks, she said, were a sign the insurgency was failing, as "you can look at the country as a whole and see that there are many parts of Iraq that are functioning quite well."[29]

It is worth noting that these remarks came in the wake of the much-touted Iraqi elections. The media was hyping the "purple finger" for all it was worth. The war was still popular in America.

Later that same month she was selling her wares on *Meet the Press*: "It is not in America's interests for the Iraqi government, the experiment in freedom and democracy, to fail." As for troop withdrawal, "That would be a mistake," she told Tim Russert. "I don't believe we should tie our hands or the hands of the new Iraqi government." Her position was "stay the course"—just like George W. Bush.[30]

Hillary's military assessment, however, was dead wrong. The war wasn't going well. In fact, the situation on the ground was deteriorating daily. Public support waned and dissent grew, especially among Democrats. Hillary had hit her stride as Queen of Hawkland, but now the times were a' changing. With her future in mind, she began to dance, first slowly, then in complete turns, until she was nearly back in the arms of her Democratic left-wing base.

Before we follow her down the twisty road toward political realignment, let's first examine just how deeply enmeshed in the war game Hillary was.

Embracing War

The speech Hillary gave on the floor of the Senate prior to her vote in favor of the war resolution is a classic. Hillary, Student Extraordinaire, was back in all her glory, complete with analysis and critique.

First, she cites the facts that "brought us to this fateful day." Second, she analyzes the plan of action others have proposed, pointing out their weaknesses. Third, she offers a suggestion that can offend no one. Fourth, she warns that once bombs begin dropping bad things can happen. Fifth, she gives three reasons for voting "yes." Next she lists what she claims are things she isn't voting for, but in reality is. Then she closes her statement with this sentence: "Saddam Hussein—this is your last chance—disarm or be disarmed." The cowboy in the White House couldn't have said it any better.

A closer look at her speech reveals just how committed Hillary was to the war when the country supported it.

The facts that she laid out in her remarks for why the country must go to war were the same ones President Bush offered. She commented on the atrocities of Saddam Hussein, cited his chemical and biological weapons, his nuclear program, and mentioned the aid and sanctuary he has provided to terrorists, including al Qaeda. She repeatedly stated that these facts are "not in doubt." She then added, "It is clear, however, that if left unchecked, Saddam Hussein will continue to increase his capacity to wage biological and chemical warfare, and will keep trying to develop nuclear weapons.... Now this much is undisputed."[31]

Contrast that statement with what she said four years later when the war was no longer popular: "I feel like he misled the Congress and the country.... I believe you could have taken the major players in this drama and they would have passed polygraphs about what they believed the threat was, because they were so obsessed with what [Saddam Hussein] had done, and the potential for what he could do."[32] She could have been one of those players!

Next in her floor speech, Hillary takes credit for her role in moving the nation toward the policy of regime change in Iraq. "In 1998 [during the Clinton years], the United States also changed its underlying policy toward Iraq from containment to regime change and began to examine options to effect such a change, including support for Iraqi opposition leaders within the country and abroad."[33]

She is referring to the Iraq Liberation Act, which was ushered into law by her husband. It set the process of "regime change" in motion and led directly to the misinformation Hillary claimed to be "undisputed." While Hillary has earned her place among the best when it comes to mental gymnastics, even with her ideological flexibility it would be nearly impossible to reconcile her support for this act and her subsequent outbursts against the Bush administration for misleading her about the war.

It worked like this: the Iraq Liberation Act appropriated funds to opposition groups such as Ahmed Chalabi's Iraqi National Congress (INC). Chalabi and his gang funneled intelligence to the White House and Congress while on the U.S. payroll to the tune of $240 million. It is this very intelligence which Hillary now decries as false.

While the attempt to effect "regime change" originated, in part, from the first Bush administration, the effort didn't really mature until the Clinton years. The Clintons supported the idea whole-heartedly. When the Iraq Liberation Act was passed with the full approval of Hillary and her husband, Chalabi thanked the authors for bestowing American largesse on the INC:

Today, October 31, 1998, is a great day for the Iraqi people. Today President Clinton signed into law the Iraq Liberation Act of 1998. The American people have given their support for the end of dictatorship and for democracy in Iraq.

The INC welcomes this courageous and historic action by President Clinton and thanks him for it. I will begin immediate consultations with leaders in the INC and others to work for a united response on how best to take advantage of the provisions of the Iraq Liberation Act. We will present a united front to maximize the chances of success. We look to President Clinton to support and work with a united INC to achieve our common goals.[34]

Funds began to flow into the coffers of Chalabi and his cronies, and the INC came into its own as a formidable lobby. Jane Mayer pointed out in the *New Yorker*:

In 1994 and 1995, Robert Baer, the former CIA officer, met Chalabi several times in Kurdistan, in northern Iraq, an autonomous area protected from Saddam by the United States. Chalabi had established an outpost in Kurdistan. "He was like the American ambassador to Iraq," Baer recalled. "He could get to the White House and the CIA. He would move around Iraq with five or six Land Cruisers."

Hundreds of thousands of dollars were flowing each month "to this shadowy operator—in cars, salaries—and it was just a Potemkin village. He was reporting no intel; it was total trash. The INC's intelligence was so bad, we weren't even sending it in."[35]

Consider these facts as you read a few comments she made when the war was no longer popular. In 2005 Hillary wrote: "I...expect the President and his Administration to take responsibility for the false assurances, faulty evidence...."[36] Then in 2006 she told a group of Princeton students: "It will not further our common goals or our American ideals if we veer from evidence-based decision-making, substituting instead ideology and arrogance."[37] It's the old gal herself.

For Hillary to complain about "false" and "misleading" intelligence after she and her husband helped build this network of deception is to reach new heights of hypocrisy. But then she probably holds the old record. Or do you think she could have forgotten how "not in doubt" and "indisputed" she claimed the evidence was when she voted for war? Oh, that's right, she was "misled." You think that's like being "brainwashed"?

Back to her floor speech.

Hillary praised dissent as "central to our freedom and to our progress, for on more than one occasion, history has proven our great dissenters to be right." It was more gratuitous than anything else—a crumb thrown in memory of her antiwar days, because when it came right down to it she moved along, leaving the dissenters to fend for themselves.

While criticizing the "unilateralism" of the Bush administration and taking credit for authoring the policy of "regime change," the senator from New York declared that she was going to cast "the hardest vote" of her life in favor of the resolution. Like a professor lecturing a class about the intricacies of U.S. foreign policy, she carefully wends her way between two positions and winds up embracing neither.

On the one hand, there are the "unilateralists," who want us to "gather such allies as we can" and launch an immediate strike. The only problem, according to Hillary, was, "If we were to attack Iraq now, alone or with few allies, it would set a precedent that could come back to haunt us. In recent days, Russia has talked of an invasion of Georgia to attack Chechen rebels. India has mentioned the possibility of a pre-emptive strike on Pakistan. And what if China were to perceive a threat from Taiwan?"

Hillary's analysis of costs and benefits, however, never considered the problems we actually now have in Iraq, such as civil war, the breakup of the country, or the possible destabilization of the region.

On the other hand, continued the senator, "others argue that we should work through the United Nations and should only resort to force if and when the United Nations Security Council approves it." This argument has "great appeal," Hillary explains, "but there are problems with this approach as well." The UN, you see, "is still growing and maturing" and "often lacks the cohesion to enforce its own mandates. And when Security Council members use the veto, on occasion, for reasons of narrow-minded interests, it cannot act. In Kosovo, the Russians did not approve NATO military action because of political, ethnic, and religious ties to the Serbs." Those "narrow-minded interests" to which Hillary so contemptuously referred are known as national sovereignty and national interests. In her view, it is unfortunate that the UN hasn't "matured" into a one-world government so it could impose its will on all its member nations, including good old Uncle Sam.

So what are we to do, Hillary? We can't go with the unilateralists because it could set a bad precedent, and we can't go with the multilaterals because those obstructionist Russians might vote "Nyet!"

Having assessed the other options, Hillary offered one of her own:

> I believe the best course is to go to the UN for a strong resolution that scraps the 1998 restrictions on inspections and calls for complete, unlimited inspections with cooperation expected and demanded from Iraq. I know that the administration wants more, including an explicit authorization to use force, but we may not be able to secure that now, perhaps even later. But if we get a clear requirement for unfettered inspections, I believe the authority to use force to enforce that mandate is inherent in the original 1991 UN resolution, as President Clinton recognized when he launched Operation Desert Fox in 1998.[38]

Let me get this right. To deal with Saddam Hussein, who in her own words is a "real threat to his people, to the region, including Israel, to the Untied States, to the world,"[39] Hillary insists we to go to the UN to get a new resolution, so we look like we asked permission. But if they won't authorize force, and they won't, we should take a watered-down resolution and then we can invade anyway—the old resolution of 1991 allows it. That's her plan? And she wants to be president?

Then she warns us, "After shots are fired and bombs are dropped, not all consequences are predictable."[40] This has got to be another classic. Hillary is about to vote for war but even before the vote she is providing herself cover from any responsibility related to the vote—wars are unpredictable, you know.

Then for additional coverage she gives us another statement of non-responsibility:

> My vote is not, however, a vote for any new doctrine of preemption, or for unilateralism, or for the arrogance of American power or purpose—all of which carry grave dangers for our

nation, for the rule of international law and for the peace and security of people throughout the world.[41]

But a "new doctrine of pre-emptive war" and "unilaterism" is exactly what she voted for! And Hillary knows it—she is just building her "it's not my fault" defense in the event the war doesn't go as planned.

The old gal was in good form that day—the master of equivocation, rationalization, and evasion at her best. But Hillary undeniably voted for war with Iraq, and did so "with conviction." Her statements of unequivocal support of President Bush's pre-emptive, unilateral strike against Iraq lasted for three years and only add to the evidence. Consider a few.

December 2003, nine months into the war and no WMDs have been found: "I was one who supported giving President Bush the authority, if necessary, to use force against Saddam Hussein. I believe that that vote was the right vote," she said to the Council on Foreign Relations. "This will not be an easy undertaking. It will require patience, and it will require continuing support of the American people . . . since failure is not an option."[42]

April 2004, thirteen months into war and no WMDs have been found, CNN's Larry King asks her if she regrets her war vote: "Obviously, I've thought about that a lot in the months since," she said. "No, I don't regret giving the president authority because at the time it was in the context of weapons of mass destruction, grave threats to the United States, and clearly, Saddam Hussein had been a real problem for the international community for more than a decade."[43]

February 2005, two years into the war and no WMDs have been found, and with escalating violence in Iraq and mounting questions at home: "We need to make sure that this new government in Iraq can succeed," she told Tim Russert. "There are lots of debates about whether we should have, how we should have, decisions that were made along the way with respect to our involvement here. But where we stand right now, there can be no doubt that it is not in America's interest for the Iraqi government, the experiment in freedom and democracy, to fail."[44]

Hillary remained close to her script for two and a half years—her vote was the right one, failure in Iraq was not an option, patience was needed, the road would be long, but it was in America's interests for the Iraqi government to succeed. She had all the rhetoric of a true hawk, but none of the heart. While I believe Hillary was comfortable in her new role as superhawk, this was not the cause to which Hillary was committed. It was a means by which she promoted the cause to which she was committed—the driving force behind this pro-war profile of hers was self-interest, not America's interest. Her vote and support for the war were precisely the credentials she needed to be a credible presidential candidate in 2008. But as the war grew deadlier with no end in sight, and the public grew more and more uneasy, so did Hillary.

The Retreat Begins

Small but significant cracks began to appear in Hillary's rhetoric in 2004. Forced to defend a war that was bringing home no good news, she resorted to old habits. She began to blame others for all that had gone wrong, all the while supporting the war.

In the spring of that year, while expressing "no regrets" for her vote, Hillary said she was as surprised as the rest of us when no "weapons of mass destruction" turned up in postwar Iraq: "The consensus was the same, from the Clinton administration to the Bush administration. It was the same intelligence belief that our allies and friends around the world shared. But I think that in the case of the [Bush] administration, they really believed it. They really thought they were right, but they didn't let enough sunlight into their thinking process to really have the kind of debate that needs to take place when a serious decision occurs like that."[45]

What exactly is she saying? That the Clinton administration, while endorsing the widely held assessment of Saddam's WMD capabilities, didn't really believe it? Or in the case that they did believe it, aren't they guilty of the same reluctance to "let enough sunlight into their thinking process"? And wasn't she the one who pronounced the facts "undisputed"? Perhaps all of the flip-flopping was making her dizzy.

Again in 2004, in a speech to the Brookings Institution, she pointed to "the fact that before the war actually began, many questions were raised about what would happen—what was the postwar Iraq plan? How many troops; for how long; how much; what was the nature of the mission?"

These questions were raised, all right, but not by Hillary. As we have seen, her greatest concern was to legitimize the policy—by getting a UN Security Council imprimatur on it.

By November 2005, support for the war had plummeted, especially among Democrats. Some party leaders were calling for immediate withdrawal of troops, others for a timetable. Potential 2008 presidential candidates John Kerry and John Edwards had repudiated their own pro-war votes, calling the war a mistake. Simply criticizing the president was no longer adequate for Hillary; her base was growing increasingly restless. She needed to get back in line with the weathervane—it had moved significantly since she last looked.

She spent the next year or so running away from any responsibility for her pro-war vote, putting as much distance between herself and the Bush administration's "mismanagement" of the war effort as possible.

"If Congress had been asked [to authorize the war], based on what we know now, we never would have agreed," she wrote in an e-mail to supporters. Insisting that she takes "full responsibility" for the vote, she gives any number of excuses—none of which were her fault. She was bamboozled into voting yes on account of "false" intelligence provided by the Bush administration. She believed the administration's assurances that they would try every means to disarm Iraq short of war before ordering a military assault and whines that "their assurances turned out to be empty ones."[46]

Packed with blazing criticism for President Bush, she abandons the "no regrets" column but doesn't quite join the "it was a mistake" gang. Rather than take responsibility for a policy she supported and voted for, Hillary flounders about in order to get back in line with her left-wing Democratic base. And for all the caterwauling and complaining about the Bush administration's lack of a plan, Hillary's policy prescriptions for a nation at war turn vague and contradictory:

> There are no quick and easy solutions to the long and drawn out conflict the [Bush] administration triggered. . . . I do not believe that we should allow this to be an open-ended commitment without limits or end. Nor do I believe that we can or should pull out of Iraq immediately.[47]

We know what she's against, but what's she for? What should we do? You'd have to parse all her postwar statements down to the last comma before we could glean a coherent meaning out of her various and sundry pronouncements.

Although she claimed for years she had no regrets about her vote in favor of authorizing the use of force against Iraq, by the winter of 2007 she was back on the Senate floor charging that President Bush "rushed us into war" and adamant she would never have taken us to war. "If I had been president in October of 2002," she said," I would have never asked for authority to divert our attention from Afghanistan to Iraq, and I certainly would never have started this war."[48]

Back to her floor speech for just one moment: "So it is with conviction that I support this resolution as being in the best interests of our nation. A vote for it is not a vote to rush to war; it is a vote that puts awesome responsibility in the hands of our president and we say to him: use these powers wisely and as a last resort. And it is a vote that says clearly to Saddam Hussein: this is your last chance—disarm or be disarmed."[49]

Hillary is remarkable—she is unrestrained by any previous position she has ever taken. She wakes up every morning with a completely clean slate. So which is it—was the nation rushed into war, or not? And why if she were president in 2002 would she never have asked for this vote if, as she said in 2002, it was "in the best interests of our nation"? And why in 2002 did she vote to give the president authority to go to war if, as she now says, she had been the president at the time she wouldn't have asked for the authority and certainly wouldn't have started this war? Is she saying she would have opposed herself?

"Oh! what a tangled web we weave, when first we practice to deceive." But not even Sir Walter Scott would believe this one.

Hillary found herself in the thorny position in early 2006. Politically she needed to throw aside her hawkish inclinations to appease her base. But at the same time her presidential ambitions demanded she maintain credibility as tough on national security. She laid out her "plan" in January 2006, repeating what she was against, and then in the same paragraph contradicting what she was for:

I do not believe that we should allow this to be an open-ended commitment without limits or end, nor do I believe that we can or should pull out of Iraq immediately. If last December's elections lead to a successful Iraqi government, that should allow us to start drawing down our troops during this year while leaving behind a smaller contingent in safe areas with greater intelligence and quick-strike capabilities. This will help us stabilize that new Iraqi government. It will send a message to Iran that they do not have a free hand in Iraq despite their considerable influence and personal and religious connections there. It will also send a message to Israel and our other allies, like Jordan, that we will continue to do what we can to provide the stability necessary to prevent the terrorists from getting any further foothold than they currently have.[50]

What and where are these "safe areas" she refers to—except permanent military bases in Iraq? While a full-fledged military occupation extended indefinitely isn't a viable option, in light of events, a withdrawal to bases—"safe areas"—implies a semi-permanent U.S. troop presence in the country. Does this not fall under the category of "open-ended commitment" conceivably "without limits or end" that she claims to oppose?

And Hillary conditions a troop drawdown on the creation of "a successful Iraqi government." Now that the Iraqi government has not lived up to our hopes, can one assume she opposes a drawdown now? This plan suggests the lady from New York may not be up to the job.

Hillary was forced to take another giant leap to the left when the campaign season began to pick up at the end of 2006. With her Democratic base fervently antiwar and Barack Obama stealing much of her left-wing constituency, the entire concept of responsibility—let alone consistency—was thrown to the wind, and Hillary began to reinvent herself in a hurry. Asked about her vote in favor of the war, she told an interviewer on NBC's *Today* show, "Obviously, if we knew then what we know now, there wouldn't have been a vote," adding, "and I certainly wouldn't have voted that way."

Is this not the Hillary of the past talking? Always confident when she has all the facts, but unable to make decisions when professional assessment and personal judgment are required. If only she had perfect knowledge in the run-up to war, then she would have figured it all out. I would hope so—but who has that? We expect our leaders to make sound judgments without it, and then to defend those decisions based on any number of factors. But Hillary has no interest in any of this. She's prefers lying low and waiting for the polls. "At a time when politicians in both parties have eagerly sought public forums to debate the war in Iraq," wrote Dan Balz of the *Washington Post*, "Senator Hillary Rodham Clinton has kept in the shadows."[51] Leadership is not one of her strengths.

Hillary resisted voicing any regrets about her pro-war vote for years—and yet, when the polls pointedly told her that this was and is a losing position with her Democratic constituents, she did a 180-degree turnaround without blinking an eye. But why shouldn't she? The purpose of her pro-war vote and those years of pro-war rhetoric was the extreme makeover—it required she have a pro-war profile. Then along came Obama and the makeover was forced to undergo a course adjustment, several in fact. What's a gal to do? With the makeover in charge, Hillary did what was demanded of her—she flipped and flopped and flipped some more.

Foreign Policy under President Clinton II

What would American foreign policy look like under President Hillary?

Of course, we can't say for sure: just look at George W. Bush. He came into office calling for a more "humble" foreign policy—and we got the doctrine of military preemption. Hillary's fervent followers are bound to be surprised, once she gets into office, as she reveals herself as more neoconnish than the neocons on the question of war and peace. It is where Hillary seems most comfortable since her days as co-president.

A major problem for Hillary, however, is her unique combination of ersatz "idealism" and a real arrogance. Both characteristics came into play when she tried to implement an Iraqi "oil trust" arrangement she supported as part of a solution to the disastrous situation in Iraq. The idea was to organize this "trust" around the concept of an equal distribution of oil wealth to all sectors of Iraqi society, by giving all the citizens "shares" in the black gold that constitutes that country's main source of future income. The goal is to lure the Sunnis into laying down their arms and integrating themselves into the Iraqi polity.

Her infamous arrogance was on full display in her interview with the editors of the *New York Daily News*, in which she expands on her frustration with the Iraqis over this issue:

> In the last month, I've seen the president of Iraq, I've seen the deputy prime minister of Iraq, I've communicated with our ambassador in Iraq, and I've asked the same question: "When are you going to get the oil deal done?" And I keep being told, "Oh, it's imminent. We have legislation. It's going to happen." Well, the last thing I heard is they're going to punt it for another eighteen months. That means [the fighting] will not end, on the Sunnis' end.[52]

Hillary is barking orders at the Iraqis, and when they fail to comply she is stunned. She doesn't understand what they are doing in Iraq, why they aren't falling all over themselves to implement the latest orders from the junior senator from New York. Don't they know she is Hillary Clinton and when she's issued a command she expects it will be carried out, just like when she was co-president?

Hillary seems confounded by all of this. But her approach to foreign policy will never work, not in Iraq, and not in any foreign country. Our friends and our enemies alike are looking constantly for that most offensive of all American traits, arrogance. A few directives from the old gal and all bets are off that Americans will be permitted to travel overseas.

No one expects politicians of any stripe to stand by their alleged convictions in spite of the political consequences, like Horatius at the bridge; however, to be so brazen about so utterly forgetting what one said yesterday, and so consistently unwilling to take responsibility even for such a serious matter as voting to send American troops into harm's way—that truly is irresponsible, unforgettable, unforgivable, and unpresidential.

As Hillary moves to the left in anticipation of a hard fight in the Democratic primaries, her true position remains a bit of a mystery. After all, if she is willing to give up long-standing positions in favor of what is—or seems to be—the more popular position at the time, then it is fair to ask: What does she truly believe? What does Hillary want when it comes to U.S. foreign policy? What would the Clinton restoration have in store for us in the realm of international affairs?

While her sharp political instincts enable her to pick up rather quickly on the popular mood and allow her to "reposition" herself accordingly, there is a general trend in her views on America's relationship to the rest of the world. The history of Hillary's evolution on the foreign policy issue is a journey away from her "progressive" roots—almost an act of contrition to make up for her radical past. Whether this is from conviction or purely political calculation is hard to say. And there is always the gender issue, which will almost inevitably have an impact on her stance.

As the first woman president, she would be compelled, both politically and psychologically, to prove herself a capable commander in chief of the armed forces. This kind of pressure is dangerous when applied to the one individual on earth whose hasty decision can plunge the world into disaster. For someone with that kind of power to have a need to "prove" herself is a dangerous situation indeed. This "tough" act can only distort the formulation of policy at the top, and it has every potential to wreak havoc in a realm where one false move can cost too many lives.

It is worth noting Hillary's own thoughts on the matter. "We need a tough-minded, muscular foreign policy, one that not only respects our allies and seeks new friends as it strikes at known enemies, but which is understood and supported by the majority of the American people."[53]

While "strikes at known enemies" may be a precise description of Hillary's personal and political life, it is a chilling prescription for a nation's foreign policy.

Chapter Five

Queen of the Amnesties

It was a rare moment. Hillary could have been sitting on the front steps shooting the breeze with a friend (you think she has ever done that?)—two old birds just talking:

"Neighborhood's changing, Hil."

"Sure is, El, and not for the better."

"Right about that, Hil."

"Why, have you seen all those illegal immigrants hanging around at the 7-Eleven down on Main?"

"Sure have—it's a doggone disgrace, and the government's doing nothing about it."

But Hillary wasn't on the front porch. She was talking with radio host John Gambling. "I am, you know, adamantly against illegal immigrants," Hillary said. That alone was a show stopper but she went on:

People have got to stop employing illegal immigrants. . . . I mean, come up to Westchester, go to Suffolk and Nassau counties, stand on the street corners in Brooklyn or the Bronx; you're going to see loads of people waiting to get picked up to go do yard work and construction work and domestic work.[1]

It was beautiful actually—a prominent Democrat had figured it out. She had seen what Americans see every day and she saw it the same way. Hillary was speaking the language of the millions who have had to confront the frightening reality that the massive invasion coming across our southern border had reached their communities, along with all its devastating consequences. While the words of the Left's leading lady sounded like a heartfelt response to the problems of illegal immigration, there can be no doubt it was Hillary the Politician who was behind them. Her shrewd instincts did not underestimate the power of the chord her comments would strike with the overwhelming majority of her audience.

Was it possible, though, even conceivable, that Hillary was going to wade into the heated national debate on illegal immigration on the side of the American people? Was she prepared to defy her party's leadership, as well as powerful ethnic lobbyists, corporate America, and her liberal democratic base on the most contentious domestic issue facing the country? It was a remarkable development.

After she smacked employers of illegal aliens, she went right for the throat of the second culprit, our inept federal government:

Clearly, we have to make some tough decisions as a country. And one of them ought to be coming up with a much better entry and exit system so that if we're going to let people in for the work that otherwise would not be done, let's have a system that keeps track of them.[2]

That was enough to put liberal Hillary squarely to the right of both President Bush and Senator John McCain, one of the Republican front runners for 2008. What would the red states do with a show down like this?

As the senator from New York, a state where more than 20 percent of the population is foreign-born, Hillary was surely aware of the problems posed by mass immigration.[3] But it was not until September 11, 2001, when terrorists brought down New York City's twin towers, that the issue of border security had Hillary's full attention. She saw firsthand, as did the nation, the real and immense danger America faces with her borders open to all who choose to come—for good or for evil.

In December 2001, Hillary challenged Canadian officials to "crack down on some of these false documents and illegals getting in." A year later, when investigations concluded that several of the terrorists had traveled through Canada en route to their final destination—New York City—Hillary lambasted the Canadian government for its lax border security.[4] But this was hardly noteworthy coming as it was from the senator of the state that took the brunt of that terrible day.

A side note: Hillary said she was "adamantly against illegal immigrants." While the quote was correctly repeated in a number of news outlets, the *New York Times,* making reference to it several years later, did Hillary the favor of changing it to "illegal immigration." The *Times* couldn't have Hillary saying what it would have labeled a xenophobic slur had it come from the mouth of a conservative.[5]

Hillary had no follow-up to this unusual foray into the enemy camp, and her liberal voting pattern remained unaltered. In fact, she was relatively silent on the topic for the better part of two years. It is unclear whether she was taken to the woodshed by the Left, or if her words were nothing more than a trial balloon. But she was back talking tough in November 2004.

In an interview with FOX's Greta van Susteren, Hillary attacked President Bush's failure to improve the nation's border security:

> I don't think that we have protected our borders or our ports or provided our first responders with the resources they need, so we can do more and we can do better... there's technology now available. There are some advanced radar systems. There are biometric and other kinds of identification systems that we've been very slow to deploy and unwilling to spend money on.[6]

This second hit into the right field of the immigration debate sent panic waves through conservative ranks. Writing for News-Max.com, Carl Limbacher, a conservative author, was the first to sound the alarm: "More than any other leader of either political party, U.S. Sen. Hillary Clinton has been focusing on immigration reform and border security—taking hard positions that appeal to frustrated Republicans in a move that could guarantee her enough support in red states to win the White House in 2008."[7]

The *Washington Times* followed with a story entitled: "Hillary Goes Conservative on Immigration," leading with, "Sen. Hillary Rodham Clinton is staking out a position on illegal immigration that is more conservative than President Bush, a strategy that supporters and detractors alike see as a way for the New York Democrat to shake the 'liberal' label and appeal to the traditionally Republican states."[8]

Then it was conservative columnist Tony Blankley's turn. In an editorial entitled "God Bless Hillary Clinton," he writes:

> ... the ever cold-blooded Miss Hillary has started to stake out a position to the right of the Republican Party. Just listen to her Pat Buchananesque defiance... [he mentions the quotations cited above]. These are hardly idle pensées coming from the Iron

Maiden from Chappaqua. Rather, it is a part, and a big part, of her calculated strategy to shed her liberal image and seize the White House from the Republicans in 2008 by attacking them on the most vulnerable part of their right flank: open borders, illegal immigration, and lax anti-terrorist security.[9]

Even my brother Pat (Buchanan) added his thoughts to the development, commenting that: "Hillary Clinton...has spoken out against illegal immigration with a forthrightness that makes Bush sound like a talking head for La Raza."[10]

With a couple of pointed remarks, Hillary had captured the attention of the Right. It mattered little what she had said or done prior to November of 2004. She was moving their way with speed and alacrity—talking the talk of an immigration hawk. The potential consequences of such a scenario were devastating for Republicans, who had no national leader with the courage to take a stand against the illegal cheap labor to which its corporate friends were now addicted. Whatever Hillary was up to—whether it was a cynical political ploy or a sincere concern—mattered little. As one Republican stalwart, who admitted a strong dislike for the Clintons, said, "If she ran on a platform of promising to do something about illegal immigration, hell, even I'd vote for her."[11]

But the question remained: What was Hillary up to? Was she really planning to stake out a position to the right of Bush and McCain on immigration that would carry her through to 2008? Or had she just let down her guard one afternoon, scrapping the talking points and telling it like it was? Then there was the question: if she was moving to the right—would her left-wing base permit it? Hillary was their lifelong sister and would be given more wiggle room than most, but this was asking a whole lot even for a Clinton.

Then it was as if someone had turned on a switch. After smoldering for years, the illegal immigration debate exploded onto the national stage, becoming at times so acrimonious that it quite literally poured into the streets of America. The battle was engaged and all were expected to take their positions. There would be no exceptions.

But in fairness to those who write that Hillary was "evolving politically" it must be acknowledged that there was a period of some months when it could be said that Lady Hillary had assumed the role of something other than a liberal on the border security/enforcement aspect of the immigration debate. But the period wasn't long, was noteworthy only for its rhetoric, and produced no action. It could be said that Hillary was somewhat of a tease, and nothing more.

A Perfect Pro-Amnesty Record

Prior to her Buchananesque outbursts, Hillary's political career was on the straight and narrow to liberal heaven (wherever that might be). There was not the slightest indication of a turn to the right on the immigrant issue—not in what she said, and not in how she voted. She was a Ted Kennedy Democrat who was making no waves.

La Raza, the largest and most powerful Hispanic lobbying organization in the country and a virtual ACLU for the illegal alien community, hosted Hillary at their 1998 national conference. Hillary at the time was the First Lady and she was a favorite of theirs. In her speech she cited a litany of all her husband had done for their community, from appointing Hispanics to high level positions to creating a toll-free line for Spanish-speaking callers to get information about educational opportunities. The list was long, if not particularly impressive. Democrats had been pandering to the Hispanic American community for years, and Bill and Hillary were no different. She even remarked that "as early as seven years from now, Hispanics will become the nation's largest minority group," adding, "Now that's very exciting news."

In her first few years in elected office Hillary's vote put her solidly in the La Raza camp. There wasn't an amnesty on which she didn't place her senatorial seal of approval. Little amnesties, medium-sized amnesties, and huge, inclusive Kennedy amnesties, it didn't matter to Hillary, she supported them all—from the amnesties for illegal farm workers to the one for illegal alien students under the age of twenty-one. Hillary even cosponsored legislation introduced by Senator Kennedy that would have granted amnesty to virtually all ten million plus illegal immigrants living in the country in 2004—and, oh yes, let's not forget their spouses and children.[12]

So while her rhetoric certainly got the attention of the Right, the Left must have been completely dumbfounded. They didn't say much at the time, and for good reason. What did they care what Hillary was saying on radio and television—in Congress she belonged to them. The Americans for Better Immigration, an immigration-reduction group that keeps tabs of all votes and grades the lawmakers accordingly,[13] gave the lady a "D-" for her overall record on immigration and an "F-" for amnesty.

What then was the tough talk all about?

Hillary, who goes to bed with a binder full of cross tabs from the latest polls, understood what a treasure chest of votes was out there for the taking. America was desperately looking for a champion on this issue and so she played with the idea a couple times. But each time she reached out to grab the ring she was likely reminded who it was who brought her to the dance. She could not break with both her corporate sponsors and the political left on so critical an issue—and expect to win the primary. There were already grumblings among the antiwar crowd for her support of the Iraq war. She couldn't risk alienating the base any further. So each time she was tempted, Hillary thought better and got back in line.

Playing to the Left

To put to rest any concern her base might have after hearing she was out late again with Buchanan and the boys, Hillary put on her Sunday best and with goodies bulging from her pockets went to break bread with La Raza a second time. In her address to their national conference in July 2005, Hillary listed one piece of legislation after another that she had introduced, was introducing, or hoped to introduce—all of which were by implication designed specifically for the benefit of the Hispanic community. She could have bored a donkey with this speech, but she had something for every Hispanic, the young and old, the educated and the dropout, the sick and the healthy, the legal and the illegal. There was even something for Hispanics who might be exposed to lead poisoning, or who had asthma, or needed help with English. And there was something for those who wired money, and for those who fight in wars alongside our troops.

This speech was "Pandering Hall of Fame" material.

I have culled from her remarks a comment worth noting, one in which the senator offers something special for those who broke our laws. It shows just how out of touch Hillary is with the hard-working men and women of Middle America:

I am a proud cosponsor of the DREAM Act. We want to make it possible for the 65,000 undocumented young people who graduate from our high schools each year to receive in-state tuition rates, and pursue their own dreams. And I hope with your help, we will make that DREAM Act a reality.

How incredibly audacious of the elite class of American legislators to call a bill that penalizes Americans citizens and legal immigrants the "Dream Act." And they wonder why they are held in such contempt by the people.

This bill would give illegal aliens the right to in-state tuition where citizens and legal residents are required to pay the full ride. At a time when millions of Americans are struggling to pay the ever-increasing costs of college education for their own children, the liberal elites want these same families to subsidize with their taxes the education of illegal immigrants, by giving them cut-rate tuition costs. But they, the citizens, have to pay the full price. Why? Because they are legal.

This bill so offends the fairness instinct of nearly all Americans that in January 2006 the people of Massachusetts, upon learning their Democratic legislature was about to adopt a similar measure, revolted. It was estimated that there would be a taxpayer-funded loss of $9,000 per illegal student in the Massachusetts university system. On top of that, those living in nearby states, some of whom actually worked in Massachusetts, would have to pay the full tuition for their own children. The outrage among the citizens of this bluest of blue states was so great that it caused hardened liberal legislators to panic, and defeat the bill themselves.[14]

Her performance before La Raza left little doubt among the crowd that Hillary was with them—they responded to her pandering with thunderous applause. But interestingly, for all she promised, Hillary kept her powder dry on the most contentious aspects of the immigration debate. As reported in the *Washington Post*, one astute attendee, Nellie Moreno of Phoenix, commented that Hillary's talk sounded like a campaign speech, but that "she was surprised Clinton did not talk about immigration, temporary guest worker programs and the border with Mexico."[15]

Hillary was still trying to keep a foot in both camps. Offering up every imaginable service known to man to the Hispanic community, she tightened her hold on this crucial voting block. But she still was not about to give up hope of making inroads into the voter-lucrative border security/enforcement camp either. All she needed to do was be tougher than Bush and McCain, not a particularly challenging assignment, but one she had to perform with care. It was a strategy that could take her back into the White House, this time as Numero Uno; or it could backfire and cause her to lose the primary. To make matters worse, immigration winds were picking up across the country and Hillary's weathervane was in a tailspin. Triangulation wasn't getting any easier. She decided to lay low awhile longer.

In the meantime, Hillary found herself another amnesty to champion: one for the illegal aliens victimized by Katrina. She joined a number of her colleagues to demand the Department of Homeland Security assure illegal immigrants their share of the relief aid without any fear of deportation. Americans wanted for crimes were not treated so kindly.

Smoked Out by House Republicans

Then in December 2005, the House Republicans took control of right field and tossed Hillary for a loop. In direct response to an increasingly angry outcry from Americans across the country, Republicans passed a tough-as-nails border security/enforcement package. La Raza and friends went ballistic and Hillary went deeper underground.

The bill was H.R. 4437, the Border Protection, Anti-Terrorism, and Illegal Immigration Control Act of 2005. It called for seven hundred miles of fencing along the Mexican border, required employers to verify workers' status using an Internet-based query system, granted local law enforcement a role in enforcing federal immigration laws, and prohibited federal grants to cities that maintain sanctuary policies for illegal aliens. The purpose of the bill was simple: the nation wanted its borders secure and the laws enforced, and they wanted it now. Republicans agreed.

The response was a sight to behold. You would have thought the House passed a measure calling on citizens to use armed resistance against illegal immigrants. The open borders crowd was apoplectic—they had the White House, the Senate, the leaders of both parties, and corporate America on their side. How in the world did these ragtag conservative House members get the upper hand? The answer was easy—Republicans had found the courage to do their job. They gave voice to the American people—passing a bill that demanded the federal government do *its* job—enforce sanctions against those who are hiring the illegal cheap labor and secure the nation's borders against terrorists, drug runners, criminals, gang members, and illegal immigrants. The nation was paying too high a price for Washington to continue its policy of doing nothing.

Hillary was in a bind. How could she oppose a border security/enforcement bill—it was where she had, albeit tentatively, placed her second foot. But the Left's reaction to the proposal was so extreme Hillary couldn't possibly break with them. Since partisan politics prohibited her from saying anything good about the Republican plan, Hillary did the next best thing—stayed low and kept her head down.

For months as this debate consumed the nation, the lady who would be president was AWOL.

According to the *New York Times*, "[Hillary] had been criticized by some immigrant activists for saying little about the issue until March 8...."[16]

The Associated Press's David Barrett wrote, "[Hillary is]... largely staying away from [the immigration] issue that has roiled

Congress in recent months and spurred a number of conflicting proposals."[17]

And she wasn't working away behind the scenes either. That idea was dispelled by Newsday.com:

[Hillary] had played a minor role in this year's Senate debate, eschewing many strategy sessions, reportedly out of deference to Sen. Ted Kennedy, the Democrats' lead negotiator. By contrast, Sen. Charles Schumer (D-N.Y.) has played a central political role.[18]

Hillary avoided the most controversial issue facing America; wouldn't so much as take a position. She had a campaign to think about. There was no telling how this issue would play out in 2008, so she did her leaderless best to wait it out. But the badgering from the Left forced her out of hiding and into battle.

In a March speech to Irish immigrants, nearly three months after the bill passed the House, Hillary took a stand. But rather than attack the principle parts of the bill—the security or enforcement provisions, Hillary created a false consequence and attacked that. In her opening salvo she lambasted Republicans for trying to create a "police state" to round up illegal immigrants, adding that it would be "an unworkable scheme to try to deport 11 million people, which you have to have a police state to try to do."[19] Not to worry that neither the bill nor any Republican had called for mass deportation, and no mention of attrition—that millions of illegal aliens would choose to return to their homelands if the rule of law were restored. But those were facts and Hillary never let them get in her way.

In this same speech, however, Hillary proposed that instead of the Republican plan for border security, we have immigration changes "based on strengthening our borders in order to make us safer from the threat of terrorism." Is she joking? The border is secure or it is not secure—and if it's not, anyone comes in, including terrorists.

A few weeks later Hillary struck again, this time introducing the Good Lord into the debate. The old gal is a piece of work—rather than debate the issue she tossed a hand grenade into the crowd.

> It is hard to believe that a Republican leadership that is consistently talking about values and about faith would put forth such mean-spirited legislation. . . . It is certainly not in keeping with my understanding of the scriptures because this bill would literally criminalize the Good Samaritan and probably even Jesus himself. . . . We need to sound the alarm about what is being done in Congress.[20]

Criminalizing Jesus—where does she get this material? She had half the preachers in America rereading the parable of the Good Samaritan. And, no, they didn't find anything about illegal aliens.

Sean Hannity asked Congressman James Sensenbrenner, the author of the House immigration bill, to address just this issue when he was a guest on FOX's *Hannity and Colmes*. Hannity asked whether the House border security bill would "punish the clergy and other organizations from assisting, or helping, or offering social services of some kind to illegal immigrants," as some in the media were reporting. Sensenbrenner called this charge a "red herring" and added:

> The people who are complaining about that have not read the bill. For over fifty years, it has been a crime to aid, and abet, and assist illegal aliens. What my amendment does is to put a knowing and willful standard in there so that those who are part of a

criminal alien smuggling ring can be more easily prosecuted and sent to jail. These are the people who get those who cross the border to carry drugs and, in some cases, they're trafficking people into prostitution or white slave rackets.[21]

The clause was never intended to be used to prosecute churches or charitable organizations, and never would be used to do so. But again, those are the facts and the lady senator could not have cared less about them.

What's more, she was too busy working on triangulating. It was becoming a full-time job.

Weeks after her two broadsides against the House bill, Hillary told *New York Daily News* columnist Michael Goodwin that she was all for building a fence along the Mexican border and she supported cracking down on employers who hire illegal aliens—exactly what the Republican plan called for. She did, however, support a guest worker system, and said she would have no problem phasing it in over "twelve to twenty-four months" after strengthening border security. Finally Hillary had a plan. It was a long, tortuous path but she had a plan. Borrowing heavily from Republicans, Hillary had put together a detailed three-step approach to illegal immigration, four steps if you throw in her support for amnesty. It lasted all of three days.[22]

Goodwin's column ran on Saturday, April 22, praising the senator and pronouncing that, "...in an interview on Friday, [Hillary] cited specific goals that could, and hopefully will, become the heart of bipartisan legislation that might actually fix this national crisis."[23] By Monday Hillary was in full retreat, her office "clarifying" what the senator actually meant to say. As for that twelve to twenty-four month lag time, "Clinton spokesman Philippe Reines seemed to back off that assertion, saying the senator would only support a lag as a last resort."[24] It was just another quick visit into right field—she came home when La Raza called.

In his column Michael Goodwin commented that, "[Hillary] seemed exasperated at being categorized" on this issue of immigration. "I'm frustrated and I'm in an uncomfortable position," she told him. "People often want to put you in an either-or category in America politics. It is difficult to stay where you are."[25] You can say that again.

The Mother of All Amnesties

In response to the tough immigration bill passed by the House, ethnic groups mobilized illegals and their supporters, sending millions into the streets of America to protest the very suggestion that America enforce her immigration laws. During the spring there were marches in hundreds of cities. The earlier protests were marked by angry, defiant protesters shouting in Spanish and carrying Mexican flags. Signs read: "Stop the Nazis," "Chicano Power," and "This is Stolen Land,"[26] with at least one depicting Congressman James Sensenbrenner, the bill's author, wearing a Nazi uniform.[27] Protest organizers changed the tone of subsequent protests but the message was the same. As Pat Buchanan wrote, it was "a show of force, a demonstration of raw street power to force the government of the United States into granting to 12 million illegal aliens, who have broken our laws and broken into our country, not only the full benefits of U.S. citizenship, but full citizenship."[28]

The Senate was up next and they gave the protesters what they wanted and then some. In late May they passed S. 2611, the Comprehensive Immigration Reform Act, dubbed the McCain-Kennedy bill. It was the most radical piece of legislation to pass either house of Congress in a generation. Had it become law, it would have reduced the nation to a welfare state within twenty years. Here are a few of the highlights:

- Granted amnesty to nearly all of the millions of illegal aliens living in the country and family members not yet here.
- Granted amnesty to the employers who had hired the illegal aliens.
- Allowed states to give in-state tuition to illegal aliens.
- Allowed amnestied illegal aliens to claim Social Security benefits for work done in the country illegally and prohibited the prosecution of these aliens for Social Security fraud or identity theft.
- Required the United States to consult with Mexico before constructing any fencing along the border and to assist Mexico in securing its southern border.
- Would have given millions of our tax dollars to immigrant rights groups, the same groups behind the protests against the Republican House bill.

In addition, the bill would have increased legal immigration exponentially, and opened our doors to thousands of additional immigrants every year under a "temporary guest worker" plan, which is nothing more than a two-step amnesty. Dr. Robert Rector of the Heritage Foundation, an architect of the welfare reform, explained, "There is nothing temporary about this program; nearly all the 'guest workers' would have the right to become permanent residents and then citizens."[29]

Take the amnesty and their families, add the guest-worker amnesty and their families, and then add the new growth in legal immigration and poof—66 million immigrants in twenty years. And this doesn't account for any new illegal immigrants—we best keep adding.[30] The cost of enacting the bill, including the benefits for which these new immigrants would qualify, would rise to $50 billion annually within ten years.[31] "In the long run, the [McCain-Kennedy] bill, if enacted," said Rector, "would be the largest expansion of the welfare state in thirty-five years."[32] And all America wanted was the borders secured and the laws enforced.

During the floor debate, a few heroic senators, led by Republican senator Jeff Sessions of Alabama, fought desperately to stop it. Hillary was not one of them. In fact, she opposed virtually every attempt to rein in the bill. When Republican senator David Vitter of Louisiana offered an amendment to strike all amnesty provisions from the bill, she voted against it. When Republican senator John Ensign of Nevada offered an amendment to keep illegal aliens from collecting Social Security, she voted against that too. When Democratic senator Jeff Bingaman of New Mexico introduced an amendment to reduce the number of immigrants who could be admitted under the "guest" worker plan, Hillary voted against it. This last amendment was one of the few that passed. Had it not, the number of mostly poor and unskilled immigrants that would flood our shores in the next twenty years would not be 66 million, it would be 103 million. Hillary had no problem with that.[33]

When the final bill came to the floor of the Senate Hillary joined sixty-one of her colleagues to vote "yea." With each vote, both on the amendments and on the final bill, Hillary defined herself as an open borders, pro-amnesty liberal, who sees nothing wrong with an emerging welfare state in this country designed to accommodate tens of millions of poor and needy foreigners to taxpayer-funded education, medical expenses, in-state tuition, English courses, social services, and Social Security benefits, even for work they did illegally. And she would make them citizens, creating a huge voting block wedded to liberal tax and spend policies. With polls showing that half of Mexico would move to the United States if given the chance and liberals offering up the country—you and I best get working, 'cause someone's going to have to pay for it.

In the end Hillary went home to the family. The "mother of all amnesties" was too much for her to resist and, besides, brother Kennedy had drafted the bill under the close supervision of Hillary's corporate friends and her La Raza pals. If it were to become law it would rival the creation of Social Security and Medicare. No liberal worth her salt would oppose such a bill.[34]

But Hillary can no longer talk with any credibility about enforcement—she voted to give amnesty to the employers of illegal immigrants. She can no longer talk with any credibility about border security—while she voted for the fence, Hillary specifically voted to require America to consult with Mexico before building security structures along our southern border.

As for all that tough talk—just the mental meanderings of a politically shrewd opportunist who knows the dangers of straying too far from home.[35]

Chapter Six

The Gender Feminist

ABOUT A MONTH AFTER THE CLOSE of her husband's impeachment trial, amid speculation she would run for the U.S. Senate, Hillary Clinton took off for Egypt with her daughter Chelsea. They made their way to the Valley of the Queens and to the mortuary temple of an ancient Egyptian ruler named Hatshepsut.

Hatshepsut, who lived in the fifteenth century BC, is a unique and revolutionary figure in the history of world leaders. She is also a sort of role model for Hillary. The daughter of Pharaoh Thutmose I, she became regent of Egypt when her husband and half-brother, Thutmose II, died, leaving as his heir a male child by another wife. But Hatshepsut was not willing to settle for the regency. As her nephew grew older, she ruled Egypt with him. But craving total power and the title to go with it, she eventually declared herself "king"—not queen—and became sole ruler of the realm.[1] She was perhaps the world's first feminist.

In some of the stone monuments carved by her slaves, Hatshepsut is depicted in men's clothing and a fake beard.

As Hillary and Chelsea toured this woman-king's temple, Hillary joked to a reporter, "Well, I am looking for another career."

She then pointed up at the temple's ceiling, painted with white stars on a field of blue. "Look," she said. "Like all things—men, women, night, day."[2]

This concept of the world as a place divided into dueling camps, where one sex is perennially pitted against the other, is never far from Hillary's mind. Just as many liberals see the world in terms of class warfare, Hillary sees it in terms of gender warfare.

Author Christina Hoff Sommers calls Hillary a "gender feminist." At an American Enterprise Institute seminar titled "Hillary Rodham Clinton as Feminist Heroine," Sommers defined this term: "Feminists can be roughly divided into two camps: equity feminists and gender feminists. Equity feminists want fair treatment of women and no discrimination. From the point of view of equity feminists (and I count myself among them) most of the major battles in the U.S. have been won. Women are not merely doing as well as men in this society; in many ways they are now doing better. But gender feminists are not celebrating. Gender feminists see women as a subordinate class, routinely tyrannized and victimized by men. Many live in a chronically offended state.

"Why do I count the First Lady with the gender feminists?" asked Sommers. "After all, she never speaks these days as a professed feminist. She is a careful politician, so you will not hear her mention 'patriarchal hegemony' or the 'gender system.' But you will find her practicing what the gender feminists preach. Like other gender feminists, she constantly exaggerates women's victim status."[3]

The day before touring Queen—or "King"—Hatshepsut's temple, Hillary did exactly that in a speech at the American University in Cairo. The speech was advertised in advance as "a major address on promoting religious tolerance and encouraging the development of civil society," but Hillary still managed to squeeze in several allusions to oppression of women, suggesting that American women, Egyptian women, and women everywhere were involved in a single global struggle for feminist liberation. Her discussion eventually settled, as it so often does, on issues of "family planning"—efforts to free women not merely from men, but also from motherhood, so they might "live up to their God-given potential."[4]

Hillary raved about the UN conference on population that had taken place in Cairo in 1994. That conference had sparked a global debate because its draft report, which was supported by the Clinton administration, attempted to establish a global right to "fertility regulation," which was defined by the World Health Organization to include abortion. The final document issued by the conferees was toned down, but to Hillary it nevertheless marked a historic milestone for women.[5]

"It was five years ago that thousands of people gathered here in Cairo for the International Conference on Population and Development," she said. "The further in time we move from that conference, the more remarkable it seems, because for the very first time I've been able to find in history, there was a world gathering which reached the conclusion that we must do more to develop the potential of all people, particularly women, if we expect to live in a prosperous, peaceful, stable world."[6]

And what did these globalists do to promote so lofty a goal? "We agreed to make family planning a right."[7] Family planning leads to world peace? Think she learned this at Yale?

At the center of this worldwide battle for reproductive rights is, of course, unlimited access to abortion. Abortion is a critical aspect of "empowering women" in the distorted world of the narcissist feminist—which explains why Hillary demands that it be available to all women, for any reason, at any time, by any method.

"Common Ground"

"Clinton Seeking Shared Ground Over Abortions," read the front-page headline in the *New York Times*.[8] The date was January 25, 2005, and the story was about a speech Hillary had given the previous day to 1,000 pro-abortionists. In it she had called on her feminist pals "to find common ground" with pro-lifers to reduce the number of abortions.[9]

"Yes, we do have deeply held differences of opinion about the issue of abortion and I, for one, respect those who believe with all their hearts and conscience that there are no circumstances under which any abortion should ever be available," she said.[10]

The *New York Times* reported that Hillary "appeared to be reaching out beyond traditional core Democrats who support abortion rights."[11]

The audience of family planners was not amused by Hillary's conciliatory gesture to the enemy. "Mrs. Clinton's remarks drew some gasps and head-shaking from those gathered here," reported the *Times*.[12]

On the surface, the implications were quite startling. Was the darling of the Left reaching across the aisle with olive branch in hand? Was the woman who blamed her husband's affairs on the vast right wing suddenly calling for a truce? Could it be? One pro-life news source took the bait, running the story under the heading: "Hillary Clinton Softens Abortion Stance."[13]

This implication of apostasy on Hillary's part caught the immediate attention of the sisterhood. They let no time pass before they were setting the record straight. NARAL Pro-Choice America president Nancy Keenan dismissed any suggestion that Sister Hillary had crossed the line. "Senator Clinton's remarks yesterday were a perfect statement of the pro-choice position," said Keenan. "She reiterated time and time again her support for *Roe*, she outlined ways to reduce unintended pregnancies."[14]

But it took Hillary's press secretary, Philippe Reines, to put the matter to rest by "clarifying" Hillary's remarks. The senator was "not attempting to remake herself...she was simply restating positions that she has set out in the past," he told the *Washington Times*.[15] The trial balloon had crashed—no matter how she voted, on the issue of abortion Hillary would not be permitted to speak softly.

But there was a revealing gem in Hillary's little sermon. It went like this: "We can all recognize that abortion in many ways represents a sad, even tragic choice to many, many women," she said.[16]

Hillary is, of course, correct. Abortion is tragic. But why? Having a bunch of unwanted cells removed is hardly a sad event, much less tragic, any more than the removal of a mole. What makes an abortion "sad, even tragic" is that an innocent unborn child loses his life because his mother can't find the love inside her to fight with all her God-given strength to protect him whatever the consequences. It's tragic, all right, for the little baby, and for the mother.

I have often said that if I did not believe that a fetus was an unborn child with all the rights associated with human life, I would stand side by side with my pro-choice friends defending the right of women to make all decisions about their bodies. And over the years, in debate after debate, it is from this premise that feminists have argued. The fetus, they would invariably instruct me, was not a child; it was nothing more than a glob of cells.

Then along came the sonogram and everyone could see for themselves that what grew inside a woman had a heartbeat, arms and legs, cute little features, and his own unique character. The glob looked and acted just like a baby. Imagine that.

It was a major blow to the sisterhood.

Now, more often than not, feminists are forced into taking the indefensible position that while they know it is a child in the womb, they still have an unrestricted right to destroy the little fella. This right, claims Hillary, empowers women. Imagine—the right to kill your unborn child gives you power. It's a chilling concept.

Her "sad, even tragic" comment is not the first indication that Hillary believes it is indeed a child that is ripped from the womb during an abortion. As early as 2003, while debating a proposed ban on partial-birth abortions, Hillary referred to the unborn child as "the child, the fetus, your baby" and said that "these children cannot live outside the womb...." As a candidate for president, Hillary delights in reminding her audiences that she has fought for the rights of children for thirty-five years. The discarded bodies of forty million aborted babies would suggest otherwise.

Hillary has spent a lifetime fighting to keep abortions legal—all of them. Hers is the most extreme position a person can have on the issue and she has championed it at every opportunity, helping to keep abortion on demand the law of the land.

"Close to Infanticide"

When the issue of partial-birth abortion first came up in the Senate in 1996, Democratic senator Daniel Patrick Moynihan of New York, who occupied the Senate seat Hillary now holds, was horrified. Moynihan was pro-choice. But he believed partial-birth abortion went way too far.

"It is as close to infanticide as anything I have come upon in our judiciary," he said.[17] Moynihan supported overriding President Clinton's veto of the ban; sadly, the veto was sustained.[18]

Seven years later, in March 2003, when a ban on partial-birth abortion again reached the Senate floor, Hillary was horrified. But she was not horrified by the details of partial-birth abortion, in which a baby's fully formed head, the only remaining part of the baby still inside the mother, is punctured with scissors. Then its brain is suctioned out to kill it before it is "born." What shocked Hillary was the timing of the vote.

How, Hillary fumed, could the Republican leadership bring this bill up during Women's History Month?

"Not only do I believe this is an inappropriate and unfortunate time for this debate to be occurring, but I find it deeply ironic that it is taking place in the month of March, Women's History Month," she said in a Senate floor speech. "Apparently, some people believe that the purpose of Women's History Month is to literally bring us back to a time in history when women had no choices."[19]

No choices? What was she talking about? Was she really suggesting that if Congress prohibited this one procedure—a form of abortion that was "close to infanticide"—that the U.S. government would be on its way to prohibiting all choices for women? Surely Hillary wasn't going there.

Oh, but she was. Banning partial-birth abortion, she argued, would put America on the road to becoming a Communist police state along the likes of the People's Republic of China and Nicolae Ceausescu's Romania.

Under the Communist dictator Ceausescu, Hillary said, the government ordered that all women must bear at least five children. "So they eliminated birth control, they eliminated sex education, and they outlawed abortions. Here is what happened to you if you were a woman in Romania during the Ceausescu regime: Once a month you would be rounded up at your workplace. You would be taken to a government-controlled health clinic."[20] (I wonder if these clinics are like the ones called for in her national health care plan.)

The women, according to Hillary, were told to disrobe, were examined by a government doctor with the secret police looking on, and if pregnant would be monitored to assure nothing happened to the pregnancy.[21] If a woman wasn't with child, "her family was fined a celibacy tax of up to 10 percent of their monthly salary."[22] (Finally, a tax Hillary doesn't support.)

Hillary then abruptly jumped from Eastern Europe to East Asia, and from compulsory childbearing to compulsory birth control, describing China's harshly enforced one-child policy. "So whether it was Romania saying you have to have children for the good of the state, or China saying you can only have one child for the good of the state, the government was telling us what we were supposed to do with our bodies."[23]

Forced to have five babies? Forbidden to have more than one? Enforced by Gestapo-like tactics? Did Hillary really believe this was where America was headed if Congress banned partial-birth abortion? In fact, she was certain of it. "I raise these issues not because they are part of the past or because they happened somewhere far away, but because I can guarantee you, standing here as a senator, if we go down this path, you are going to have the same kind of overzealous prosecutors and police officials doing the very same kind of things in this country."[24]

So much for "common ground"—when the U.S. Senate considered prohibiting the most extreme form of abortion, an act seen as the first cousin of infanticide by her predecessor, a liberal pro-choice Democrat, Hillary didn't say she understood his views, much less the views of those who oppose all abortion.

No, before she voted against the ban on partial-birth abortion, the radical Wellesley feminist who always lurks beneath the surface of Hillary's otherwise carefully staged Senate persona burst forth—ranting.

But as a way to soften the rants, she did open and close them with a line she stole from her husband. When she was recognized to speak, the immediate issue on the floor was an amendment to the partial-birth abortion ban sponsored by Democratic senator

Tom Harkin of Iowa. It said that the sense of the Senate was that the Supreme Court had correctly decided *Roe v. Wade*, the case that overturned the abortion laws of every state and established abortion on demand as a so-called "right." "I thank my friend from Iowa, I thank him for introducing this important sense-of-the-Senate resolution amendment that will reaffirm *Roe v. Wade*, making it clear that the policy of this Senate is for abortion to be legal, safe, and rare," she said.[25]

Bill Clinton had first used this "legal, safe, and rare" line in his 1992 presidential campaign.[26] But again, it implicitly concedes that abortion takes a human life. Otherwise, why would she care if it were rare?

One particular exchange during the debate offers a chilling glimpse into the inner sanctum of Hillary's cold heart. Senator Rick Santorum, a supporter of the ban on partial-birth abortion, had brought on to the Senate floor drawings that showed a perfectly formed baby being killed in a partial-birth abortion. Hillary used Santorum's charts to argue that partial-birth abortion needed to remain legal to kill imperfect babies.

"I am also concerned about some of the visual aids that have been used by some of my colleagues," she said. "They show a perfectly formed fetus, and that is misleading. Because if we are really going to have this debate, then we should have a chart that demonstrates the tragic abnormalities that confront women forced with this excruciatingly difficult decision. Where are the swollen heads?"[27]

To his credit, Santorum would not let Hillary get away with this argument. Bluntly put, she was saying partial-birth abortion was needed as a form of euthanasia or eugenics for malformed babies. When she finished her speech, Santorum moved in for the kill:

Hillary: "Does the senator's legislation make exceptions for serious life-threatening abnormalities or babies who are in such serious physical condition that they will not live outside the womb?"

Santorum: "No, if..."

Hillary: "That is the point."

Santorum: "I understand the senator's point. I guess my point in rebuttal is that if you want to create a separation in the law between those children who are perfect and those children who are not..."

Hillary: "No..."

Santorum: "Please, let me finish. If a child is not perfect, then that child can be aborted under any circumstances. But if that child is perfect, we are going to protect that child more.... What the senator from New York is asking me to do is separate those who are somehow not the way our society sees people as they should be today and put them somewhat a peg below legal protection than the perfect child.... No, I do not have an exception in this legislation that says if you are perfect, this cannot happen to you; but if you are not perfect, yes, this can occur. The senator is right, I do not."[28]

Hillary had no rational response. Senator Santorum had caught her advocating extermination of less than perfect babies. Even in the case of a genetic disorder or other abnormality, there is no justification to deliberately kill the child before nature is able to take its course.

Hillary's political instincts were triggered; she sensed she had backed herself into a dark and ugly corner. At that point she cut the debate short. "To respond, if I could, to the senator from Pennsylvania, my great hope is that abortion becomes rarer and rarer."[29] She then added, "I want the record to be very clear that I value every single life and every single person." Let the record show that that's a lie.

Hillary fought to keep legal a brutally inhumane procedure that, in her own words, kills "children." She calls abortion "tragic," saying she wants it to be "rare" to somehow immunize herself from the political fallout of her extreme position. Bottom line: Hillary knows partial-birth abortion is a horrific procedure that results in "infanticide." She knows abortion kills children. But this knowledge in no way interferes with her insistence that women have unfettered access to both.

Hillary is so committed to fight alongside the feminists on the far left that she doesn't care about the body count or what it has done to her soul. Given this uncompromising commitment, it is not surprising that she has compiled a perfect pro-abortion voting record according to NARAL Pro-Choice America.[30] Whether the issue is providing tax dollars to organizations that perform or promote abortions overseas, rejecting appellate and Supreme Court nominees whom NARAL does not trust to uphold *Roe v. Wade*, or preserving the ability of people to sneak someone else's child across state lines for an abortion, when the Culture of Death calls, Hillary never fails to do its bidding.

"To March, or Not to March?"

"To March, or Not to March?" That was how one headline described one of the first great political questions facing Hillary's 2000 U.S. Senate campaign.[31]

The march at issue was New York City's St. Patrick's Day Parade, which is sponsored by the Ancient Order of Hibernians (AOH), a Catholic fraternal organization. Like most marches, AOH's parade is an exercise in free speech. Its express purpose is to celebrate the saint responsible for converting Ireland to the Roman Catholic faith, which, as is well known, does not approve of homosexual activity. Accordingly, while AOH welcomes individual gays and lesbians to march in its parade, it does not allow a gay rights advocacy group called the Irish Lesbian and Gay Organization (ILGO) to march under its own banners. This AOH policy has survived a court challenge[32] and has made the parade the object of a boycott by some Democratic New York politicians seeking the favor of gay rights groups.

Thus the parade presented a dilemma for Hillary's first senatorial campaign. On one side were gay rights activists, part of her natural left-wing constituency and an important fund-raising base. On the other were Irish Catholics, a large, traditionally Democratic constituency in New York State.

To march, or not to march? To stand with traditionalist Irish Catholics or with gay rights groups? That was the question. Typically, Hillary tried to stand in both places at the same time. No saint, she proved to be incapable of physical bi-location.

The controversy started on December 7, 1999, when a group of gay activists threw a fund-raiser for Hillary in Manhattan. One of the guests at the private event asked the First Lady what she thought of her husband's "don't ask, don't tell" policy, which allows gays to serve in the military as long as they don't publicly declare they are gay or engage in homosexual activity. She said she disagreed with her husband's policy and favored allowing gays to serve openly in the military.

The *New York Times* heard about Hillary's remarks and double-checked it with her campaign. Hillary confirmed her opposition to "don't ask, don't tell." "Gays and lesbians already serve with distinction in our nation's armed forces and should not face discrimination," she said in the statement. "Fitness to serve should be based on an individual's conduct, not their sexual orientation."[33]

The day after this story ran on the front page of the *Times*, Hillary held a press conference in Manhattan with a group of Irish American leaders to express her support for the peace process in Northern Ireland. A reporter asked her if she would participate in the annual St. Patrick's Day Parade. Considering her audience, Hillary gave exactly the answer you would expect from a politician accustomed to marching on both sides of the street.

"I would hope so," she said. Then, referring to the group of Irish Americans who had joined her for the press conference, she added, "As long as I've got a lot of good company, I would certainly go marching in the St. Patrick's Day Parade."[34]

Gay rights activists who had just been toasting her now started roasting her.

"We would be greatly disappointed if any candidate for the United States Senate participated in a parade that was not inclusive," Kevin Finnegan, president of the Gay and Lesbian Independent Democrats, told the *New York Post.*[35]

"We would urge all people of conscience to stay away from the parade as long as it is excluding certain Irish groups," said Brendan Fay, co-chair of a gay Irish group called the Lavender and Green Alliance.[36]

"Clinton needs to make her stand now," said Anne Maguire, a leader of ILGO. "She either supports lesbians and gay men in New York, or she actively supports the bigots who tell us we can't be Irish and gay at the same time."[37]

Hillary waffled. Her spokesman, Howard Wolfson, told the *New York Times* that she had made no definite plans to march in the parade, unmistakably carving out room for the First Lady to cave to the pressure from ILGO and dump the Hibernians. "It wasn't a firm commitment that she made," said Wolfson. "I think she said she hoped to, and we will revisit the issue when we get closer to St. Patrick's Day. We'll deal with Christmas first."[38]

That Sunday, Harold Ickes, a senior advisor to Hillary's campaign, appeared on CBS's *Face the Nation.* Under questioning by host Bob Schieffer, Ickes seemed to suggest that Mrs. Clinton would not march in the St. Patrick's Day Parade unless it was made "inclusive."

Schieffer: "Is she going to march in the St. Patrick's Day Parade? Because as you know, with your background in New York politics, this is a very controversial area because the Order of Hibernians do not allow gay people to march in that parade. And now her— or gay groups—her—her gay supporters are telling her now, 'Don't march in this parade.' Is she going to?"

Ickes: "Well, Bob, she hopes to. And she hopes that the parade will be inclusive, I remind you that Pat Moynihan, Ed Koch, Peter Vallone, Rudy Giuliani, many others, marched in that parade. She hopes to, but she hopes it'll be inclusive."

Schieffer: "Well, what does that mean, though? Does that mean if it's not inclusive, if they can't march, the gay folks can't march with their banners, that she won't—won't march?"

Ickes: "Right. At her—at this point, she hopes to march and she hopes it will be inclusive and that's where we are."[39]

Two weeks went by and still no decision. The controversy, however, was not going away. On December 21, ILGO's Anne Maguire spoke to the *Irish Voice*, an Irish American weekly. "We've sent a letter to Hillary," said Maguire. "Most Democrats don't march and haven't done so since 1992 because they see the parade as supporting exclusion. Already they [the Clinton campaign] are backtracking; the campaign manager told me that it was not a definite plan for her to march. We would be very surprised if she marched."[40]

But the Hibernians weren't letting Hillary off easy either. "I certainly do agree that she should march," said Jack Irwin, former president of the New York State chapter of AOH. "The courts have ruled that gays can march, but not under their own banner. I think that should suffice."[41]

Frank Durkan, chairman of Americans for a New Irish Agenda, echoed these sentiments, telling the *Irish Voice*: "I think that she should march and she will, the parade is for those who wish to honor St. Patrick."[42]

Meanwhile, gay activists began planning a counter St. Patrick's Day Parade in the Woodside neighborhood of Queens. They intended to hold it almost two weeks before St. Patrick's Day, and ILGO and other gay rights groups would be participating. Stella O'Leary, president of the Irish American Democrats, came to Hillary's rescue, suggesting she march in both. "Yes, she should march and in both parades, with the gays in Woodside, Queens, and in the St. Patrick's Day Parade," O'Leary told the *Irish Voice*.[43]

The parade problem nearly stumped the would-be senator. It took her two months to finally decide on the big one; more time was needed for the gay one. She would be in the Hibernians' traditional parade. It was a cold-blooded political calculation. "We can't throw away 15 percent of the New York State vote on this issue," a "Democratic source" told the *Irish Voice*. The paper explained: "A recent statewide poll showed Hillary trailing her likely Republican opponent, New York City mayor Rudolph Giuliani, badly among ethnic Catholics. However, campaign officials place great importance on this vote as a key swing constituency, thus their reluctance to antagonize them on the march issue."[44]

The same report said Hillary had not yet decided to march with the gays in Queens. That march was "opposed by many longtime Woodside residents; the Clinton camp is taking no position at this time," said the paper.[45] Where were her pollsters when she needed them?

When the day came, however, Hillary marched in Queens. But that was not enough to placate some gay activists. Anne Maguire of ILGO accused her of "trying to have it both ways."[46] What a thing to say about Hillary!

Later that year, Hillary marched without controversy in New York's gay pride parade, saying afterward it was "one of the greatest thrills in my life.... I've never seen anything like that."[47]

Marching with the gays paid off. That July, the leading New York State gay political group, the Empire State Pride Agenda, and the leading national gay political group, the Human Rights Campaign (HRC), simultaneously endorsed her Senate campaign. "Mrs. Clinton is the clear leader on every single issue of importance to the lesbian and gay community," Tim Sweeney of the Empire State Pride Agenda told reporters.[48]

Once safely elected, Senator Hillary did not disappoint these gay rights groups. The Human Rights Campaign scores the voting record of every senator in each two-year session of Congress. Hillary received a 100 percent rating from HRC in her first Congress and an 88 percent in each of the following two Congresses, failing to vote the HRC line on only one issue. In the last two Congresses, the group asked all senators to cosponsor the Permanent Partners Immigration Act, which would grant same-sex partners the same immigration rights as spouses of citizens. Only thirteen senators have agreed to sponsor this bill; Hillary was not among them.[49]

In 2001, after she had been elected to the Senate and years before she would be facing the voters again, Hillary was quick to turn down the stuffy St. Patrick's Day Parade in Manhattan. Pleading a scheduling conflict, she attended another parade in Syracuse—one in which gay groups were allowed to march under their own banners.

Former New York mayor Ed Koch, a champion of gay rights and longtime marcher in the St. Patrick's Day Parade, saw right through her act.

"Hillary's excuse of a scheduling conflict is ridiculous," wrote Koch. "The obvious reply was 'unschedule the conflict and resolve it in favor of New York City's St. Patrick's Day parade.' She would not. This is particularly unacceptable since, when she needed Irish and Roman Catholic support last year when she was running, she marched. She also marched in the Gay Pride Parade and asked that I march with her, as I did. Let this be the last time she insults the Irish and the Catholics."[50]

The crusty old pol doesn't much like being used, does he?

A Wink and a Nod to Same-Sex Marriage

On the all-important issue of a federal marriage amendment Hillary has marched in step with the gay Left while simultaneously posing as a defender of traditional marriage.

In the midst of the parade controversy, when her campaign was fretting about the Irish Catholic vote, Hillary announced she was against same-sex marriage. "Marriage has got historic, religious, and moral content that goes back to the beginning of time, and I think a marriage is as a marriage has always been, between a man and a woman," she said at a January 11, 2000, press conference.[51]

At the same time, she let it be known that she also favored legal domestic partnerships, and her campaign spokesman made clear that in Hillary's view these partnerships should have exactly the same legal status, if not the same name, as marriage. "She never used the phrase marriage," the spokesman said, "but she said same-sex unions should be recognized and that same-sex unions should be entitled to all the rights and privileges that every other American gets."[52] He was describing something, the *Times* reported, that Hillary had said at the same private fund-raiser thrown for her by gay groups where she first said she opposed "don't ask, don't tell."

The spokesman also said that Hillary supported the Defense of Marriage Act (DOMA), signed by her husband, which was designed to prevent states from being forced to recognize same-sex marriages contracted in other states, as would have been required under the Constitution's Full Faith and Credit Clause.

With a foot solidly in both camps, Hillary was in perfect form.

Events soon conspired, however, to unmask Hillary's two faces on marriage. In 2003 the Supreme Court ruled anti-sodomy laws unconstitutional, and Massachusetts's highest court ruled that under the state's constitution same-sex marriage was a "right." Now all that stood between the Massachusetts decision and all other states being forced to recognize same-sex marriages per- formed in Massachusetts was DOMA.

But some constitutional scholars and many Democratic politi- cians argue that DOMA is unconstitutional, because Congress lacks the authority to limit the scope of the Full Faith and Credit Clause. A Supreme Court decision overturning DOMA on these grounds, or a decision overturning a state ban on same-sex marriage based on the Equal Protection Clause of the Fourteenth Amendment, would instantly make same-sex marriage a "right" in all fifty states.

The best way to prevent this is a marriage amendment to the U.S. Constitution that strips judges of the power to overrule marriage law decisions made by state legislatures or voters.[53]

In 2004 Congress considered just such an amendment. Defeating it became the premier cause of gay rights groups. Hillary had to decide: Was she for the gay activist groups and thus for opening the door to making same-sex marriage a "right"? Or was she for protecting the traditional marriage laws of the states? She could not be both. But she sure tried.

Hillary ended up siding with the gay activists. But her argument against the marriage amendment in her Senate floor speech was pure Clintonian double-speak. The woman who once derisively compared marriage and family to slavery and life on an Indian reservation (in the *Harvard Educational Review*) now spoke effusively of traditional marriage.[54] The woman who voted to sustain *Roe v. Wade*, which overturned the abortion laws of all fifty states, now adamantly defended states' rights. The one-time Wellesley feminist now delivered a stinging diatribe against divorce and bearing children out of wedlock. She delivered her pro-marriage sermon with evangelical zeal.

"I believe marriage is not just a bond, but a sacred bond between a man and a woman," she said. "I have had occasion in my life to defend marriage, to stand up for marriage, to believe in the hard work and challenge of marriage. So I take umbrage at anyone who might suggest that those of us who worry about amending the Constitution are less committed to the sanctity of marriage, or to the fundamental bedrock principle that exists between a man and a woman, going back into the midst of history as one of the foundational institutions of history and humanity and civilization, and that its primary, principal role during those millennia has been raising and socializing children for the society into which they become adults."[55]

If the Senate was really concerned about marriage, she said, maybe it should be "trying to amend our Constitution to take away at the very first blush the idea of no-fault divorce...maybe try to write an amendment to the Constitution about custody matters....Perhaps we should have amended the Constitution to mandate marriage."[56]

After passionately defending the sanctity of marriage, she concluded the amendment wasn't needed to protect it. "The DOMA law that was enacted already protects states from having to recognize same-sex marriage licenses issued in other states," she explained, ignoring the specific reason the amendment was proposed: DOMA can, and probably will, be swept aside by the Supreme Court if not backed up by a constitutional amendment.[57]

The vote Hillary cast to defeat the marriage amendment was exactly what the Human Rights Campaign wanted. They liked it so much that they triple-weighted it on their Senate score card that year. Two years later, when the marriage amendment came up on the Senate floor again, Hillary again voted against it. This time she skipped the sermon.

In her trademark fashion, Hillary offered lip service to traditionalists while using her votes to advance the agenda of the cultural Left.

But it was her rhetoric that was on the minds of many in a 2006 meeting she had with several dozen gay leaders. Recalling her previous characterization of marriage as historically an exclusively heterosexual institution, one attendee challenged Hillary's statement that she was "against same-sex marriage on moral, religious, and traditional grounds," adding, "I found that incredibly hurtful."[58]

Caught cold in her deceitful rhetoric, Hillary claimed she had "evolved" since then. "Obviously my friends and people who spoke to me—we've had many long conversations and I think—and which I believe—that the way that I have spoken and I have advocated has certainly evolved and I am happy to be educated and to learn as much as I can."[59]

At this same meeting "[Hillary] indicated she would not oppose efforts by Eliot Spitzer, the odds-on favorite to become the new governor, to enact a same-sex marriage law in New York."

That about completes the flip, doesn't it?

Hillary's Village

When preparing for the birth of her daughter, Hillary did what many women have done and certainly would have been expected of her. As revealed in *It Takes a Village*, Hillary read everything she could get her hands on about having a baby. But it wasn't enough.

Left alone in her hospital room to nurse her newborn, Hillary panicked. "There I was, lying in my hospital bed, trying to figure out how to breast-feed," she wrote. "I had been trained to study everything forward, backward, and upside down before reaching a conclusion. It seemed to me I ought to be able to figure this out. As I looked on in horror, Chelsea started to foam at the nose. I thought she was strangling or having convulsions. Frantically, I pushed every buzzer there was to push."[60]

The nurse appeared promptly. She assessed the situation calmly, then, suppressing a smile, said, 'It would help if you held her head up a bit, like this.'"[61] That was all it took.

As I read this unenlightened report on Hillary's earliest moments with Chelsea, my first thought was that it fell into that category of information best known as "need to know," and I didn't need to know. Surely there was a purpose for this ridiculous anecdote. I read on.

Turns out this anxious moment of Hillary's and the many others that followed drove Hillary to leap to the conclusion that there is another, previously undetected, role for government—teaching parents to be good parents. Who knows what she thinks we have been doing in this country for the past two hundred plus years. But that never crosses her mind. She has a baby, is overwhelmed with concerns—and suddenly we all need the government to tell us how to do it.

Hillary's insecurity was clearly triggered with childbirth—she must have felt more dependent on experts than ever, having no confidence in her own judgment and wanting desperately to do everything right for her daughter. But this is not the case for most women. They quickly develop maternal instincts and learn to read the child and his needs as no one else can.

Hillary assumes that most women are like her—lacking in the knowledge and the confidence to care for a newborn and raise a child. She doesn't give women their due. For centuries, young, often uneducated women have been marrying and having babies. And they have been remarkable figures in the lives of their families. Where did they learn how? They drew on the strength and power that was within them. Government doesn't know of or have such resources.

It is a Samoan custom, Hillary writes, for expectant mothers to return to their mothers' village to give birth. They would be joined by the mother-in law or a sister-in-law. "With their collective experience as parents, they helped ease the transition into parenthood by showing how it was done."

Hillary then explains, "In our own American experience, families used to live closer together, making it easier for relatives to pitch in during pregnancy and the first months of a newborn's life. Women worked primarily in the home and were more available to lend a hand to new mothers and to help them get accustomed to motherhood."[62]

But now, "people and programs to help fledging parents are few and far between, even though such help costs surprisingly little."

What is she talking about? Does she not know that mothers travel across the country every day to be with daughters and daughters-in-law when a newborn arrives, that relatives and friends take in siblings for weeks at a time, and neighbors provide food and car-pools in such times of need? The system is in place, and what's more, women aren't needy people—we take care of ourselves, our families, our friends, and our neighbors. What is so lacking in Hillary and the gender feminists that they can't see this?

She goes on, "We are not giving enough attention to what ought to be our highest priority: educating and empowering people to be the best parents possible."[63]

Now she's getting to her real point: "Education and empowerment start with giving parents the means and the encouragement to plan pregnancy itself." Out of nowhere she takes us from help-ing parents be parents to keeping them from being parents. She then gives a real-life example of one of the "best models for doing this."

"I'm reminded of a particular clinic I visited in a rural part of Indonesia," she says. "Every month tables are set under the trees in a clearing, and doctors and nurses hold the clinic there. Women come to have their babies examined, to get medical advice, and to exchange information. A large posterboard chart notes the method of birth control each family is using, so that women can compare problems and results. This clinic and thousands like it around the country provide guidance that has led mothers to devote more time and energy to the children they already have before having more. The fathers, I was told, have also been affected by the presence of the clinic. They are more likely to judge their parental role by the quality of life they can provide to each child than by the number of children they father."[64]

Hillary—a women who wants to be president—is proposing our government establish a sort of roving neighborhood clinic open on the weekends so couples can grab a cup of coffee and share information about their method of birth control with neighbors and friends before heading off to the Little League game.

Hillary presents this Indonesian birth control clinic as an ideal institution in her "village." "This community clinic program, which is funded by the government and supported by the country's women's organizations and by Muslim leaders," exclaims Hillary, "is a wonderful example of how the village—both the immediate community and the larger society—can use basic resources to help families."[65] It's all about family planning—feminists funded by government, and thus determining what's best for the villagers.

But when she explains her views on the "village," just as when she explains her views on abortion and marriage, Hillary tries to have it both ways. She wants people to believe she is promoting the conservative values of Middle America when in fact she is promoting an extreme agenda that would use the power of government to reeducate people to behave in accordance with her own feminist values.

She will vigorously deny this, of course. She already has. When Senator Bob Dole accurately noted at the 1996 Republican National Convention that Hillary's "village" was in fact "big government," Hillary feigned umbrage. "In his acceptance speech at the Republican Convention, he had attacked the premise of my book, *It Takes a Village*," Hillary writes in *Living History*. "He mistakenly used my notion of the village as a metaphor for 'the state' and implied that I, and by extension Democrats, favor government intrusion into every aspect of American life."[66]

But Dole was not mistaken. Hillary is *It Takes a Village* in the flesh. She offers something for everyone, taking up both sides of a debate at different times and different places. Then she's on record as having been both for and against most everything—the war, illegal immigrants, same-sex marriage. She does the same in *It Takes a Village*.

In the opening chapters Hillary describes her own family. It was a traditional family: a man and a woman joined together in bringing children into the world and raising them. Hillary describes her parents as playing the traditional roles of breadwinning father and stay-at-home mother.

"My mother and father did what parents do best: They dedicated their time, energy, and money to their children and made sacrifices to give us a better life," she writes. "In 1994, the Carnegie Corporation issued a comprehensive report, Starting Points, which details the conditions that are undermining the development of America's youngest citizens—its infants and toddlers. In the report, the child development expert Dr. David Hamburg, the Carnegie Corporation's president, describes the ideal landscape in which to plant a child: an 'intact, cohesive nuclear family dependable under stress.' That description calls to mind the family in which I grew up," adds Hillary.[67]

She also highlights the need for parents to spend as much time as possible with their children, to be their first teachers. "For good or ill, our families and the environments in which we live are the backdrop against which we play out our entire lives," she writes. "Families shape our futures; our early family experiences heavily influence, and to a degree determine, how we forever after think and behave."[68]

This is good stuff—committed parents creating strong families to provide secure and loving homes for their children—so what was Bob Dole talking about? The rest of the book, that's what.

Once Hillary dispenses with the conservative verbiage necessary to give her cover with Middle America, she starts to build her village. And the blocks she uses are all government-issued. Every way you turn, there is a government program to cover almost every aspect of your child's life. But there is no other way for Hillary—she believes government knows best, they are the experts on what people need. It goes right to the heart of

Hillary's insecurity. She is the one who needs the rules on how to raise children—what to teach them and how to discipline them. These are decisions that require judgment and Hillary is incapable of that. Government institutions are like advisors to her—they direct and instruct. And Hillary assumes the rest of us are like her.

Note also that it is foreign governments that most inspire Hillary, as they tend to be so wonderfully engaged in the lives of their citizenry.

Here are a few things you'll find in Hillary's village:

- Universal health care. "Examples of the village at work can be found in countries where national health care systems ensure access to pre- and post-natal care for mothers and babies," she writes. "Many people believe that we cannot guarantee health care to all because of the cost. In fact, a sensible universal system would, as in other countries, end up costing us less."[69] Hillary doesn't explain how the quality of America's health care became the envy of the world.
- "Parent education" featuring "home visitors." Hillary describes a Hawaiian state program called "Healthy Start," in which parents are screened at the hospital when their children are born to see if the government should send "visitors" to their home. The program is now voluntary, but Hillary has devised a way to change that: "While Healthy Start operates on a consensual basis, states might also consider making public welfare or medical benefits contingent on agreement to allow home visits or to participate in other forms of parent education," she writes. And what else? You guessed it: all other nations are ahead of America in making this little intrusion into family life a reality. "It is interesting to note that all Western European countries provide some form of home health visitors," she says.[70]

As an example of how valuable home visits are, Hillary tells the story of an American friend of hers who was living in England when her baby was born. The woman's mother had hoped to be with her for the occasion but became too ill to travel. According to Hillary, "Like me, she found that the reading she had done, interesting as it was, left her with lots of unanswered questions. When the nurse came knocking at her door, my friend pulled the startled women inside and began babbling at her: 'Why won't she sleep for more than an hour? Will she ever open her eyes? Do you think she can hear me?'"

Let me get this straight. Hillary wants to create an entire government program so some yuppie can ask a government-paid nurse making house calls if her newborn can hear her? Am I hearing this right? Why didn't she just call her mom, like the rest of us do?

Women have been having babies since the time of Adam, and women have been helping other women with babies almost that long. So why is it Hillary and her smart friends can't do what millions of less-educated women do every day and do so with grace and confidence?

More government-funded goodies for the village:

- Government programs to tell children what to eat. "The U.S. Department of Agriculture, which oversees the school lunch programs, has started Team Nutrition, a partnership between the federal government, states, school districts, farmers, and businesses to promote healthy food choices in homes and schools and in the media."[71]
- Government-funded television. "As with many other social changes of the past fifty years, the children hardest hit by the negative impact of the media, television in particular, are those in low-income families," writes Hillary. "That's why public television, which has consistently provided educational

programming for children, deserves our tax dollars and charitable contributions."[72]

- Government-funded preschool/day care starting at three or younger. "Imagine a country in which nearly all children between the ages of three and five attend preschool in sparkling classrooms, with teachers recruited and trained as child care professionals," writes Hillary. "Imagine a country that conceives of child care as a program to 'welcome' children into the larger community and 'awaken' their potential for learning and growing." Here comes another foreign model for her American "village." "It may sound too good to be true, but it's not," she says. "When I went to France in 1989 as part of a group studying the French child care system, I saw what happens when a country makes caring for children a top priority. More than 90 percent of French children between ages three and five attend free or inexpensive preschools called *écoles maternelles*. Even before they reach the age of three, many of them are in full-day programs."[73] This is good?

Hillary is so excited about little tykes spending their days in regimented classrooms. But kids should be home horsing around with siblings and friends. These are the years that you develop a sense of belonging, of where you fit in the family; you feel the love and learn the rules, and the strength of these feelings are the roots of your security. None of this happens in school.

Why not introduce government incentives that would allow more mothers of children under five to stay home? Because Hillary knows that the first five years are the formative ones, and these children are her target. "Clearly, schools and day care centers, where many children are first introduced to people from a variety of backgrounds, have an important role to play in shaping attitudes and expectations," she writes. "At the Washington Beech Community Preschool in Roslindale, Massachusetts, director Ellen Wolpert has children play games like Go Fish and Concentration with decks of cards adorned with images—men holding babies, women pounding nails, elderly men on ladders, gray-haired women on skateboards—that counter predictable images."[74] Bingo.

There, in a nutshell, is what the village is all about. Hillary's endgame is to indoctrinate children as early as possible with the values of the sisterhood. The purpose of the village is to replace traditional values instilled by parents with feminist values drilled in by government-paid babysitters. The village children would never know a traditional nuclear family, that ideal unit Hillary pays lip service to in the conservative section of her book. How could they, if in their infancy these little ones were turned over to government nannies for proper nurturing? In the interest of women's liberation, Hillary reduces family life to a technocratic enterprise in which parents and professional day care providers are interchangeable and in which the government establishes the required curriculum and produces the teaching manuals to go along with it. She puts her faith in government over those to whom God gave the children, the parents.

It is worth taking a look at the belief system Hillary wants injected into our kids.

The World of the Ya-Ya Sisterhood

The first tenet of the sisterhood is that motherhood isn't all it's made out to be. In fact, Hillary and the gang find it a rather limiting affair, one that has caused too many women to miss out on life's more thrilling experiences. They have a warning: "Beware: motherhood could be dangerous to your God-given potential."

In *It Takes a Village* Hillary writes, "Most of the women my mother knew stayed home because society expected them to, and they aligned their own expectations with society's, even if they wished they had different choices."[75] "My generation lost good mothers and dedicated community volunteers among women who did not see a way to combine their work life with making a home and nurturing a family."[76]

It is time to grow up. Hillary is treating women as if they are a bunch of half-wits who were sold a bill of goods by society. The women she is referring to made choices just like the rest of us. If there are more choices now, that's life—but, like men, women need to take responsibility for their decisions and not blame society for a life that isn't what it could have been. Whining is not an acceptable response to your circumstances. Most women know that. Gender feminists don't; oppression is their middle name.

Here's another snippet of Hillary's deep-seated beliefs on motherhood: In a speech to a second UN conference on population she remarked, "By giving individuals and couples the freedom to choose the spacing and number of children, women not only gain more control over their lives, they contribute more to their families and their communities."[77] That sentence is worth a second read. Hillary is actually suggesting that if women have many children they are not doing right by their families and communities. What a shallow, empty world in which she lives. Does she not know that one of the greatest gifts mothers can give their children is siblings; that, for some, a chaotic house packed full of kids can be the happiest place on earth? Does she really believe that a mother of eight would be able to contribute more to her families and her community had she just aborted a few or been more careful? Does she not know that millions of women consider each child a gift from God and limiting them doesn't sound too grateful? And as for reaching your "God-given potential," there is no comparison between motherhood and a professional life. The Good Book tells us that the way to Heaven is service—that's what moms do all day, every day. The rewards are unmatched in this life, and I suspect in the next as well.

Hillary doesn't have any inkling of the blessing a boatload of kids can be for everyone involved. Consider the contemptuous stereotyping of large families as dysfunctional that she offers up in *It Takes a Village:*

- "I remember a six-year-old girl I tutored in reading at an elementary school in Little Rock. I'll call her Mary. She lived in a tiny house with six siblings, her parents, and an assortment of other relatives, who came and went unpredictably. There was so much commotion in the evenings that she was rarely able to sleep for longer than a few hours, and she was always tired. She seemed uncomfortable talking, but she didn't want to read either."[78]
- "A friend of mine told me about a visit she made to a family with five children. Down in the basement, she could hear the two teenage boys and their buddies singing along to the latest 'gangsta' rap CD. On the first floor, the six-year-old and the eight-year-old were slouched at either end of the couch, motionless in front of the screen, 'surfing' the channels. . . . In an upstairs bedroom, their twelve-year-old sister was watching an 'R'-rated video with a friend. It was a clear case of media assault. When my friend gently raised the issue of the poison that was pouring into those children's minds, her harried hostess could only say, 'Look, I'm doing my best.'"[79]

Hillary even slips in an unflattering allusion to the large family that produced her own maternal grandmother, a woman who abandoned Hillary's mom when she was just a small girl.

- "I'm still amazed at how my mother emerged from her lonely early life as such an affectionate and levelheaded woman. She was born in Chicago in 1919. Her father, Edwin John Howell, Jr., was a Chicago firefighter, and his wife, Della Murray, was one of nine children from a family of French Canadian, Scottish, and Native American ancestry. My maternal grandparents were certainly not ready for parenthood. Della essentially abandoned my mother when she was only three or four, leaving her alone all day for days on end with meal tickets to use at a restaurant near their five-story walk-up apartment on Chicago's South Side."[80]

All this could have been avoided, I guess, if only these poor women had been "empowered"—able and willing to prevent or abort some of those kids.

While Hillary often calls attention to her lifelong dedication to the battle for women's rights, it should be noted that she is referring to the collective form of the word "women." As individual women go, all women are not equal. There exists a certain feminist elitism at the core of Hillary's vision. In *Living History* she describes various wives of the heads of state and a female head of state she met as First Lady. Invariably she mentions education and profession—in Hillary's mind, this is what makes the woman.

- "Suzanne [Mubarak] has a master's degree in sociology and has been an energetic advocate for improved opportunities and education for women and children in Egypt.... "[81]
- "Queen Noor... an American-born Princeton graduate... has a degree in architecture and urban planning, was working as Director of Planning for Royal Jordanian Airlines.... "[82]
- "[Prime Minister] Benazir Bhutto, a brilliant and striking woman then in her mid-forties, was born into a prominent family and educated at Harvard and Oxford."[83]
- "A soft-spoken Italian-born women, Sonia Gandhi had fallen in love with Rajiv... when they were students at Cambridge University in England."[84]

- "Tony and Cherie [Blair], both barristers, the English term for trial lawyers.... A mother of three in 1997 when her husband became Prime Minister, Cherie continues her legal work...."[85]
- "[Wife of Brazil's president] Ruth Cardoso, a sociologist, assumed a formal position in her husband's government working...."[86]
- "Bernadette [Chirac] is an elegant, cultured woman who since 1971 had been a local elected official from the constituency in the Correze region. She was the only presidential spouse I knew who had been elected on her own."[87]
- "[Wife of Chile's president] Marta Larrachea de Frei, was a First Lady after my own heart. Assisted by a professional staff she tackled issues ranging from microfinance to education reform."[88]
- "[Nania Yeltsin] had been a civil engineer who had worked on water systems and then was thrust into the treacherous waters of Russian politics. From the beginning she was personable and articulate about children and their health care needs."[89]
- "Flavia Prodi of Italy, a serious and thoughtful academic...."[90]

One lonely First Lady made it into the book as nothing more than a mother—she must have absolutely nothing worthy of commendation on her résumé.

- "[Jolanta Kwasniewska, the president of Poland's wife] and I are mothers of only daughters, and that made for animated discussions of the perils and pleasures of raising them."[91]

Hillary never misses an opportunity to mention education—including the name of the institution if it's Ivy League or the foreign equivalent—and the professional careers of these women. But this is not what made these women noteworthy. If a woman is a queen it's because she's married to the king. Not because she went to Princeton. Just like Hillary, these women are famous, for the most part, because of their husbands. So Hillary goes out of her way to tell the world they are more than that—they are significant people in their own right, they are educated and professional women. Being a wife and mother just doesn't do it for Hillary. Those two roles don't lend themselves too much worth in her world of significant and "empowered" women.

When it comes to women and families, Hillary's biases are indeed rooted in the gender feminism Christina Hoff Sommers accurately describes. To Hillary, a woman who stays home and dedicates herself to raising her children is a woman who has succumbed to the victimization of a male-dominated world. She therefore portrays working women in a better light than stay-at-home moms and favors smaller families over larger ones because large families might trap women longer in the home, longer in the demeaning tasks of motherhood, keeping them from being "liberated."

Summarizing her remarks to the UN Conference in The Hague, the *Feminist Daily News* reported that Hillary said that "empowering women and children is in the world's best interest, given that woman who are empowered and educated will actively seek to limit their childbearing."[92]

My mother was educated, but not too empowered, thank goodness—I am the seventh of nine children. Brother Pat, as number three, had a fighting chance but I would have never made it. I suspect Hillary might see real value in an "empowered" Mrs. Buchanan, especially if she limited herself to just two kids. But what about Rose Kennedy? Jack, the second of nine, would probably have made the cut, but Robert shared my position as number seven. He and baby brother Ted didn't have a prayer of a chance.

I don't know about Rose Kennedy, but my mom would have succeeded in anything she did. She chose, though, to stand at the helm of a large Catholic family and the world is a better place for it. It is sad that feminists who claim to be committed to the rights of women can't appreciate that women like my mom made their choice, had all the children they were meant to have, and became giants in the lives of their families and their communities. What's more, they had no regrets and taught their children to do the same.

Hillary's Heaven

Let's go back to where we started this chapter—with Hillary in Cairo.

In her speech at the American University in Cairo, Hillary spoke of visiting the Egyptian Museum, where many artifacts of the pharaohs—including "King" Hatshepsut—are kept. "As I walked through the museum the other day, with the wonderful guidance of some experts who were with my daughter and me, I saw the kinds of things that a pharaoh or a noble person would want to bring with him into the next world—everything that was essential as we embark on the final journey of this life," said Hillary. "They believe that they were preserving what was necessary so that they could live in the future and the next life to come. And I thought to myself, what would we take with us? We know so well that we will not, we believe, have use for food or clothing, so what tangible things would we take? Probably none, now. But what about the intangibles, what of values ...?"[93]

Then Hillary enlightens us as to what these might be.

"We would want to take those values, those institutions that can really stand the test of time," she said.[94] Since we are heading for eternity she's got a point.

She then elaborates a bit. "So we would want, I believe, to bring with us institutions that would permit us to make this journey into the future, one that we could navigate with some sense of certainty about the direction we are taking." Institutions? She wants to take institutions to Heaven? So we have direction in our next life?

Let me get this right. Hillary wants to head off to Heaven armed with universal day care for preschoolers, family planning clinics, unrestricted abortion, same-sex partnerships, and all the other values and institutions of her village? I don't want to be anywhere near those pearly gates when she arrives.

Admittedly much of this speech was incoherent ramblings of one sort or another, not unusual for Hillary. And maybe she was thinking about teleporting to the future rather than getting to Heaven. You can decide for yourself—it is in the appendix of this book. But whatever she meant to say, she clearly stated what it is she values most in life. She let us know that in her mind what needs to be passed on to future generations are governmental institutions to guide them, an economy to provide for them, and a civil society.[95] There was no mention of God, family, or country.

Chapter Seven

For the Common Good

IMAGINE THE EXCITEMENT among liberal activists when Hillary won the New York Senate seat. One of their own, a champion of their causes, a woman who risked her political reputation fighting for universal health care, taking a seat at the table. They had a right to celebrate. Hillary wasn't just another reliable liberal vote—she was much more—why, she was the Jesse Helms of the Far Left. They believed, as well they should have, that they had a new "go-to guy," as Jesse had been for conservatives for decades, someone you could always rely on to make the case, and then fight to the end—win, lose, or die. What's more, Hillary brought a national audience and enormous political clout with her. She was a Superstar, a freshman Superstar, and she was theirs. It was indeed a grand victory for the Left.

But before long their expectations came tumbling down. Their plan was not her plan. She was not about to use this new perch of hers for the cause, unless you meant her cause. And the two were certainly not the same—not anymore. Hillary had no intention of spending her political capital fighting losing ideological battles as she had done so often in the past. She had more important things to do, had set a loftier goal for herself—she needed to become president. Her complete focus had to be on remaking herself into that mold. So she threw courage to the wolves and embraced a cautious, careful, small-step approach to legislating—much to the chagrin of the rank and file.

"Afraid to offend, she has limited her policy proposals to minor, symbolic issues—such as cosponsoring legislation to ban flag burning" wrote Markos Moulitsas, the founder of the political blog Daily Kos. "She doesn't have a single memorable policy or legislative accomplishment to her name."[1]

The *Atlantic*'s Joshua Green made a similar observation and presented it to Hillary during an interview. "I suggested that for all she'd been busy doing in the Senate, I couldn't find an instance where she had taken a politically unpopular stance or championed a big idea, like healthcare reform, that might not yield immediate benefits but was the right thing to do." He continued, "Interviews with colleagues and observers seemed to imply an unspoken disappointment that her talents promised a record of more height and substance than she had displayed."

In response to this line of criticism Hillary immediately referred to her work on behalf of victims of the September 11 terrorist attack. Green cut her short, remarking that that hardly fell within the category of brave and unpopular. She quickly moved to her second line of defense, "I voted against every tax cut." Green added just as quickly, "But you're a Democrat!"[2]

When Hillary took office she chose to leave the leading up to others—too many risks and the makeover plan called for none of that. But she did do the minimum required of a good liberal Democrat—she voted right. The makeover came first, but if there was no conflict with it, Hillary voted left. As a result Hillary has bragging rights to one of the most left-wing voting records in the U.S. Senate today.

The conservative National Taxpayers Union, a group dedicated to smaller government, gave Hillary a 12 percent average for the six years of her first term in the Senate—right down there with her tax-and-spend friends Senators Kennedy, Dodd, and Biden. And for those who have any doubt as to whose bidding Hillary does in the Senate, let me introduce you to Americans for Democratic Action (ADA). Here is how they describe their rating system: "Since ADA's founding in 1947, the Annual Voting Records have served as the standard measure of political liberalism. Combining twenty key votes on a wide range of social and economic issues, both domestic and international, the Liberal (LQ) provides a basic overall picture of an elected official's political position." Hillary received a 95 percent rating all six years with the exception of 2005. She recived a 100 percent that year. Need I say more?

Yet at a press conference in November of 2006, right after the Democrats had won control of the Congress, Hillary had the audacity to pose as a centrist: "We are ready to roll up our sleeves and work with our Republican counterparts. Our country works best when we govern from the vital, dynamic center."[3] The dynamic center? Hillary has only spent vacation time there—when she was trying to get her war position tailored to the electorate— then a hurricane hit and she's still spinning.

To get a better idea of just how far left Hillary's record places her, consider her position on several big government items.

Health Care

Her efforts in 1993 to nationalize America's health care system were such a colossal disaster, one might think Hillary would be whistling a different tune about now. But that would be foolish.

She is as committed today to socializing medicine in America as she has ever been. Hillary claims her massive government takeover of the health care industry was the only way to control the rising costs; but far more important to her, it put the state in control of that much more of society.

In fairness, the lady is not shy about making her intentions known. She raised the issue in her speech to the Democratic Convention in 2000. "You may remember I had a few ideas about health care." She then added, "I've learned a few lessons since then. But I haven't given up on the goal."[4] More recently, in November 2006, she remarked, "Health care is coming back. It may be a bad dream for some."[5]

Nightmare is more like it—especially if it is created in the likeness of the monstrosity she proposed as co-president. To raise just a few of the finer points of her earlier attempt to restructure America's health care system: Hillary would have federalized the nation's teaching hospitals and required everyone to carry national identification cards containing computer chips embedded with their confidential medical information.[6] For those who dared violate the rules, the consequences were financially ruinous, as reported in a 1999 column by Tony Snow. Maximum fines included:

- $5,000 for refusing to join the government-mandated plan (Could we still call America the land of the free? It might be a stretch.)
- $5,000 for failing to pay premiums on time (If it happens twice they send out Bruiser and Roscoe to work over your knees.)
- Fifteen years for doctors guilty of receiving "anything of value" in exchange for helping patients bypass the bureaucracy (Making it a crime right up there with child molestation.)

- $10,000 a day for faulty physician paperwork (Don't let that groaning patient in the next room disturb you, Doc.)
- $50,000 for unauthorized patient treatment (Who do these doctors think they are? Doctors?)
- $100,000 a day for drug companies that mess up federal filings"[7] (Would that be like overlooking $100,000 in cattle future profits on an IRS form?)

This health care plan was a thing of beauty for Hillary—socialized medicine enforced by a totalitarian government.

Large businesses would have likely survived in Hillary's brave new world but small businesses, the backbone of the nation, were at risk. And this powerful constituency raised the alarm—putting all on notice that Hillary's plan had dire consequences for them. Her response was pure Hillary—she simply could not be "responsible for every undercapitalized small business in America."[8] She proved equally indifferent to the complaint that her plan severely restricted patient choice. When a woman commented she didn't want to get assigned to a plan not of her choosing, Hillary answered, "It's time to put the common good, the national interest, ahead of individuals."[9]

So firm is her commitment to total government control that in 2003 when the Medicare prescription drug bill was introduced in the Senate, a mammoth $400 billion entitlement proposed by President Bush and endorsed by Senator Kennedy, Hillary voted against it. Why? Because, according to CNN's Judy Woodruff, Hillary didn't believe it went far enough. It only covered 50 percent of most drug costs after the deductible, but the real stake in the heart for Hillary was that it had a private sector aspect to it. "I believe it should be in Medicare," Hillary explained.[10]

With other 2008 presidential hopefuls now calling for massive new health care coverage, the old gal isn't about to let one of them get to her left. She paid too high a price staking out this territory to let anyone get near her property line. Hillarycare will be back, repackaged just like its creator, but it will be back, you can bet on it.

Education

Ronald Reagan is often quoted as saying that government wasn't the answer, it was the problem. Hillary takes just the opposite point of view. As stated years ago she believes the purpose of the state is "to use its means of acquiring tax money, of making decisions to assist us in becoming a better, more equitable society as it defines it."[11] The all-wise government determines the kind of society we should be, and then they enforce it. But to effect the necessary change they need to control the education of the children.

Hillary understands this perfectly and as we saw in an earlier chapter, she advocates government funded and regulated early head start and head start programs—to get to the kids as early as possible. Higher education is already owned and operated by the left, so she sees government's role as simply subsidizing it for all students legal or illegal. As for elementary and secondary schools, Hillary supports an ever-expanding role for big brother. Whatever the latest effort is to get government more involved, from Goals 2000 to the most expensive federal education bill of all, No Child Left Behind, Hillary can be counted on to champion it.

It doesn't seem to matter to Hillary, or anyone in Washington for that matter, that there's not a shred of evidence that the billions of dollars that have been poured into education have given us better educated kids. But that doesn't mean the money hasn't had an impact. As the federal government has become increasingly involved in our schools, the curriculum has changed—away from knowledge-based academics, where the focus was on reading, writing, and arithmetic, and toward an ideological curricula based on attitudes, values, beliefs, and behaviors—an area that had previously been the responsibility of parents.[12] Education hasn't improved, but the indoctrination is coming along just fine.

Behind the new curricula is the powerful National Education Association, with whom Hillary is in lock step. They are pro-abortion, pro–gay rights, support public schools programs "from birth through age eight," and claim every child has the right to "freely available information and knowledge about sexuality."[13]

The NEA demands the right to teach children sex education, including diversity of sexual orientation and gender identification, incest, and homophobia.[14] And on these subjects their teachers have proven quite proficient. Unfortunately, that's not always the case when teaching reading, writing, and arithmetic—or science or history. One would think that assuring the nation that its children would have qualified teachers would be a primary concern of the NEA. But it's not so. They are too busy wailing about the right to take their left-wing agenda into the classroom and protecting their inept teachers from testing.

It was on this latter issue—testing of teachers—that Hillary was forced to break with the NEA—politics required she do so, at least publicly. It happened in Arkansas when Hillary was named by her husband to be the chair of the Education Standards Committee, which was formed "to recommend sweeping educational reforms."[15]

The Arkansas State Supreme Court had ruled that the state's system of financing education was unconstitutional. Property taxes had been the source of school funding and, according to the courts, this posed an unfair disadvantage to the state's poorer communities. In *Rewriting History*, Dick Morris describes in-depth discussions and subsequent polls that led to the decision to finance the state's education by increasing the sales tax by 1 percent. What Morris's polls had assured the Clintons was that the public would accept the tax if—and only if—they believed the quality of the schools would actually improve.[16]

They decided to propose the tax increase along with serious educational reforms that would be well received by parents across the state. The job of Hillary's committee was to come up with the reforms.

The committee decided to adopt strict new mandatory education guidelines, as well as introduce standardized tests for students and mandatory testing of teachers. In Hillary's own words: "Though this enraged the teachers' union, civil rights groups, and others who were vital to the Democratic Party in Arkansas, we saw no way around the issue. How could we expect children to perform at national levels when their teachers sometimes fell short?"[17] Exactly, Hillary, how could you?

A Tennessee study concluded that the competence of a teacher can affect the performance of students by as much as 50 percent.[18] Hilary had no choice. If the plan was to have any semblance of success, it had to challenge the powerful teachers' union. And their anticipated outrage would help convince the public the Clintons were serious about improving the quality of education in Arkansas. Bill's re-election was what was at stake. Hillary did what had to be done—she demanded all teachers be tested.

According to the original plan, the teachers were to be tested on their basic knowledge and skills. If they failed the test, they would be permitted to take it again two years later. If they failed a second time, they were to be discharged from teaching. But the first test results were alarming: one-half of all the teachers had failed. To make matters politically worse, minority teachers flunked in even larger numbers.[19]

If these results had been released, the teachers' union, minority groups, and parents would have all gone ballistic. The state would have been on its ear—but the underlying cause of Arkansas' failing schools would have been on the front pages for all to see. Only then could the system have been fixed—only then could the children of the state have a fighting chance at a decent education. As

David Horowitz puts it, "Since Arkansas is one of the poorest states in the union, a failing school system meant that its disadvantaged children would be denied the only opportunity they would ever get to lift themselves out of poverty and into a better life."[20]

The children of Arkansas were depending on Hillary, the woman who claimed to be their champion. But when they needed her the most, when they needed her to be strong for them, she couldn't do it—political expediency wouldn't allow it.

With test results in hand, Hillary and Bill called their old friend Dick Morris and asked him to poll Arkansas voters to determine the politically acceptable level of failure for the teachers—it was determined that the public expected about a 10 percent failure rate. And so it was. The Clintons cooked the books and announced that 10 percent of Arkansas teachers had failed the testing. Hillary and Bill won, the teachers won, the taxpayers got skunked, and the kids lost what could well have been their only ticket out of poverty.[21]

Today Hillary is opposed to testing teachers unless they are the new ones, fresh out of school.[22] She knows poor teachers are at the root of the problem; she said as much in *Living History* when she explained why she proposed testing them in the first place. But she isn't about kids, she's about politics. Hillary took on the NEA when it was politically expedient for her to do so, and then folded when that was politically expedient. Now it is politically expedient that she return to their fold—she has a presidential campaign to consider.

Hillary has long ago forgotten those kids in Arkansas. Since then she has become an important person on the world stage, at least in her mind. In a speech to the Council on Foreign Relations in 2004, Hillary didn't call for better education for all Americans. That would have been embarrassingly provincial. Hillary, the senator from New York, upped the ante and "unveiled legislation designed to provide universal basic education for all children throughout the world."[23] Match that, Senator Kennedy.

How arrogant she is. To expect Americans to pay billions of dollars funding Third World educational systems when so many of our own children lack the first-class education they deserve. Proposing "education for all" is so cheap a stunt, it does nothing but draw praise onto herself. Think how much more she would have accomplished had she fired those lousy teachers in Arkansas.

Tax and Spend

In June 2004 Hillary found herself at a Democratic fund-raiser in San Francisco, speaking to the crowd of high rollers. "Many of you are well enough off that...the [Bush] tax cuts may have helped you," she said. "We're saying that for America to get back on track, we're probably going to cut that short and not give it to you." Then she added this little gem: "We're going to take things away from you on behalf of the common good."[24] Bet the drinks were flowing after that.

In this rare moment of intellectual honesty, Hillary used the same expression that popped out of her mouth years earlier when under pressure to defend her health care plan: "It's time to put the common good, the national interest, ahead of individuals."[25]

And how was it that she defined the role of government some years earlier? "To use its means of acquiring tax money, of making decisions to assist us in becoming a better, more equitable society as it defines it."[26]

Hillary's view of government is simple. It is to remold society. It can do so by coercion, as in the case of health care; by indoctrination, as in the case of education; or by redistributing the wealth through tax and spend policies. It is pure, unadulterated socialism, the type that is forced upon a people by their government.

The Reverend Don Jones, Hillary's spiritual advisor from her high school days and a lifetime confidant, confirms that this indeed is at the core of Hillary's beliefs. "My sense of Hillary is that she realizes absolutely the truth of the human condition, which is that you cannot depend on the basic nature of man to be good and you cannot depend entirely on moral suasion to make it good," the Reverend told the late Michael Kelly. "You have to use power. And there is nothing wrong with wielding power in the pursuit of policies that will add to the human good. I think Hillary knows this. She is very much the sort of Christian who understands that the use of power to achieve social good is legitimate."[27]

Hoping to go to Heaven on our dime, Hillary has put her religion into practice in the U.S. Senate. A passionate taxer, she views tax cuts as evil. She often quotes the late Senator Moynihan, who accused Republicans of wanting to "starve the federal government, to prevent it from being able to do anything other than national defense."[28] And she doesn't hesitate to add her own indictment, charging that the Bush tax cuts were "funded by kicking 500,000 children out of after-school programs,"[29] and blaming them for everything from the recession of 2001 and the depletion of the surpluses in Social Security and Medicare, to threatening the safety of our homeland.[30]

"Will ending the dividend tax make air travel safer?" she rhetorically asked the students at John Jay College. "Will it secure our nuclear power plants? Will it keep a dirty bomb out of New York harbor? Will ending the tax on dividends save one police officer or firefighter his or her job? In short, will it make America safer?"[31]

You have to wonder why Hillary becomes so exercised over efforts to let hardworking Americans keep more of their money. The wording of her response to the demise of a 2006 bill designed to permanently eliminate the estate tax is instructive; "Repeal of the inheritance tax would have set aside $1 trillion so that the small fraction of millionaires and billionaires in this country would pay nothing when they transfer their huge estates to their heirs."[32]

"Set aside?" Who exactly was setting anything aside? And why does she believe you should be taxed when you die? What kind of deal is that—as if you don't already have enough problems dying with all that money. ("It is easier for a camel to go through the eye of a needle, than for a rich man to enter into the kingdom of Heaven." Mark 10:25)

But in Hillary's mind, these moneys are set aside—they are sitting there waiting for her to get to the White House. This sizable chunk makes for a fine rainy day fund for that village of hers, and those rotten Republicans are trying to take it away from her.

But as committed a taxer as Hillary is, it's no match for the spender in her. After only a year in office she was reported to have been the biggest spender of taxpayer money for a freshman senator in history.[33]

During her first two years in office she sponsored or cosponsored 169 bills that would have increased spending by $124 billion, and not a one that would have reduced it. The following couple years the old gal outdid herself, sponsoring or cosponsoring 211 bills that would have increased spending and three bills that would have reduced it, for a total net cost of $378 billion, giving her the silver medal for the category "top spenders in the U.S. Senate" during the period.[34]

Then there is Citizens against Government Waste, a non-partisan watchdog group, which gave Hillary an average score for her first term in office of 10 percent—which puts her smack into the "hostile to the taxpayer" column. She even had the honor of sharing CAGW's "Porker of the Year" award with her colleague Senator Schumer in 2005, for their duel efforts to get federal development moneys for upper-class Westchester County, New York.[35] In April 2006, Hillary returned to her home town to address the distinguished members of the Economic Club of Chicago. In her long and boring presentation, Hillary called for a government-driven economy that would rebuild America. Tax cuts, she said, "are not the cure-all for everything that ails the American economy. It takes the right tax system and the right investments, including infra-structures.... We need investments, decisions, and policies that only all of us acting together through our government can make to set the stage for the future prosperity."[36]

There she goes again—all things must go "through the government."

And as for the rich, Hillary had little good to say: "America did not build the greatest economy in the world because we have rich people. Nearly any society has some of those." Clearly they are in the crosshairs. In an article covering the speech, entitled "Waking Up to Hillary's Big-Government Nightmare," Larry Kudlow wrote: "Without exactly saying it, [Hillary] clearly implied tax hikes on the rich and a large-scale redistribution program worthy of any centrally planned economy." Kudlow describes Hillary's goals of "a middle class life, education, health care, transportations, and retirement" as "nothing more than a massive dose for government spending and regulating—a sure prescription for humongous taxes and a declining economy."[37]

This was the 2006 version of Hillary. To the core she is a tax and spend liberal of the highest order.

Lipstick on the Pig

In spite of what is unquestionably an extremely liberal voting record on all major issues, with the exception of her war vote—which she now attributes to having been "misled"—Hillary markets herself, somewhat successfully, I might add, as a centrist. Those who conspire to perpetuate this fraud point to her cosponsoring a bill to ban flag burning, or her legislation to keep violent videos out of the hands of children, or her support of faith-based initiatives. Some go so far as to suggest her participation in congressional prayer groups and the fact she occasionally dons a cross are further proof of legitimate conservative credentials.

To even suggest Hillary has middle to right leanings is utterly absurd—her Senate votes fly in the face of such a claim. The sheer flimsiness of her dalliances with the Right are so shallow and insignificant they bring to mind that expression "nothing more than lipstick on a pig"—it's still very much a pig.

I think this goes exactly to the point my friend Ed Rollins made, "Hillary Clinton is tough, intelligent, effective, ruthless, and committed to undoing everything accomplished by Ronald Reagan. Anyone who underestimates her does so at their peril."

In the field of fiscal and trade policies Hillary has performed a similar act. On the stump she calls for a balanced budget and a reduction in the trade deficit; talks about wanting "made in America" to always stand for something, addresses the plight of our manufacturing sector, and warns "we are in the midst of an American jobs crisis."[38] She even voted against the Central America Free Trade Agreement (CAFTA), despite her husband's support of free trade measurements when he was president. All this plays well with the workers of America, who feel abandoned by the Democratic Party.

But on the other hand she calls us "global citizens";[39] praises her husband for putting America on the "right course to a globalized and integrated world"; and remarks that "a single, unified world is a perspective we Democrats have not successfully made clear."[40] Hardly the language of the economic populist that her earlier remarks are intended to suggest. But it does fit the profile of a pandering politician aware that nearly half of all independent voters, a critical voting block for Hillary, are fed up with the free trade policies of the past, believing they are at the root of the massive exportation of American jobs and the stagnant wages of our workers at home.[41]

This same block of voters expect the nation to balance the budget—again Hillary has solid verbiage to suggest that she is with them—a true deficit hawk. But while she calls for a balanced budget and supports a pay-as-you-go approach to spending, Hillary votes for nearly every spending bill that comes across her desk. The level of taxes needed to support her spending sprees would bankrupt the nation. I doubt this is what those voters have in mind.

When studying Hilary you can not make any conclusions from the words she uses—they are simply tools to deceive. And what's more, a few comments and an isolated vote doesn't turn a born internationalist into a champion of America's working people, any more than mentioning the name of God makes her a member of the vast right wing.

The Evidence Is In

We have completed our examination of Senator Hillary on the issues and the evidence is irrefutable. Her votes consistently support the agenda of the Left, unless that vote can be better used to promote her presidential ambitions.

Hillary has toned down her appearance, her rhetoric, her attitude, and her approach as part of the makeover. But she did not forget where she came from. Liberal activists had wanted her to be an outspoken and formidable leader in the Senate of the United States; she chose instead a more reserved and cautious persona. It was what the makeover required. But Hillary has sent a clear and unambiguous signal to her left-wing friends that they can always count on her. On only one issue—the war on Iraq—has she endangered her relationship with them, and she is now beating a retreat—and blaming George W. Bush for that miscalculation.

When all is said and done, what does Hillary believe? For what does she stand? In what direction would she take the nation if she were the president?

First and foremost, Hillary is an ardent and radical feminist. Of all the liberal causes of her past, this is the one most deeply rooted. She does not just represent radical feminists; she is one of them. Their agenda is her agenda, and as president she will promote both here and abroad the empty ideals and distorted values of this failed and fading movement.

Second, Hillary adheres to the tenet "from each according to their ability, to each according to their need." She is a big government, tax and spend liberal who can match the best of them. Her vision of the role of government in the lives of its citizens is nearly limitless, as is her willingness to take from them whatever she needs to support her village.

Third, Hillary is an internationalist who will glory in her role on the world stage and expect American taxpayers to pay for education and welfare programs for women and children around the world. She supports amnesty for illegal aliens and would open our borders to tens of million of additional foreign workers. Moreover, she would provide them and their families with medical expenses, education costs, and a pathway to citizenship. In other words, she will be as generous as she can be with *your* money, spending it here and abroad.

Finally, when it comes to war, what does Hillary believe? As president will she reserve the use of our military for those situations in which America's vital interests are threatened? Or will she see another role for them in this increasingly dangerous world? In short, would Hillary, as president, use the power and might of the U.S. military to force some Third World leader to get in line? I believe she would. For two reasons.

First, Hillary has not been a card-carrying member of the antiwar movement for years. And if there were any residual commitment she felt to its principles it was not enough to override the compelling interest of her own ambitions. She voted for war for no better reason than that it was in her personal interest, not because it was in America's interest. Time and again the liberal media give her political aspirations as the explanation for her pro-war vote, and amazingly many on the Left find this completely acceptable. I doubt the families of those who gave life or limb are as understanding of her contemptible and callous disregard for the well-being of our soldiers. But then the tide turned on Hillary and presidential ambitions required that she too turn—this time against that war, and so she has.

Second, Hillary is about power—and our bombs are power, the greatest power on earth. She felt that power when she instructed her husband to drop them on Serbia. Why would she hesitate to do it again?

Chapter Eight

The Stepford Candidate

T HERE IS AN EXCITEMENT in presidential politics not unlike that in a boxing match. As each candidate steps into the ring the crowd gives him the once-over—assessing if he has the strength, the punch, the footwork, and the fortitude to go the distance. They watch as he hits some issues, dances around others, and takes a few blows to the body. In the early rounds they continue to size him up, but the real test comes when the pounding gets bloody—can he sustain the beating long enough to get to another round? If the candidate can find his voice and hit his natural stride quickly enough, he'll grow more confident with each round. That's when the crowd will know this one's ready for prime time.

Politics is great theater—exhilarating, exhausting, and infinitely gratifying for those who brave the arena, and ever so entertaining for those on the sidelines.

Hillary has had fifteen years of experience on the national stage. She has had great success and felt the warmth of praise, and she has stumbled and fallen and felt the sting of criticism. But through all these years of battle Hillary has never been kept down. While her failures have made her more hesitant and certainly less daring, she has always returned to the arena to face another day. Whatever one's feelings are toward her, there is no denying that Hillary is a battle-tested, prime-time-ready, tough and formidable candidate who knows how to play the game and is ready and willing to be as ruthless as necessary to win.

Why then was an extreme makeover necessary? Among the 2008 presidential candidates Hillary has the most experience, as much knowledge, the keenest sense of politics, and an organization that is unrivalled. What's more, makeovers aren't free. There are consequences for candidates who try to reposition themselves on issues in the opening round of a campaign; the "wishy-washy, flip-flopping opportunist" label is guaranteed to follow. And if the makeover is intended to disguise the character or personality of a candidate, good luck. Under pressure the real McCoy will invariably return to the scene.

The firm of Clinton & Clinton, however, must have determined that the risk was worth it, that parts of Hillary—temperament, character, beliefs, style, or some combination thereof—had to be altered to fit some arbitrary mold of what a presidential candidate needs to look like. And the depth of the problem must have been severe, considering they signed her up for a political lobotomy. No part of Hillary was designated off-limits. For six years Hillary has been under the knife, so to speak, as the experts attempted to transform her from that spirited and divisive left-wing media darling who made such good right-wing copy into a more serious national figure—moderate in temperament, style, politics, and tone.

The question is: Has it worked? Is the 2008 edition of Hillary more likely to be president than the earlier versions?

The answer is an unqualified yes—she has won two statewide elections in the last six years, held the office of senator, and added immensely to her knowledge of the nation and the world. Whether she needed a makeover to accomplish any of this is doubtful; her superstar status and incredibly weak opponents had as much to do with her election victories as anything. But there is no doubt Hillary is the odds-on favorite to win the nomination of her party, and most indicators point to a 2008 Democratic takeover of the presidency. Bottom line: Hillary is the woman to beat if you are running for president in 2008.

However, a surprising number of roadblocks are popping up as Hillary attempts to navigate her way back to the White House, seemingly in spite of the extensive planning and complete transformation of the candidate. But some of the most serious obstacles Hillary faces are actually the result of the makeover. What a bit of twisted fate it would be if the extreme makeover Hillary underwent to capture the highest office in the land contributed in a significant way to her failure to do so.

Hillaryland

By all accounts, Hillary's costly campaign organization is impressive in both size and quality. Considering her compulsive need for advisors for everything from shoe color to message, this was to be expected. But too many advisors in a campaign are like too many cooks in the kitchen. There needs to be a single boss and a few trusted aides to have an effective operation. With so many chiefs in its camp, Hillaryland may well be headed to internecine warfare at the first sighting of bad polls.

There is a second trap into which a huge and heavily financed campaign will often fall. In an effort to control everything that happens—leaving nothing to chance—the consultants strip a campaign, and the candidate, of any sense of spontaneity.

This is not lost on Democrats. As one Democratic advisor told me of Hillary, "Hillary is extremely smart and competent. If she will just trust her own instincts...if she is too dependent on her consultants that will be her downfall."

Take, for instance, Hillary's message. To guarantee it is in line with what the public wants to hear, her advisors poll endlessly and glean from pages and pages of cross-tabulations not only what she should say, but how she should say it. But no matter how good the message, if it is artificially produced it loses the human element and rings hollow.

A message from the heart, on the other hand, creates a bond between the voter and a candidate. The genuine candidate imparts something of himself in the process and triggers in the voter a sense of attachment that is nearly impossible to break.

But since Hillary has always had difficulty communicating with her heart, you might argue, it makes no difference. Not so. The senator from New York, the former First Lady of the United States, was never a robot. She is now. Her consultants have so over-programmed her that there is nothing warm, natural, or authentic left. They turned her into a Stepford candidate. After purging the personality and eliminating the natural range of human emotions, her makeover artists turned her into their image of the perfect female candidate for president—frozen face and all. She looks, acts, and talks the part of the main character in some low-budget Hollywood production called *Madam President*.

None of this is missed on those who might one day vote for her. Maureen Dowd of the *New York Times* writes that "[Hillary] is overproduced and overscripted."[1] Liberal blogger Markos Moulitsas described the new and improved Hillary as a "heartless, passionless machine"[2] and *Slate*'s Jacob Weisberg noted that "it's hard not to find Hillary a bit inhuman."[3]

This makeover is hurting Hillary. As David Corn of *The Nation* told me, she is going to have a hard time with Democrats. "She seeks power more than she confronts it. That alienates her, to a degree, from the passionate base of the party that hungers for widespread change."

And that is indeed the case. At least one feminist leader has already responded to the makeover by breaking ranks with the Stepford candidate. Abortion rights champion Kate Michelman endorsed Hillary's primary opponent John Edwards, explaining, "I know the difference between those who advocate as a political position and those who understand the reality of women's lives."[4] (Whiny women and wimpy insults—the sisterhood can be unbearable sometimes.)

"Artificial," "inhuman," "robotic," "heartless," "cold," "calculating," and "overproduced" are words commonly used to describe the newly made-over Hillary. While surely not the intent of the makeover, they are its natural consequence. She willingly turned her public persona over to others to control and manipulate. As a candidate, Hillary will never find her voice or hit her natural stride—and she will never acquire the confidence of candidates who do. She never gave herself that chance, so insecure she was about being herself. And now it's too late. Her addiction to advisors has taken over her life. She does and says nothing more and nothing less than what they direct, leaving nothing particularly interesting about Hillary left.

Is It Over Yet?

Campaigns are intended to be about the future; from a field of candidates the public chooses the leader for tomorrow. A new face with fresh ideas will often catch the attention of the public for just this reason. While a seasoned veteran may win, the newcomers are always a welcomed distraction from the old war horses—often generating much of the excitement and energy in a race.

Freshness by its very nature attracts interest and is an invaluable asset for any candidate. But it is difficult to maintain in a lengthy, drawn-out race. Most candidates tend not to wear well over the long haul. The public gets weary of seeing them and tires of hearing the same old sound bites.

The lack of anything remotely fresh presents a significant problem for Hillary. Even before she decided to run for president, Hillary was nearly universally known and nearly as many people had formed an opinion about her. While the sheer force of her celebrity status creates an atmosphere of excitement around her, it remains to be seen if this will translate into support for her presidential ambitions. As actress Kathleen Turner observed, Americans "don't want a celebrity woman president."[5] The polls suggest Ms. Turner knows what she is talking about. In a Marist February 2007 national poll, 43 percent of Americans said they would "definitely not consider voting for her."[6]

In fairness, Hillary could not have run as a new face—she is an old-timer, embedded into our national consciousness during her turbulent years as First Lady. But she could have done a few things to bring a greater sense of freshness to her presidential effort. And it would have been to her benefit to have done so.

Instead, she deepened the public perception that she has been running for president forever. (Then again, maybe she has.)

In her first years in the Senate, Hillary's makeover artists wisely instructed her to lie low, to get out of the public limelight. Americans had seen enough episodes of the Arkansas soap opera to last a lifetime. Hillary had worn them down, exhausted them with her constant anger and troubled presence. The advisors employed the "out of sight, out of mind" tactic of politics, giving Americans a break from the old gal and hoping they would forget the past. And they did. After a few years Hillary was reintroduced as a softer, kinder version of her former self; Americans were intrigued and gave the new Hillary the benefit of the doubt. That part of the makeover plan worked like a charm—her approval numbers rose and remain high.

But Hillaryland abandoned this strategy way too early. While her 2006 reelection campaign would have drawn national attention under any circumstances, Hillaryland made the conscious decision to maximize it. She had no discernible primary opposition and her Republican opponent never so much as posed a threat. Instead of running a good strong campaign that would have assured her of a solid victory, Hillary turned her reelection campaign into $46 million presidential warm-up. Her game plan was to overwhelm the 2008 opposition—start early, lock up the talent, build a powerhouse of a team, win her Senate race by a landslide, then storm the Democratic primary with such force as to virtually clear the field.

In so doing she turned her presidential campaign into a marathon. Never a good idea for any candidate, but especially not for Hillary.

First, Hillary doesn't wear well. As Karl Rove put it, there is a "brittleness about her."[7] This is a deadly quality for a candidate. Americans rank likeability as one of the most important factors in choosing a candidate. As the campaign drags on, Hillary's act will grow old, and as pressure builds it will become increasingly difficult to hide the angry person who lurks beneath the makeover. And when that lady, with whom we are all too familiar, begins to make cameo appearances, the public will gain greater respect for the insight of Karl Rove.

Hillaryland is surely aware that deep in the crevices of America's collective mind reside repressed memories of the torturous affair we had with the Hillary of old. Each day she is in our line of vision, the chances increase that these memories will be awakened. When the old gal peeks out from beneath the makeover—if for only a minute—the public consciousness will be stirred and at some point people will begin to recall the chant of years ago: "Is it over yet? Please, let it be over." It is unlikely they will then vote for four more years.

It would have been far more prudent for Hillary to have kept her campaign shorter, lending it some freshness as a new and improved Hillary introduced herself. But that's a one-act play— one Hillary has risked turning into a Greek tragedy.

I Am Woman, Hear Me Whine

According to at least one national poll, America has caught up with the rest of the free world. It is ready to elect a woman president. A December 2006 *Los Angeles Times*/Bloomberg poll found that only 4 percent of registered voters would not vote for a woman president.

Unfortunately for Hillary it isn't that easy. She is not just a woman running for president. She is also a Democrat and she is running for president in a time of war. Since the Vietnam War, Hillary's party has carried the stigma of being weak on national defense. And while the nation may be ready for a woman president, it does not mean Americans are ready for a female commander in chief during a time of war. Hillary accurately assessed this situation and recognized that it was doubly important to acquire solid pro-military credentials before throwing her bonnet into the ring.

And so she did.

As mentioned earlier, Hillary wrangled her way onto the prestigious Armed Services Committee and took numerous trips to the war zones of Afghanistan and Iraq. Then, to seal the deal, the lady voted for and supported the invasion of Iraq. It was a safe bet. The public was overwhelmingly behind the president's preemptive war and it was a grand opportunity for Hillary to prove once and for all that she had shed those antiwar rags she once donned so proudly.

The makeover dictated a pro-war stance and Hillary performed her duties with real fervor. But after years of playing with fire, Hillary finally got burned. The war vote that at the time looked to be a gift turned into the greatest barrier she now faces to winning the nomination. While being a woman is not the detriment she thought it might be, the vote she cast in part because she was a woman may well be.

The makeover artists made two assumptions as they planned Hillary's presidential bid. Both proved to be completely wrong. First, they believed that Hillary's strongest primary opponents would come from right-leaning Democrats—Mark Warner, possibly. So they moved Hillary to the right with conservative-lite rhetoric, the war vote, and a few minor issues. This made her vulnerable on her left flank and created a void large enough to attract both John Edwards and Barack Obama.

Second, as she was considered an icon of the Left, her advisors believed Hillary could wander toward the Right without repercussions. They underestimated the strength and commitment of the antiwar activists.

Washington Post reporter Harold Meyerson explained Hillary's dilemma. While Bush continues to pursue a military solution in Iraq, the war will become increasingly unpopular in this country. "Bush will drive the nation toward the Democrats, and Democrats toward their most credible champion of ending the U.S. occupation. Hillary Clinton is not high on that list."[8] She would have been at the top had she not voted for war.

While Hillary's gender has proved troublesome on the foreign policy front, it could well be the principle strength of her campaign on other fronts. And Hillary is mining it for all it's worth.

Candidate Hillary is not running for president as a sitting U.S. senator or an accomplished public servant who happens to be a woman. Hillary is running for president *as* a woman, selling her sex as a significant asset of her candidacy. She is offering women in America a "Madam President." Her campaign is quick to point out that 54 percent of the 2004 presidential voters were women, and it is working to increase that turnout in 2008. Her campaign is focusing on the "caring issues" of education, heath care, and retirement,[9] and the candidate is making comments like: "We've never had a mother who ever ran or was elected president."[10]

In addition, Hillary is traveling the country on a heavily orchestrated "listening tour," carrying on insipid "conversations" and "chats" with audiences that are predominantly women. It's enough to set the cause of women back a generation. In these "talking forums" Hillary directs most of her questions to women and regularly raises commonly held female grievances like: "I don't think I am the only woman here who thinks you have to work harder."[11] (Please, not four years of a Whiner in Chief. We'll all be begging for a good sex scandal.)

Hillary's strength is without question among Democratic women, and she is counting on her sisters for victories in both the primary and the general election. But if she keeps up this pathetic pandering to women, she won't have a single self-respecting man left in her camp. And while many women may say, "You go, girl," millions of others will pause long enough to consider the nation. When they do, they'll turn, take a second look at Hillary, see nothing but a parody of a candidate, and then they'll find themselves a good man to vote for.

Bill, Standing by His Woman

Political analysts will tell you that in a Democratic primary Bill is an enormous asset for Hillary. He enjoys a 63 percent approval rating overall according to a February 2007 Gallup poll, and those numbers are even stronger among Democrats and Independents.[12] He can raise his wife hundreds of millions of dollars, build her an impressive list of endorsements, and deliver whole communities into her column. At least that was the plan. They are a powerful team and he expects his friends and advisors to be there for Hillary as they were for him. What's more, Bill has a vested interest in her success—he too wants to return to the center of power.

But consider the remarks of Clinton's old Hollywood buddy David Geffen, who abandoned his Clinton loyalties and endorsed Barack Obama. "He's a reckless guy," Geffen said of Bill. He "gave his enemies a lot of ammunition to hurt him and to distract the country." He went on: "I don't think anybody believes in the last six years, all of a sudden Bill Clinton has become a different person." Geffen believes that if Republicans are digging up dirt on Bill, they'll hold it until Hillary is nominated, then drop it.[13] If this happened it could destroy Hillary's hopes of returning to the White House.

This part of the Bill equation is anything but beneficial to Hillary. Already there exists a wealth of concern among Democrats that Hillary on her own is not electable. This concern is fueled by polls such as the Marist poll cited earlier, in which 43 percent of Americans said they would not even consider voting for her.[14]

Referring to the former First Lady as an "incredibly polarizing figure," Geffen then raised the character issue. Recalling Clinton's Marc Rich pardon, he said, "Yet another time when the Clintons were unwilling to stand for the things that they genuinely believe in. Everyone in politics lies, but they do it with such ease, it's troubling."[15] (Amazing: even Clinton-loving liberals have repressed memories. It could be a banner year for psychologists.)

For the purpose of Hillary's presidential campaign, Bill and Hillary may well be inseparable—"two for the price of one," as she claimed many years ago. Hillary has her own baggage, as David Geffen kindly points out, but she also carries his.

With strong political winds behind them, Democrats know that the 2008 presidential campaign is theirs to lose. So they are more motivated than ever to give Americans a nominee for whom they can vote with confidence. No matter how strong Bill is in the polls, if the party fears his personal affairs will again spill into the tabloids and make their way back onto cable television, they will walk away from Hillary. They know Americans are not interested in viewing four more years of the private lives of the miserably unhappy couple from Arkansas. In this regard, Bill adds heavily to Hillary's primary problems.

There is another problem Bill causes Hillary. Together they give the appearance of a political dynasty—and Americans don't like dynasties. There is something inherently anti-democratic about them. By constantly evoking Bill's name, promising to continue the policies of his administration, and physically campaigning with him, Hillary reinforces this concept. Twenty years of nothing but Presidents Bush-Clinton-Bush-Clinton doesn't play well in Peoria—and, therefore, doesn't bode well for Hillary.

Hillary may see unfairness in all this. After all, Bill couldn't have been president without her. While it is also true that Hillary could never be president without Bill, it may be that she can't be president with him, either. If that should be the case, it should make for some lively pillow talk.

Hillary's Obama Nightmare

Imagine Hillary during one of those sleepless nights we all have. As an accomplished political strategist, one who is intent on returning to the White House, she likely walks through imaginary scenarios in which things go wrong, then constructs ways to prevent them from happening. With these thoughts on her mind, she drifts into the world of dreams where all her concerns float together into a single glob of semi-conscious thought. Her sleep suddenly becomes restless—the glob begins to grow and develop until finally it is a fully grown man masquerading as her primary opponent—the ultimate anti-Hillary candidate. Hillary awakens frightened and agitated, consoled only by the realization that she was having a nightmare, that the monster she had created in her subconscious was not real, it was only her imagination playing a nasty little game on her. Of this she is certain—real people don't have names like Obama.

Barack Obama may have a crazy name but he is without question the made-to-order candidate to bring Hillary down.

Hillary's strengths as a candidate are that she is smart, possesses star power, and has claim to a historic first if elected. But Obama matches her on every point and then raises the ante. He is brilliant, an overnight superstar, and also has claim to a first if elected. In addition Obama is fresh, genuine, comfortable with himself, and immensely likeable.

The excitement and energy Obama generated when he threw his hat into the ring is a clear indication that he could well capture the hearts of the Democrats. He is the future and Hillary can't compete with that. She has been around too long—and anyway, winning hearts isn't her thing. She prefers the overpowering, dominating approach to campaigning. Effective as that may be, it can be beaten by a campaign that touches the hearts of the voters.

On experience Hillary has Obama cold. But self-interest has driven so much of Hillary's experience that she has left her base feeling somewhat used. What's more, she abandoned her base when she voted for war and then held the position for years. Obama, on the other hand, opposed the war from the get-go and is perceived to be a true believer in a year when Democrats are looking for the real thing—not a jaded, made-to-order politician. In short, Hillary is someone they can vote for; Obama is someone they can love.

Then there is the African American community. Their vote is critical in the Democratic primary, especially in the key state of South Carolina, where they make up nearly half of primary voters. Bill is beloved in this community, even to the point that he was dubbed "the first black president" by novelist Toni Morrison. Add the fact that 59 percent of the black vote is cast by women and it is understandable that Hillary expected this vote to fall solidly in her column. Then along came Obama. A member of Congress who is an African American woman gave her assessment of this development's impact on Hillary's campaign: "If her base is black women, it vanishes down to zero" with Obama in the race, she told *Newsweek*. Obama is married to an African American woman, a fact of critical importance to these women.[16] Can Hillary really expect to do any better with black men?

Obama's strengths aren't the only factor undermining Hillary's efforts. Her reactions to him are quite revealing. In her mind, he is an inexperienced upstart without a shred of an agenda who had the audacity to get in her way. He triggers her arrogance.

Likewise, every single Democrat who abandons her for Obama will enrage Hillary. The old gal knows the only way to guarantee loyalty is to punish the disloyal, and she will be tempted to do so immediately. He triggers her anger and vindictiveness.

And she certainly isn't going to stand by and let the happy, hopeful Obama spoil her plans. She has to go mean.

Consider how many sightings there were of the old Hillary—all within weeks of Obama's announcement.

First we saw her keen sense of entitlement inflamed. Jonathan Alter reported in *Newsweek* in December 2006 that "Hillaryland is in a 'how dare he' frame of mind, insisting the wet-behind-the-ears senator doesn't have the standing to crash her party."[17]

Then it was her notorious temper: After Obama announced and David Geffen agreed to throw him a Hollywood fund-raiser, a friend of the senator's is reported to have said, "Hillary is livid."[18] That's our old Hillary—angry as ever.

Then we saw a glimpse of her anger as she released her rapid-response wolves to publicly deal with the Hollywood betrayal. After Geffen's remarks about the ease with which the Clintons lie were made public, Hillary's spokesmen bypassed the offending Geffen and aimed their fire directly at Obama. "While Senator Obama was denouncing slash and burn politics yesterday, his campaign finance chair was viciously and personally attacking Senator Clinton and her husband. If Senator Obama is indeed sincere about his repeated claims to change the tone of our politics, he should immediately denounce these remarks, remove Mr. Geffen from his campaign and return his money." This may have been just a little practice volley to give Obama a taste of what's to come. As one of my friends, a senior Democratic official said, "When Hillary finishes with him, Obama isn't going to know what color he is."

Obama has put Hillary into a terrible bind. She dedicated over six years of her life remaking herself and building the greatest political machine ever assembled. Her name was so big and her organization so powerful that her nomination was considered inevitable. No one, it was thought, could stop the juggernaut. Then along came Obama.

What is Hillary to do? She has only two weapons in her arsenal: politically overpowering or personally destroying. But Obama's campaign exploded onto the scene and gained enormous strength and momentum in its opening weeks. Overpowering it is not an option. She must destroy him.

But the downside is enormous.

If she destroys the Left's new love, will they come back home to her or will they never forgive her, turning their back on her forever?

Her second problem is that if she moves to destroy Obama, America will know who did it—they'll see the familiar markings of the cold, calculating, ruthless woman destroying the reputation of yet another innocent person simply because he got in the way of her pursuit of power. The extreme makeover will be shattered, her cover blown—the old Hillary will be back in all her glory. But Americans vote for people they like and they have seen more than enough of that old gal to know there is nothing likeable about her.

Obama may or may not be able to go the distance, but he is the one guy who can sure keep Hillary from crossing the line.

Chapter Nine

Unfit to Serve

W E'VE BEEN ENTRUSTED with a precious gift by our founding fathers, and just as they sacrificed and fought to pre-
serve it, it is our duty and honor to do the same. We see the
country we love drifting away from the values and principles upon
which it was founded—the very same that made it a great and
good country. We cannot stand on the sidelines and watch the
nation slip away. In many ways our nation is at a crossroads in history, and the next president will greatly determine the kind of
country we will become. It is, therefore, more important than ever
that we get this election right.

Hillary has determined that she is the one for the job and she
has dedicated six years of her life preparing. This is fair enough.
But she has chosen an unacceptable way to get ready for the highest office in the land—she has used these years to reinvent herself
so that she might reach the top on wings of deceit.

Hillary knew she couldn't successfully run for president as herself. She needed a fill-in—someone dramatically different than she to be the candidate. It was for this purpose that she underwent an extreme makeover. It is the made-over version of Hillary who is the current candidate. But it is not the made-over version who will be our president.

The junior senator from New York wants us to see her in a new light and she wants us to forget the woman she was. While she has a moral obligation to be honest with the voters, to tell us truthfully who she is, what she believes, and where will she take this great nation of ours, she will not.

And so the responsibility falls upon each citizen to find out which of the women associated with this tightly wrapped package is the one who would be president if candidate Hillary were to be elected. And they need to do so now—before any votes are cast. The consequences of doing less are too grave to consider.

Hillary's makeover has been extreme—it had to be. That alone should raise the alarm. Who is it she so desperately wants to hide from the public and what kind of president would she be? You now have the answers. For one last minute, let us reflect upon them and consider how they might impact her performance as president and commander in chief.

The most frightening aspect of this woman is that she lies. She lies about everything and she lies about anything. There is no other way to say it. Her word means nothing. Hillary simply can never be trusted. As president she will not be limited or encumbered by the truth. She never has been and she never will be. It is just who she is.

Candidate Hillary talks of having a "responsibility gene." If that be the case, then it came from the pool of excessively recessive genes. Hillary never takes responsibility—not for her words, her actions, or her troubles. She blames others for any and all difficulties in which she finds herself—from her vote on war with Iraq to the investigations that once plagued her. And she is a card-carrying member of NAV, the National Association of Victimhood. As president, she will dismiss criticism as the mean-spirited ranting of some group like the vast right wing or the troglodyte club of Middle America. The fault or problem will not be hers—it never has been. Hillary has never been a stand-up woman, and will never be a stand-up president.

The real Hillary suffers from severe insecurity. Having never learned to deal with it directly, she has succumbed to its powers. Her lack of confidence in her own abilities has driven her to become dependent upon hordes of experts, advisors, and even gurus. She cannot lead—she is simply incapable of doing so. As president she will follow—it may be polls or people—but she will always be following.

And while Candidate Hillary is all about moderation, President Hillary will be all about extremism. The makeover presents a Hillary who is softer and more appealing to Middle America. But don't let the smiles and pleasantries fool you. Hillary has the heart of a hardened feminist. She embraces the policies and philosophies of the Far Left on all significant social issues—abortion, gay marriage, or putting two-year-olds in all-day, government-run schools. The sisterhood will be celebrating endlessly if Hillary returns to the White House—they know she will never disappoint them.

In addition, Candidate Hillary campaigns as a common sense, fiscally responsible advocate of the balanced budget. But her lack of confidence in her own judgment and her addiction-like dependence on the advice of others has convinced Hillary that the rest of us are as insecure as she is—she can't think for herself, so that means to her that none of us can either. And thus we need the government to tell us what to do. She believes it is in the best interests of Americans to have the government guiding and instructing them in nearly all aspects of their lives. Just as she lacks faith in herself, Hillary lacks faith in the ability of others to do right by themselves, their families, and their communities. She believes the deep resources and extensive expertise of Big Brother are essential in assuring the proper outcome. President Hillary will be anything but moderate in her governing. Just as her Senate record portends, she will reign over a massive expansion of government and she will expect Americans to pick up the tab. After all, it is "for the common good."

All the while Hillary was undergoing her extensive reinvention, one important thing did not change: to whom she delivered the goods. She always went home when it was time to vote. Her ADA rating gives her one of the most solid liberal records in the U.S. Senate and is proof enough that Hillary will be the same as president. She will spend like a President Ted Kennedy, handle environmental concerns like a President Al Gore, push the gay agenda like a President Barney Frank, and advocate for feminist causes like a President Hillary Clinton. None of this bodes well for the nation.

While she bounces around on the issue of Iraq and talks tough about military action elsewhere, it can't be certain what she would do if she had the power. It depends on how beholden she'll be to the antiwar wing of her party, if she's able to recapture their loyalties and win the election. The question is, will this leftward pull be enough to counter the powerful urge coming from within her to prove to the world that it is she, Hillary, who is the commander in chief of the greatest army on earth? This kind of tug of war can endanger the nation and is yet another warning that Hillary should never hold the office of the presidency.

Hillary is unfit to be president of our great country. She doesn't have the leadership qualities required for the office, the heart needed to inspire the nation to greatness, or the insight to know a failed policy when she sees it. And what's more, we can't risk placing our future in the trust of any more of her gurus.

These are the facts and America needs to be warned. The extreme makeover of Hillary Rodham Clinton is a fraud and for the sake of the nation must be exposed—because what's lurking behind is dangerous to the health and security of the nation.

It is your job to spread the word.

Chapter Ten

Twelve Questions the Media Should Ask Hillary Because America Has a Right to Know

1. *Given the title of the Iraq war bill, can you explain why you did not understand that the vote you cast was a vote for war with Iraq?*

   Senator Clinton, you have said that in October of 2002 when you voted for the measure entitled "A Joint Resolution to Authorize the Use of United States Armed Forces Against Iraq" you did not foresee this vote giving the president authority to invade Iraq. You believed it was a vote for diplomacy.[1] Given the title of the Iraq war bill, can you explain why you did not understand the vote you cast was a vote for war with Iraq?

2. *Senator Clinton, you say you were "misled" by President George W. Bush into supporting the Iraq war. Governor George Romney said he was "brainwashed" into supporting the Vietnam War. Can you explain the difference between*

being "misled" and being "brainwashed"?

Due to the perception that mental strength, consistency, and plausible explanations should be prerequisites for a would-be commander in chief, Governor George W. Romney's 1968 presidential bid was derailed by his comment that he had been "brainwashed" by American generals into supporting the Vietnam War. Senator Clinton, you say you were "misled" by President George W. Bush into supporting the Iraq war. Can you explain the difference?

3. *Senator Clinton, why do you find it difficult to take a stand and keep it? Is this not the very essence of leadership?*

   Senator, in April of 2006 you told a reporter the following: "I'm frustrated and I'm in an uncomfortable position.... People often want to put you in an either–or category in American politics. It can be difficult to stay where you are."[2] Senator Clinton, why do you find it difficult to take a stand and keep it? Is this not the very essence of leadership?

4. *As you believe in state-funded health care, have you considered how the cost to the taxpayer of your generous health care policy will play in concert with your generous immigration policy?*

   Senator Clinton, in May of 2006 you voted to increase the number of immigrants allowed into the U.S. from 19 million to 103 million (an increase of 84 million immigrants in twenty years). As you believe in state-funded health care, have you considered how the cost to the taxpayer of your generous health care policy will play in concert with your generous immigration policy?

5. *Would you support a bill that would introduce government regulation of child discipline?*

The California legislature is considering banning the spanking of children less than three years of age. Would you support this or any other bill that would introduce government regulation of child discipline? If so, on what grounds do you support allowing the state to limit the rights of parents to choose the best method of discipline for their children?

6. *What have you done to cause your integrity to be so harshly called into question?*

    Senator Clinton, consider the following comments made about you:

    - Bill Safire of the *New York Times* has called you a "congenital liar."[3]
    - Maureen Dowd wrote "[Bill and Hillary] have chose tactics over truth with such consistency that it's impossible to accept anything they say."[4]
    - A friend of yours, David Geffen, recently said: "Everybody in politics lies, but [Bill and Hillary] do it with such ease, it's troubling."[5]

    These statements represent the Right, the Left, and a friend. What have you done to cause your integrity to be so harshly called into question?

7. *Why would you lie and place your daughter so close to having a tragic story of her own on September 11?*

    In an interview on national television, Senator, right after September 11, you said your daughter Chelsea was out jogging near the towers and that she actually heard the planes hit. This was not true. Your daughter was in an apartment a safe distance away. Thousands of Americans have truly tragic stories related to that day. Why would you lie and place your daughter so close to having a tragic story of her own?

8. *Do you believe that your dependence on the input of others in both your professional and personal life has influenced your belief that it is in the interest of the citizens to have government instructing them in their professional and personal lives?*

   Senator, throughout your life you have always surrounded yourself with numerous advisors and experts. Do you believe that your dependence on the input of others in both your professional and personal life has influenced your belief that it is in the interest of the citizens to have government instructing them in their professional and personal lives?

9. *Is it not hypocritical to hold your opponents to far higher standards than yourself?*

   Senator, you called for one of your opponents to return the money raised for him by Hollywood producer David Geffen. Mr. Geffen's crime was to call you and Bill liars. However when the *New York Times* reported that you accepted $157,000 from a company owned by John Burgess, "a disbarred New York lawyer with a criminal record for attempted larceny and patronizing a sixteen-year-old prostitute,"[6] you refused to join the many other politicians and return his donations. Is it not hypocritical to hold your opponents to far higher standards than yourself?

10. *What do you have against the traditional family?*

   In March of 2004, you voted against the Unborn Victims of Violence Act, a bill which defined a violent attack against a pregnant woman as a crime against both the mother and the unborn child. In 2001 you voted against the marriage penalty tax, which was designed to eliminate or significantly reduce the additional tax burden created by lumping together spousal income. What do you have against the traditional family?

11. *Having failed as co-president during your husband's administration, why should the voter believe you would do better as president?*

   Your co-presidency was marked by scandals, investigations, a grand jury appearance, and a botched attempt to nationalize our health care system, a policy outrightly rejected by Americans. Having failed as co-president, why should the voter believe you would do better as president?

12. *Senator Clinton, why did you believe an extreme makeover was necessary?*

   There is much talk in the media that you have "reinvented" or "recreated" yourself. You and your staff have used the word "evolved" to describe this process. Senator Clinton, why did you believe an extreme makeover was necessary?

Acknowledgments

I AM NOT THE WRITER in the family, and so after several chapters I decided to ask the advice of my good friend Terry Jeffrey, for whose opinion I have always held the utmost respect. I asked him to read through several early chapters and let me know his verdict: Should I stop while still ahead or plow through to the end? Not only did he offer sound advice and many strong suggestions, but Terry also lightened my spirits with the strength of his encouragement.

I also want to thank another good friend, Justin Raimondo, who willingly shared with me his vast knowledge of foreign policy and answered all my questions without ever calling the tutorial over.

In addition, the help and research done by aspiring attorney Chad Burchard was invaluable, as was the constant support of my assistant Marcus Epstein. Marcus kept the trains running in my office when I would go to the mountains of West Virginia to write undisturbed for days at a time. Rosemary Jenks, a valued friend, agreed to review parts of the manuscript. Her suggestions were excellent and each was incorporated into the text.

The book would never have made it past the first two chapters had it not been for the hard work of my dear friend Sharon Korchnak. Her research was an indispensable part of this effort, but even more important were those long hours of "Hillary talk" when I would call her in the wee hours of the night. She was always there, always upbeat, and always positive. You can't ask more of a friend.

I would also like to thank my Democratic friends who willingly shared with me their insight into Hillary, but who, for the sake of their careers, have asked to remain unnamed.

And finally I must acknowledge the steady hand of my editor, Miriam Moore, who never hesitated to guide me back onto the beaten path when she found I was aimlessly wandering. This was more often than I would like to admit, but she was always right.

Appendix A

Wellesley College 1969 Student Commencement Speech

Hillary D. Rodham
May 31, 1969

I am very glad that Miss Adams made it clear that what I am speaking for today is all of us—the 400 of us—and I find myself in a familiar position, that of reacting, something that our generation has been doing for quite a while now. We're not in the positions yet of leadership and power, but we do have that indispensable task of criticizing and constructive protest and I find myself reacting just briefly to some of the things that Senator Brooke said. This has to be brief because I do have a little speech to give. Part of the problem with empathy with professed goals is that empathy doesn't do us anything. We've had lots of empathy; we've had lots of sympathy, but we feel that for too long our leaders have used politics as the art of making what appears to be impossible, possible. What does it mean to hear that 13.3 percent of the people in this country are below the poverty line? That's a percentage. We're not interested in social reconstruction; it's human reconstruction. How can we talk about percentages and trends? The complexities are not lost in our analyses, but perhaps they're just put into what we consider a more human and eventually a more progressive perspective. The question about possible and impossible was one that we brought with us to Wellesley four years ago. We arrived not yet knowing what was not possible. Consequently, we expected a lot. Our attitudes are easily understood having grown up, having come to consciousness in the first five years of this decade—years dominated by men with dreams, men in the civil rights movement, the Peace Corps, the space program—so we arrived at Wellesley and we found, as all of us have found, that there was a gap between expectation and realities. But it wasn't a discouraging gap and it didn't turn us into cynical, bitter old women at the age of 18. It just inspired us to do something about that gap. What we did is often difficult for some people to understand. They ask us quite often: "Why, if you're dissatisfied, do you stay in a place?" Well, if you didn't care a lot about it you wouldn't stay. It's almost as though my mother used to say, "I'll always love you but there are times when I certainly won't like you." Our love for this place, this particular place, Wellesley College, coupled with our freedom from the burden of an inauthentic reality allowed us to question basic assumptions underlying our education. Before the days of the media orchestrated demonstrations, we had our own gathering over in Founder's parking lot. We protested against the rigid academic distribution requirement. We worked for a pass-fail system. We worked for a say in some of the process of academic decision making. And luckily we were in a place where, when we questioned the meaning of a liberal arts education there were people with enough imagination to respond to that questioning. So we have made progress. We have achieved some of the things that initially saw as lacking in that gap between expectation and reality. Our concerns were not, of course, solely academic as all of us know. We worried about inside Wellesley questions of admissions, the kind of people that should be coming to Wellesley, the process for getting them here. We questioned about what responsibility we should have both for our lives as individuals and for our lives as members of a collective group.

Coupled with our concerns for the Wellesley inside here in the community were our concerns for what happened beyond Hathaway House. We wanted to know what relationship Wellesley was going to have to the outer world. We were lucky in that one of the first things Miss Adams did was to set up a cross-registration with MIT because everyone knows that education just can't have any parochial bounds any more. One of the other things that we did was the Upward Bound program. There are so many other things that we could talk about; so many attempts, at least the way we saw it, to pull ourselves into the world outside. And I think we've succeeded. There will be an Upward Bound program, just for one example, on the campus this summer.

Many of the issues that I've mentioned—those of sharing power and responsibility, those of assuming power and responsibility have been general concerns on campuses throughout the world. But underlying those concerns there is a theme, a theme which is so trite and so old because the words are so familiar. It talks about integrity and trust and respect. Words have a funny way of trapping our minds on the way to our tongues but there are necessary means even in this multi-media age for attempting to come to grasps with some of the inarticulate maybe even inarticulable things that we're feeling. We are, all of us, exploring a world that none of us even understands and attempting to create within that uncertainty. But there are some things we feel, feelings that our prevailing, acquisitive, and competitive corporate life, including tragically the universities, is not the way of life for us. We're searching for more immediate, ecstatic and penetrating mode of living. And so our questions, our questions about our institutions, about our colleges, about our churches, about our government continue. The questions about those institutions are familiar to all of us. We have seen heralded across the newspapers. Senator Brooke has suggested some of them this morning. But along with using these words—integrity, trust, and respect—in regard to institutions and leaders we're perhaps harshest with them in regard to ourselves.

Every protest, every dissent, whether it's an individual academic paper, Founder's parking lot demonstration, is unabashedly an attempt to forge an identity in this particular age. That attempt at forging for many of us over the past four years has meant coming to terms with our humanness. Within the context of a society that we perceive—now we can talk about reality, and I would like to talk about reality sometime, authentic reality, inauthentic reality, and what we have to accept of what we see—but our perception of it is that it hovers often between the possibility of disaster and the potentiality for imaginatively responding to men's needs. There's a very strange conservative strain that goes through a lot of New Left, collegiate protests that I find very intriguing because it harkens back to a lot of the old virtues, to the fulfillment of original ideas. And it's also a very unique American experience. It's such a great adventure. If the experiment in human living doesn't work in this country, in this age, it's not going to work anywhere.

But we also know that to be educated, the goal of it must be human liberation. A liberation enabling each of us to fulfill our capacity so as to be free to create within and around ourselves. To be educated to freedom must be evidenced in action, and here again is where we ask ourselves, as we have asked our parents and our teachers, questions about integrity, trust, and respect. Those three words mean different things to all of us. Some of the things they can mean, for instance: Integrity, the courage to be whole, to try to mold an entire person in this particular context, living in relation to one another in the full poetry of existence. If the only tool we have ultimately to use is our lives, so we use it in the way we can by choosing a way to live that will demonstrate the way we feel and the way we know. Integrity—a man like Paul Santmire. Trust. This is one word that when I asked the class at our rehearsal what it was they wanted me to say for them, everyone came up to me and said "Talk about trust, talk about the lack of trust both for us and the way we feel about others. Talk about the trust bust." What can you say about it? What can you say about a feeling that permeates a generation and that perhaps is not even understood by those who are distrusted? All they can do is keep trying again and again and again. There's that wonderful line in East Coker by Eliot about there's only the trying, again and again and again; to win again what we've lost before.

And then respect. There's that mutuality of respect between people where you don't see people as percentage points. Where you don't manipulate people. Where you're not interested in social engineering for people. The struggle for an integrated life existing in an atmosphere of communal trust and respect is one with desperately important political and social consequences. And the word "consequences" of course catapults us into the future. One of the most tragic things that happened yesterday, a beautiful day, was that I was talking to woman who said that she wouldn't want to be me for anything in the world. She wouldn't want to live today and look ahead to what it is she sees because she's afraid. Fear is always with us but we just don't have time for it. Not now.

There are two people that I would like to thank before concluding. That's Ellie Acheson, who is the spearhead for this, and also Nancy Scheibner who wrote this poem which is the last thing that I would like to read:

My entrance into the world of so-called "social problems"
Must be with quiet laughter, or not at all.
The hollow men of anger and bitterness
The bountiful ladies of righteous degradation
All must be left to a bygone age.

And the purpose of history is to provide a receptacle
For all those myths and oddments
Which oddly we have acquired
And from which we would become unburdened
To create a newer world
To transform the future into the present.
We have no need of false revolutions
In a world where categories tend to tyrannize our minds
And hang our wills up on narrow pegs.
It is well at every given moment to seek the limits in our lives.
And once those limits are understood
To understand that limitations no longer exist.
Earth could be fair. And you and I must be free
Not to save the world in a glorious crusade
Not to kill ourselves with a nameless gnawing pain
But to practice with all the skill of our being
The art of making possible.

Appendix B

Excerpts of Liz Carpenter Lecture Series Remarks by First Lady Hillary Rodham Clinton

University of Texas
Austin, Texas
April 7, 1993

... But what Ann Richards talked about is what I want to expand on in my remarks leading into the panel discussion with all of these distinguished panelists and with questions from many of you that I understand were submitted. Because the problems that she alluded to are not just American problems; they are not just governmental problems. We are at a stage in history, I would suggest, in which remolding society certainly in the West is one of the great challenges facing all of us as individuals and as citizens.

And we have to begin realistically to take stock of where we are, stripping perhaps away the romanticism that Governor Richards referred to, to be able to understand where we are in history at this point and what our real challenges happen to be.

And I say that it is not just an American problem. Because if one looks around the Western world; if one looks at Europe; if one looks at the merging democracies, at Asia; if one looks certainly here in North America, you can see the rumblings of discontent, almost regardless of political systems, as we come face to face with the problems that the modern age has dealt us.

And if we take a step back and ask ourselves, "Why is it in a country as economically wealthy as we are despite our economic problems, in a country that is the longest-surviving democracy, there is this undercurrent of discontent—this sense that somehow economic growth and prosperity, political democracy and freedom are not enough? That we lack, at some core level, meaning in our individual lives and meaning collectively—that sense that our lives are part of some greater effort, that we are connected to one another, that community means that we have a place where we belong no matter who we are?" And it isn't very far below the surface because we can see popping through the surface the signs of alienation and despair and hopelessness that are all too common and cannot be ignored. They're in our living rooms at night on the news. They're on the front pages; they are in all of our neighborhoods.

On the plane coming down, I read a phrase in an article in the newspaper this morning talking about how desperate conditions are in so many of our cities that are filled with hopeless girls with babies and angry boys with guns. And yet, it is not just the most violent and the most alienated that we can look to. The discontent of which I speak is broader than that, deeper than that. We are, I think, in a crisis of meaning. What do our governmental institutions mean? What does it mean to be educated? What does it mean to be a journalist? What does it mean in today's world to pursue not only vocations, to be part of institutions, but to be human?

And, certainly, coming off the last year when the ethos or selfishness and greed were given places of honor never before accorded, it is certainly timely to ask ourselves these questions.

One of the clearest and most poignant posings of this question that I have run across was the one provided by Lee Atwater as he lay dying. For those of you who may not know, Lee Atwater was credited with being the architect of the Republican victories of the

'70s and the '80s; the vaunted campaign manager of Reagan and Bush; the man who knew how to fight bare-knuckled in the political arena, who was willing to engage in any tactics so long as it worked and he wasn't caught at it.

And yet, when Lee Atwater was struck down with cancer, he said something which we reprinted in *Life* magazine, which I cut out and carry with me in a little book I have of sayings and Scriptures that I find important and that replenish me from time to time, that I want to share with you.

He said the following:

Long before I was struck with cancer, I felt something stirring in American society. It was a sense among the people of the country, Republicans and Democrats alike, that something was missing from their lives—something crucial. I was trying to position the Republican Party to take advantage of it. But I wasn't exactly sure what it was. My illness helped me to see that what was missing in society is what was missing in me. A little heart, a lot of brotherhood.

The '80s were about acquiring—acquiring wealth, power, prestige. I know. I acquired more wealth, power and prestige than most. But you can acquire all you want and still feel empty. What power wouldn't I trade for a little more time with my family? What price wouldn't I pay for an evening with friends? It took a deadly illness to put me eye-to-eye with that truth, but it is a truth that the country, caught up in its ruthless ambitions and moral decay, can learn on my dime.

I don't know who will lead us through the '90s, but they must be made to speak to this spiritual vacuum at the heart of American society—this tumor of the soul.

That to me will be Lee Atwater's real lasting legacy, not the elections that he helped to win.

But I think the answer to his question—"Who will lead us out of this spiritual vacuum?"—the answer is "all of us." Because remolding society does not depend on just changing government, on just reinventing our institutions to be more in tune with present realities. It requires each of us to play our part in redefining what our lives are and what they should be.

We are caught between two great political forces. On the one hand we have our economy—the market economy—which knows the price of everything but the value of nothing. That is not its job. And then the state or government which attempts to use its means of acquiring tax money, of making decisions to assist us in becoming a better, more equitable society as it defines it. That is what all societies are currently caught between—forces that are more complex and bigger than any of us can understand. And missing in that equation, as we have political and ideological struggles between those who think market economics are the answer to everything, those who think government programs are the answer to everything, is the recognition among all of us that neither of those is an adequate explanation for the challenges confronting us.

And what we each must do is break through the old thinking that has for too long captured us politically and institutionally, so that we can begin to devise new ways of thinking about not only what it means to have economies that don't discard people like they were excess baggage that we no longer need, but to define our institutional and personal responsibilities in ways that answer this lack of meaning.

We need a new politics of meaning. We need a new ethos of individual responsibility and caring. We need a new definition of civil society which answers the unanswerable questions posed by both the market forces and the governmental ones, as to how we can have a society that fills us up again and makes us feel that we are part of something bigger than ourselves.

Now, will it be easy to do that? Of course not. Because we are breaking new ground. This is a trend that has been developing over hundreds of years. It is not something that just happened to us in the last decade or two. And so it is not going to be easy to redefine who we are as human beings in this post-modern age. Nor will it be easy to figure out how to make our institutions more responsive to the kind of human beings we wish to be.

But part of the great challenge of living is defining yourself in your moment, of seizing the opportunities that you are given, and of making the very best choices you can. That is what this administration, this president, and those of us who are hoping for these changes are attempting to do.

I used to wonder during the election when my husband would attempt to explain how so many of the problems that we were confronting were not easy Democratic/Republican, liberal/conservative problems. They were problems that shared different characteristics, that we had to not only define clearly, but search for new ways of confronting.

Then someone would say, "Well, you know, he can't make up his mind," or "He doesn't know what he wants to say about that." When instead what I was hearing and what we had been struggling with for years is how does one define the new issues? How do we begin to inject some new meaning? How do we take old values and apply them to these new—for many of us— undreamed of problems that we now confront? And that is what all of us must be engaged in in our own lives, at every level, in every institution with which we interact.

Let me just give you some examples. If we believe that the reconstruction of civil society with its institutions of family, friendship networks, communities, voluntary organizations are really the glue of what holds us together; if we go back and read deToqueville and notice how he talked over and over again about the unique characteristics that he found among Americans and rooted

so many of those in that kind of intermediary institution of civil
society that I just mentioned, then we know we have to better
understand what we can do to strengthen those institutions, to
understand how they have changed over time, and to try to find
meaning in them as they currently are.

That's why the debate over family values over the last year,
which was devised for political purposes, seemed so off point.
There is no—or should be no—debates that our family structure is
in trouble. There should be no debate that children need the stability, the predictability of a family. But there should be debate
over how we best make sure that children and families flourish.
And once that debate is carried out on honest terms, then we have
to recognize that either the old idea that only parental influence
and parental values matters, or the nearly as old idea that only
state programmatic intervention matters, are both equally falla-
cious. Instead we ought to recognize what should be a common-
sense truth—that children are the result of both the values of their
parents and the values of the society in which they live. And that
you can have an important..... (End of side one of tape.)

(In progress) ... how best to make sure parental values are the
ones that will help children grow and be strengthened, and how
social values equally must be recognized for the role they play in
how children feel about themselves and act in the world. And then
we can begin to have what should be a sensible conversation about
how to strengthen both. That's the kind of approach that has to
get beyond the dogma of right or left, conservative or liberal.
Those views are inadequate to the problems we see.

Any of you who have ever been in an inner city, working with
young people as I have over the years, will know as I do the heroic
stories of parents and grandparents who, against overwhelming
odds, fight to keep their children safe—just physically safe; and
who hold high expectations for those children; whose values I
would put up against any other person in the country, but who

have no control over the day-to-day violence and influence that comes flooding in the doors of that housing project apartment; and who need a society that is more supportive of their value than the one they currently have.

Equally, all of us know the contrary story of families with enough economic means, affluent enough to live in neighborhoods that are as safe as they can be in our country today, so they have the social value structure of what we would hope that each child in America could have in terms of just basic kinds of fundamental safety and physical well-being, but whose parental values are not ones to promote a childhood that is a positive one, giving children the chance to grow up to achieve their own God-given potential. So that the presence of values of society are not enough, either.

There are so many examples of how we have to think differently and how we have to go beyond not only the traditions of the past, but unfortunately for many of us, well-held and cherished views of the past; and how we have to break out of the kind of gridlock mentality which exists not just in the Congress from time to time, but exists as well in all of us as we struggle to see the world differently and cope with the challenges it has given us.

Yet I am very hopeful about where we stand in this last decade of the 20th century, because for all of the problems that we see around us, both abroad and at home, there is a growing body of people who want to deal with them, who want to be part of this conversation about how we break through old views and deal with new problems. And we will need millions more of those conversations.

Those conversations need to take place in every family, every workplace, every political institution in our country. They need to take place in our schools, where we have to be honest about what we are and are not able to convey to our children; where we have to be honest about the conditions which are confronting so many of our teachers and our students day in and day out; where we have to be honest that we do have to set high expectations for all children and we should not discard any because of who they are or where they come from.

And where we need to hold accountable every member of the educational enterprise—parents, teachers and students. Each should be held accountable for the opportunity they have been given to participate in one of the greatest efforts of humankind, passing on knowledge to children. And we have to expect more than we are currently getting.

We also need to take a hard look at other institutions. As Governor Richards said, we are in the midst of an intensive effort of trying to determine how we can provide decent, affordable health care to every American. And in that process we have to ask hard questions about every aspect of our health care system. Why do doctors do what they do? Why are nurses not permitted to do more than they do? Why are patients put in the position they're in?

But to give you just one example about how this ties in with what I have said before about how these problems we are confronting now in many ways are the result of our progress as we have moved toward being modern men and women: Our ancestors did not have to think about the many of the issues we are now confronted with. When does life start; when does life end? Who makes those decisions? How do we dare impinge upon these areas of such delicate, difficult questions? And, yet, every day in hospitals and homes and hospices all over this country, people are struggling with those very profound issues.

These are not issues that we have guidebooks about. They are issues that we have to summon up what we believe is morally and ethically and spiritually correct and do the best we can with God's guidance. How do we create a system that gets rid of the micromanagement, the regulation and the bureaucracy, and substitutes instead human caring, concern and love? And that is our real challenge in redesigning a health care system....

So every one of our institutions is under the same kind of mandate. Change will come whether we want it or not, and what we have to do is to try and make change our friend, not our enemy. But probably most profoundly and importantly, the changes that will count the most are the millions and millions of changes that take place on the individual level as people reject cynicism; as they are willing to take risks to meet the challenges they see around them; as they truly begin to try to see other people as they wish to be seen and to treat them as they wish to be treated; to overcome all of the obstacles we have erected around ourselves that keep us apart from one another, fearful and afraid, not willing to build the bridges necessary; to fill that spiritual vacuum that Lee Atwater talked about. . . .

Let us be willing to help our institutions to change, to deal with the new challenges that confront them. Let us try to restore the importance of civil society by committing ourselves to our children, our families, our friends; and to reaching out beyond the circle of those of whom we know, to the many others on whom we are dependent in this complex society; and understanding a little more about what their lives are like and doing what we can to help ease their burdens. . . .

Appendix C

Excerpts of Address by the First Lady of the United States of America, Hillary Rodham Clinton, at the American University in Cairo

Cairo, Egypt
March 23, 1999

... Egypt has a special place in the imagination of people throughout the globe. Certainly Americans are reminded of our ties to Egypt every single day. Just look at the back of our dollar bill. It carries two symbols—symbols that have their roots in the symbolism of ancient Egypt. We have an eagle that could look, if you squint, like a falcon, like a descendant of the kind of symbolism that one sees in the Egyptian Museum and that I'm looking forward to seeing in Luxor. Certainly, the idea of soaring high, as high as one can go, looking down on the earth arrayed below is one that has special meaning for people everywhere. But we also have on the back of that dollar bill the pyramid, representing man's triumph over death, not with physical life but with the ideas, the values, and the history that one leaves behind.

As I walked through the museum the other day, with the wonderful guidance of some experts who were with my daughter and me, I saw the kinds of things that a pharaoh or a noble person would want to bring with him or her into the next world—everything that was essential as we embark on the final journey of this life. They believe that they were preserving what was necessary so that they could live in the future and the next life to come.

And I thought to myself, what would we take with us? We know so well that we will not, we believe, have use for food or clothing, so what tangible things would we take? Probably, none now. But what of the intangibles, what of the values, what of those things that we cannot necessarily hold in our hand but we leave to our children and our grandchildren?

I was reminded of that as I visited some of the sights here in Cairo. The mosques that I have seen—mosques that have survived earthquakes, water damage, hot desert winds—and are still standing because they have been lovingly cared for and are now being restored by successive generations. They, too, symbolize, not in a material way, but in a very deep and profound way, what we want to carry with us, what we may not be able to pack in a box, but which may mean more than anything we could pack—a priceless material value passed on.

What would we bring with us today? While we stand at a pivotal, and some might even say paradoxical moment in history, an end of a century, an end of a millennium, a time of great promise and opportunity, we can also see as we look around us, a time of anxiety and even of fear at the pace of change that is engulfing us. We would want to bring with us those values, those institutions that can really stand the test of time. We would want to bring with us our human awareness, our knowledge of the past, so that we could be better prepared to navigate through the future.

My husband often says that there is no constant in the world anymore, except the constant of change. And that our challenge as human beings—Egyptians, Americans—is to make change our friend, to understand how to harness and deal with the forces that have been unleashed primarily by technology, but also by changing political and economic forces.

So we would want, I believe, to bring with us institutions that would permit us to make this journey into the future, one that we could navigate with some sense of certainty about the direction we are taking. We'd want to bring an economy that provides opportunities for all people—not only those lucky enough to be in this beautiful and historic hall—but everyone, everyone who could in his or her way be prepared for that journey. We'd want to bring with us a society in which we not only are consumers, but also citizens, where we recognize the role of spirituality in our lives, not just materialism; in which we would be equipped as best we can, as imperfect beings to be prepared to imagine a better world, not to retreat inward to the past as is the temptation in a time of change.

At the White House, we are attempting to mark the passage of this time by trying to think of ways that we can honor the past and imagine the future. How can we honor this past that is with us, that we have survived in this century? And how can we take from the past what we need? How do we challenge ourselves to address the top questions that have always been with human beings but which today because of the conditions around the world, seem even more pressing?

I often think of society with a very simple metaphor: a three-legged stool. One leg is the government, one leg is the economy, and one leg is what we call civil society. Now, obviously, we could not sit on that stool if there were only two legs or even just one. We could not sit on it if one leg was much more powerful and longer than the other two. Creating that balance in society among these principal institutions that govern and in many ways define our lives together is something we are constantly striving to achieve.

We know we need governments—effective, competent, functioning governments that can do what individuals cannot do for themselves and can do what market economies cannot do or produce, governments that protect our freedoms and defend our lives, respect human rights and the rules of democracy.

But even a government, no matter how well functioning, cannot in and of itself create citizens. The free market economy can create jobs and wealth and consumers and it needs to unleash the potential that is within so many people to have a better economic life for themselves. But the market economy, which can do many things, cannot create citizens. Only civil society, that third leg of the stool, can fulfill that important challenge.

So I want for just a few minutes to concentrate this morning on that third leg of civil society, of citizenship. Because if we are imagining this journey, a journey that the pharaohs took into the next world, a journey which we take while living into the world being created around us, we need to bring with us functioning, effective, competent governments that know their limits, but can produce the kinds of services that citizens need and we need to bring with us the unleashed power and energy of a free market economy that can take someone selling in the bazaar and give him as good a chance for the future just as the head of the largest corporation.

But when it comes to civil society, that is a constant act of creation. Because creating citizens who understand democracy, who protect democracy, who appreciate the human rights of themselves and others, can only be done in the space that exists between the government and the economy, the space that, after all, really makes life worth living, the space we create in our families, the space that we fill with the associations we freely choose, the space that is the quality of life as we measure it.

We know what we mean sometimes by civil society, but we can't always describe it. We know that it is that element of human association and existence that really defies description because, at the end of the day, it is what makes life worth living.

So how do we nurture this civil society? In our religious associations, with the freedom of the expression of our religious beliefs, with the spirituality that we choose to follow, with the voluntary associations, even the soccer clubs we support, we are creating civil society.

It has never been more essential because we have never had more people living in democracies than we have now at this point in human history. And living in democracies forces us to confront some issues that in the past we didn't have to think about. Government made those decisions for us, a planned economy made those decisions for us, or in the case of some societies, anarchy basically abdicated the space that both government and an organized economy should fill.

And so here we are at the end of this century, thinking about how we will make this journey and wondering to ourselves how we create more, stronger civil societies. I think that there are several lessons that we have been learning around the world as we look to see how we better prepare for the future. First, we know now we have to invest in all people, in their education, in their health care, in providing the credit and economic opportunity to them that allow individuals, both alone and together, to live up to their God-given potential.

It was five years ago that thousands of people gathered here in Cairo for the International Conference on Population and Development. The further in time we move from that conference, the more remarkable it seems, because for the very first time I've been able to find in history, there was a world gathering which reached the conclusion that we must do more to develop the potential of all people, particularly women, if we expect to live in a prosperous, peaceful, stable world.

So instead of mechanistically focusing on just one aspect of our life, with respect to population control, a broader view was taken, a more human view that said: "No, we need to look at the entire person, we need to respect the entire woman, we need to educate the minds as well as care for the bodies, we need to provide opportunities so that people feel that they have a future that they can invest in."

With the entire world listening, the results of that conference sent a clear, clarion call. No nation can move forward if half of its citizens are fed last or least, uneducated, under-educated, overworked, denied credit and health cares, subjected to violence inside or outside of the home or are otherwise left behind.

We agreed to a set of goals. We agreed to make family planning a right. We agreed to reduce infant, child, and maternal mortality. We agreed to make education a right for all, not a privilege for the few. And I want to congratulate Egypt publicly, as I congratulated President Mubarak yesterday morning, on the progress that has been made in this country in meeting those fundamental goals. I have been privileged to see just a few of the examples of that progress over the last day and a half, and I expect to see more in the days to come....

Think if you will, about the values you would take to the next world. What would you pack if you were to go? If a tomb were to be built for you today and you didn't bring any of the seed that you needed or the clothes that you would wear, what would you take with you?

I hope that all of us think about that as we approach the end of this century. I hope among the values we take and the lessons that we've learned are to respect the dignity of all individuals, and particularly, to give women and girls the rights and responsibilities of citizenship, to work to make sure that our societies are balanced with functioning, effective governments, strong and vibrant economies and civil societies that bring people together, not drive them apart.

I hope we will bring with us our respective religious beliefs and faiths and we will also bring with us the tolerance and respect we should have for others. As we move into that uncharted terrain of the next century, navigating our small boats, I hope we will recognize that we are blessed indeed, to live at the end of this century—the most violent in human history—because I hope we will have learned how to honor the past, rejecting the lessons of history we do not need to take with us anymore, and carrying the ones we should value and hold dear as we work to create a better present and future for ourselves and our children.

When Dr. Gerhart introduced me, he referred to Um Kalthoum. I was told of a line in one of her famous songs, "I am the people, I am the people," she sang. "I do not know an impossible." Those are words that we should think about as well.

This extraordinary country and its citizens have proven over thousands of years that the impossible can be rendered possible and I look to you to continue to demonstrate that, not only here at home, but abroad as well. It would be a tragedy of great dimension were we to lose this opportunity in human history to do more to realize our own humanity and to create the conditions that will enable us, well into the next century, to look back and say, "I lived my life as well as I could, I made my contributions. And when I left on my final journey, I hope I left behind those values and ideals that will enable people to live more peacefully, with prosperity, respect, dignity, and tolerance well into the future." . . .

Notes

Introduction
SHEDDING THE LIBERAL LABEL

1. Raymond Hernandez, "For the Moment, Mrs. Clinton Looks Like the Candidate to Beat," *New York Times*, November 4, 2004.

2. Raymond Hernandez, "As Clinton Shifts Themes, Debate Arises on Her Motives," *New York Times*, February 1, 2005.

3. Dan Balz, "Clinton Is a Politician Not Easily Defined," *Washington Post*, May 30, 2006.

4. Donald Lambro, "Hillary's Handicaps," *Washington Times*, July 13, 2006.

5. Markos Moulitsas, "Hillary Clinton: Too Much of a Clinton Democrat?" *Washington Post*, May 7, 2006. Http://www.washingtonpost.com/wp-dyn/content/article/2006/05/05/AR2006050501717_pf.html.

6. Joshua Green, "Take Two," *The Atlantic*, November 2006.

7. Jann Malone, "Hillary's Hair Is More Fun than Health Care," *Richmond Times Dispatch*, March 10, 1996.

8. Adam Nagourney, "Baffled in Loss, Democrats Seek Road Forward," *New York Times*, November 7, 2004.

9. Karen Tumulty, "Ready to Run," *Time*, August 28, 2006.

10. Jonathan Chait, "Clinton's Character Gap," *Los Angeles Times*, May 28, 2006.

11. Lois Romano, "Beyond the Poll Numbers, Voter Doubts about Clinton," *Washington Post*, July 13, 2006, A01.

12. Beth Fouhy, "Clinton Outlines Legislative Priorities," Associated Press, November 13, 2006.

Chapter One
THE PERSONALITY

1. Joshua Green, "Take Two," *The Atlantic*, November 2006.

2. Ibid.

3. Ibid.

4. Karen Tumulty, "Ready to Run," *Time*, August 28, 2006.

5. Michael Kelly, "New Hope for Nice Guys," *Jewish World Review*, August 3, 2000.

6. Hillary Rodham Clinton, *Living History* (New York: Simon & Schuster, 2003), 111.

7. Tony Snow, "Queen Tut?" *Jewish World Review*, July 8, 1999.

8. Green, "Take Two."

9. Clinton, *Living History*, 39.

10. Ibid.

11. Ibid., 41.

12. Ibid., 31.

13. Ibid., 41.

14. Ibid., 40.

15. Ibid., 39.

16. Ibid., 41.

17. Ibid.

18. Green, "Take Two."

19. Clinton, *Living History*, 144.

20. Ibid., 133–44.

21. Ibid., 115.

22. Dick Morris, *Rewriting History* (New York: Regan, 2004), 114.

23. Dick Morris, "Hillary Will Never Retreat," *Jewish World Review*, June 19, 2006.

24. Clinton, *Living History*, 21–22.

25. Barbara Olson, *Hell to Pay* (Washington, DC: Regnery, 1999), 32.

26. Clinton, *Living History*, 23.

27. Olson, 46–47.

28. Saul Alinsky, *Rules for Radicals* (New York: Random House, 1971), 30.

29. Ibid., 130.

30. Alinsky, 133.

31. R. Emmett Tyrrell and Mark Davis, *Madame Hillary* (Washington, DC: Regnery, 2004), 109.

32. Olson, 312.

33. Ibid., 311.

34. Francis Clines, "White House Plays Down a New-Age Visitor," *New York Times*, June 24, 1996.

35. John Ankerberg and John Weldon, *Encyclopedia of New Age Beliefs* (Eugene, OR: Harvest House Publishers, 1996), 221.

36. Ibid.

37. Craig Branch, "Jean Houston," *The Watchman Expositor*, http://www.watchman.org/profile/hustnpro.htm.

38. Tom Knott, "Hillary Should Widen Talks With Choir Silent," *Washington Times*, June 27, 1996.

39. Craig Branch, "Jean Houston."

40. Jennifer O'Connell, "Succour for Suckers," *Sunday Business Post*, February 1, 2004.

41. Bob Woodward, *The Choice* (New York: Simon and Schuster, 1996), 132.

42. Clinton, *Living History*, 93.

43. Ibid., 138.

44. Ibid., 43.

45. Ibid., 111.

46. Ibid., 112.

47. Ibid., 501.

48. Ibid., 137.

49. Ibid., 136.

50. Ibid., 139.

51. Ibid.

52. Ibid., 394.

53. Ibid., 141–42.

54. Ibid., 324.

55. Ibid., 169.

56. Ibid., 239.

57. Ibid., 491.

58. Ibid., 180.

59. Morris, 23.

60. Michael McAuliff, "Muscle of the Hil Machine," *Daily News*, December 10, 2006.

61. Hillary Rodham Clinton, *It Takes a Village* (New York: Simon & Schuster, 1996), 22.

62. Morris, 61–62.

63. Clinton, *Living History*, 441.

64. Ibid., 444.

65. Ibid., 443.

66. Olson, 66.

67. Green, "Take Two."

68. Ibid.

69. Clinton, *Living History*, 248.

70. Tyrrell and Davis, 101.

71. Michael Kelly, "Blame Hillary," *Jewish World Review*, July 15, 1999.

72. Martha Brant and Evan Thomas, "First Fighter," *Newsweek*, January 15, 1996.

73. Olson, 314.

Chapter Two

CHARACTER

1. Michael K. Frisby and Bruce Ingersoll, "First Lady Turned $1,000 Investment in Commodities into a $98,000 Profit," *Wall Street Journal*, March 30, 1994.

2. Dick Morris, *Rewriting History* (New York: Regan, 2004),155.

3. Ibid.

4. Barbara Olson, *Hell to Pay* (Washington, DC: Regnery, 1999), 141.

5. Morris, *Rewriting History*, 157.

6. Olson, *Hell to Pay*, 163.

7. Ibid.,164

8. Ibid.,160–161

9. Morris, *Rewriting History*, 161

10. Hillary Rodham Clinton, *Living History* (New York: Simon & Schuster, 2003), 86.

11. Morris, *Rewriting History*, 163.

12. PBS, "Once Upon a Time in Arkansas," *Frontline* online. Http://www.pbs.org/wgbh/pages/frontline/shows/arkansas/docs/recs.html.

13. Olson, *Hell to Pay*, 165.

14. William Safire, "Blizzard of Lies," *New York Times*, January 8, 1996.

15. Richard Benedetto and Susan Page, "Poll: 51% hold poor opinion of first lady," *USA Today*, January 17, 1996.

16. Olson, *Hell to Pay*, 240.

17. Hugh Sidey, "The Presidency: What the Barber Knew," *Time*, November 6, 2003.

18. Olson, *Hell to Pay*, 244.

19. Media Research Center, October 19, 2000; Morris, 175.

20. FOX News, *Special Report with Brit Hume*, October 18, 2000. Http://www.mediaresearch.org/cyberalerts/2000/cyb20001019.asp.

21. Olson, *Hell to Pay*, 273.

22. Ibid.

23. Ibid., 272.

24. Andrew Ross, "Are the Clintons' Fingerprints all over 'Filegate'?" Salon.com. Http://www.salon.com/news/news960627.html.

25. "Hyman selectively quoted, distorted *NYT* editorials on Clinton FBI files scandal," Media Matters, February 22, 2006. Http://www.mediamatters.org/items/200602220008.

26. *Cara Leslie Alexander et. al. v. Federal Bureau of Investigation*, Civil No. 96-2123 (Washington, D.C. 1999).

27. Olson, *Hell to Pay*, 272.

28. "Hyman selectively quoted, distorted *NYT* editorials on Clinton FBI files scandal."

29. Olson, *Hell to Pay*, 94.

30. Morris, 199.

31. Olson, *Hell to Pay*, 197.

32. Morris, 200.

33. Harold Johnson, "Missing Person—Paula Jones has accused Bill Clinton of sexual harassment," *National Review*, April 18, 1994.

34. Morris, 220.

35. John King, "Willey v. Clinton: Who's Lying?" CNN.com, March 16, 1998. Http://www.cnn.com/ALLPOLITICS/1998/03/16/Clinton.willey/.

36. Susan Schmidt, "Starr Probing Willey Allegations," *Washington Post*, November 1, 1998, A8.

37. John King, "Willey v. Clinton: Who's Lying?"

38. *Hannity & Colmes*, FOX News, June 10, 2003.

39. Miriam Horn, "Feminists don't know what to think," *U.S. News & World Report*, September 28, 1998.

40. Clinton, 110.

41. Ibid., 109.

42. Ibid., 194.

43. Ibid.

44. Ibid., 444.

45. Ibid., 443.

46. Ibid., 445.

47. Morris, 60.

48. Ibid., 12.

49. Ibid., 180.

50. Barbara Olson, *Final Days* (Washington, DC: Regnery, 2001), 66–68.

51. Morris, 181.

52. Ibid., 180.

53. Clinton, 439.

Chapter Three

THE WOMAN WHO WOULD BE PRESIDENT

1. Joshua Green, "Take Two," *The Atlantic*, November 2006.

2. Barbara Olson, *The Final Days* (Washington, DC: Regnery, 2001), 69.

3. Hillary Rodham Clinton, *Living History* (New York: Simon & Schuster, 2003), 272.

4. "Bhutto appeals swiss money laundering charge," Reuters, August 14, 2003.

5. Clinton, *Living History*, 441.

6. Ibid., 466.

7. Art Moore, "Court brief alleges crime by Hillary," WorldNetDaily.com, January 12, 2007. Http://www.worldnetdaily.com/news/article. asp?ARTICLE_ID=53740.

8. Ibid.

9. "Trial Focuses On Hillary Clinton Hollywood Fundraiser," KTVU.com, May 8, 2005. Http://www.ktvu.com/news/4464776/detail.html.

10. Green, "Take Two."

11. Ibid.

Chapter Four
THE REBIRTH OF PRINCESS PEACENIK

1. Hillary Rodham Clinton, *Living History* (New York: Simon & Schuster, 2003), 31.

2. Ibid., 32.

3. Ibid.

4. "Hillary Clinton's Palestinian Vision," *Washington Times*, May 8, 1998.

5. Steven Menashi, "Israel's New Best Friend," *American Enterprise*, December 12, 2001. Http://www.theamericanscene.com/pubs/tae121201. html.

6. William Douglas and Matthew McAllester, "Put on the Spot: Hillary Met with Furor over Statehood, Arafat's Wife's Remarks," *Newsday*, November 12, 1999.

7. William A. Orme Jr., "While Mrs. Clinton Looks On, Palestinian Officials Criticize Israel," *New York Times*, November 12, 1999.

8. Menashi, "Israel's New Best Friend."

9. Ibid.

10. Transcript, *The McLaughlin Group*, July 28, 2000. Http://www. mclaughlin.com/library/transcript.asp?id=158.

11. Kristen Lombardi, "Hillary Calls Israel a 'Beacon of Democracy,'" *Village Voice*, December 11, 2005.

12. Menashi, "Israel's New Best Friend."

13. Clinton, *Living History*, 38.

14. Ibid., 36–37.

15. Ibid., 35.

16. Ibid., 35.

17. Ibid., 45–46.

18. Ibid., 169.

19. PBS, "Waco: The Inside Story," *Frontline*, 1995. Http://www.pbs.org/wgbh/pages/frontline/waco/timeline.html.

20. Gail Sheehey, *Hillary's Choice* (New York: Random House, 1999), 345.

21. "Hillary Clinton Likens Kosovars' Plight to Holocaust," Kosovo Crisis Center, May 15, 1999. Http://www.alb-net.com/kcc/051599.htm#3.

22. John Laughland, "The Final Death Toll in Kosovo? It's Sinking Fast," *The Spectator*, November 4, 1999.

23. Justin Raimondo, "Osama in the Balkans," Antiwar.com, October 29, 2001. Http://www.antiwar.com/justin/pf/p-j102901.html.

24. "False Hopes in Kosovo," Reuters, November 1, 2006.

25. Transcript, *CNN Late Edition with Wolf Blitzer*, August 29, 2004. Http://transcripts.cnn.com/TRANSCRIPTS/0408/29/le.00.html.

26. "Floor Speech of Senator Hillary Rodham Clinton on S.J. Res. 45, A Resolution to Authorize the Use of United States Armed Forces Against Iraq." Http://clinton.senate.gov/speeches/iraq_101002.html.

27. NBC News, Transcript, *Meet the Press*, December 7, 2003. Http://www.msnbc.msn.com/id/3660558/.

28. "Hillary Clinton: No Regret on Iraq Vote," CNN.com, April 21, 2004. Http://www.cnn.com/2004/ALLPOLITICS/04/21/iraq.hillary/.

29. "Clinton Says Insurgency Is Failing," USAToday.com, February 19, 2005. Http://www.usatoday.com/news/world/iraq/2005-02-19-iraq-senators_x.htm.

30. NBC News, Transcript, *Meet the Press*, December 7, 2003.

31. Clinton, "Floor Speech of Senator Hillary Rodham Clinton on S.J. Res. 45," October 10, 2002. Http://www.clinton.senate.gov/~clinton/news/statements/details.cfm?id=268851.

32. Joshua Green, "Take Two," *The Atlantic*, November 2006.

33. Ibid.

34. Laurie Mylroie, "Clinton Signs Iraq Liberation Act," *Iraq News*, November 1, 1998, http://www.fas.org/news/iraq/1998/11/01/981101-in.htm.

35. Jane Mayer, "The Manipulator," *New Yorker*, July 6, 2004. Http:// www.newyorker.com/fact/content/articles/040607fa_fact1?040607fa_fact1.

36. Hillary Clinton, "Letter to Constituents," November 29, 2005. Http:// www.clinton.senate.gov/issues/nationalsecurity/index.cfm?topic=iraqletter.

37. Hillary Clinton, "Remarks of Senator Hillary Rodham Clinton at Princeton University's Woodrow Wilson School of Public and International Affairs," November 18, 2006. Http://www.senate.gov/~clinton/news/ statements/details.cfm?id=250529.

38. Hillary Clinton, "Floor Speech of Senator Hillary Rodham Clinton on S.J. Res. 45,"October 10, 2002. Http://www.clinton.senate.gov/speeches/ iraq_101002.html.

39. Ibid.

40. Ibid.

41. Ibid.

42. "Remarks by Senator Hillary Rodham Clinton" (Transcript), Council on Foreign Relations, December 15, 2003. Http://www.cfr.org/publication/ html?id=6600.

43. "Hillary Clinton: No Regret on Iraq Vote."

44. NBC News, Transcript, *Meet the Press*, February 20, 2005. Http://www. msnbc.msn.com/id/7003226/.

45. "Hillary Clinton: No Regret on Iraq Vote."

46. Hillary Rodham Clinton, "Letter to Constituents on Iraq Policy," November 29, 2005. Http://www.clinton.senate.gov/issues/nationalsecurity/ index.cfm?topic=iraqletter.

47. Ibid.

48. Hillary Clinton, "Senator Hillary Clinton Speaks on Iraq on the Senate Floor," February 7, 2007. Http://www.clinton.senate.gov/news/statements/ details.cfm?id=268851.

49. Clinton, "Floor Speech of Senator Hillary Rodham Clinton on S.J. Res. 45."

50. Hillary Clinton, "Remarks of Senator Hillary Rodham Clinton at Princeton University's Woodrow Wilson School of Public and International Affairs."

51. Dan Balz, "Hillary Clinton Crafts Centrist Stance on War," *Washington Post*, December 12, 2005.

52. Hillary Rodham Clinton, "Where I Stand on Iraq," *New York Daily News*, October 12, 2006.

53. "Remarks by Senator Hillary Rodham Clinton (Transcript)," Council on Foreign Relations, December 15, 2003.

Chapter Five
QUEEN OF THE AMNESTIES

1. "Hillary Eyes Immigration as Top 2008 Issue," NewsMax.com, November 21, 2004. Http://www.newsmax.com/archives/ic/2004/11/21/233417.shtml.

2. Ibid.

3. Sam Roberts, "Immigrants Swell Numbers Near New York," *New York Times*, August 15, 2006. Http://www.nytimes.com/2006/08/15/nyregion/15minority.html?ex=1313294400&en=9ccbc874d5cf0bc4&ei=5090.

4. "Hillary Eyes Immigration as Top 2008 Issue," NewsMax.com, November 21, 2004. Http://www.newsm ax.com/archives/ic/2004/11/21/233417.shtml.

5. "N.Y. Times Alters Hillary Clinton's Immigration Quote," NewsMax.com, July 14, 2005. Http://www.newsmax.com/archives/ic/2005/7/14/125858.shtml.

6. "Senator Hillary Clinton Goes 'On the Record' (Transcript)," November 18, 2004. Http://www.foxnews.com/story/0,2933,138948,00.html.

7. Ibid.

8. Charles Hurt, "Hillary Goes Conservative on Immigration," *Washington Times*, December 13, 2004. Http://washingtontimes.com/national/20041213-124920-6151r.htm.

9. Tony Blankley, "God Bless Hillary Clinton," *Washington Times*, December 15, 2004.

10. Patrick J. Buchanan, "A National Emergency," WorldNetDaily.com, August 29, 2005. Http://worldnetdaily.com/news/article.asp?ARTICLE_ID46019.

11. "Hillary Eyes Immigration as Top 2008 Issue."

12. "All Immigration Votes of Senator Hillary Clinton," NumbersUSA.com, March 15, 2007.

13. "Immigration-Reduction Report Card: Hillary Clinton," Americans for Better Immigration. Http://grades.betterimmigration.com/view_history. php3?District=NY&VIPID=896.

14. Mac Johnson, "A major victory against illegal immigration—in Massachusetts?" HumanEvents.com, January 16, 2006. Http://www. humanevents.com/article.php?id=11613.

15. Darryl Fears, "Hillary Clinton Draws Applause from Hispanics," *Washington Post*, July 19, 2005. Http://www.washingtonpost.com/wp-dyn/ content/article/2005/07/18/AR2005071801530_pf.html.

16. Nina Bernstein, "Mrs. Clinton Says G.O.P.'s Immigration Plan Is at Odds With the Bible," *New York Times*, March 23, 2006.

17. Devlin Barrett, "Sen. Clinton Slams GOP Immigration Bill," Associated Press, March 8, 2006.

18. "Clinton's Immigration Positions Draw Criticism," Newsday.com, April 25, 2006.

19. Devlin Barrett, "Sen. Clinton Slams GOP Immigration Bill," Associated Press, March 8, 2006.

20. Bernstein, "Mrs. Clinton Says G.O.P.'s Immigration Plan Is at Odds with the Bible."

21. FOX News, *Hannity and Colmes*, "Sensenbrenner on Immigration Reform Battle," March 30, 2006. Http://www.foxnews.com/story/ 0,2933,189688,00.html.

22. Michael Goodwin, "Border Battler: Hillary Wants to Build a U.S.-Mexico Fence First—And She's Right," *New York Daily News*, April 22, 2006.

23. Ibid.

24. Glenn Thrush, "Clinton's immigration positions draw criticism," Newsday.com, April 25, 2006. Http://www.newsday.com/news/ nationworld/nation/ny-ushill254716161apr25,0,2823929.story.

25. Michael Goodwin, "Border Battler: Hillary Wants to Build a U.S.-Mexico Fence First—And She's Right," *New York Daily News*, April 22, 2006.

26. Michelle Malkin, "Racism Gets a White Wash," JewishWorldReview. com, March 29, 2006. Http://www.jewishworldreview.com/michelle/ malkin032906.php3.

27. FOX News, *Hannity and Colmes*, "Sensenbrenner on Immigration Reform Battle," March 30, 2006. Http://www.foxnews.com/story/0,2933,189688,00.html.

28. Patrick J. Buchanan, "No Amnesty, No Deal, Mr. President," National Border Patrol Council, December 7, 2005. Http://www.nbpc.net/amnesty/no_deal.htm.

29. Robert Rector, "Senate Immigration Bill Would Allow 100 Million New Legal Immigrants Over the Next Twenty Years," The Heritage Foundation, May 15, 2006. Http://www.heritage.org/Research/Immigration/wm1076.cfm.

30. Ibid.

31. Panel Discussion, "Implications of the Hagel-Martinez Amnesty Bill," Center for Immigration Studies, June 15, 2006.

32. "The Exorbitant Costs of Amnesty," Editorial, *Washington Times*, May 16, 2006. Http://www.washtimes.com/op-ed/20060515-101029-1501r.htm.

33. Rector, "Senate Immigration Bill Would Allow 100 Million New Legal Immigrants Over the Next Twenty Years."

34. Ibid.

Chapter Six
THE GENDER FEMINIST

1. Janet Kutner, "She Who Must Be Obeyed Art Review: Exhibition at Kimbell Sheds Light on First Great Female Ruler in History," *Dallas Morning News*, August 27, 2006; Grace Glueck, "The Woman Who Ruled Egypt as King, Not Queen," *Dallas Morning News*, March 31, 2006; Vibhuti Patel, "The Feminine Kingdom: Hatshepsut Promoted Peace, Prosperity and Great Art," *Newsweek*, April 10, 2006; Robert Buckman, "From Queen to Pharaoh: Texas exhibit brings life to Hatshepsut," *Washington Times*, November 21, 2006.

2. Sandra Sobieraj, "Reporter's Notebook: Mrs. Clinton, Tourist—Or Guide," Associated Press, March 24, 1999.

3. "Hillary Rodham Clinton as Feminist Heroine," American Enterprise Online, April 7, 2000.

4. United States Information Agency, "Egypt: Address of Hillary Clinton at American University in Cairo," *Africa News*, March 25, 1999.

5. John Lancaster and Boyce Rensberger, "Cairo Delegates Come to Terms; Abortion Text Approved; U.S. Immigration Policy Faulted," *Washington Post*, September 13, 1994; Alan Cowell, "Vatican Says Gore Is Misrepresenting Population Talks," *New York Times*, September 1, 1994; "U.N. Population Conference Held in Cairo; Delegates Set Stabilization Strategy; Other Developments," Facts on File, September 22, 1994.

6. "Egypt: Address of Hillary Clinton at American University in Cairo."

7. Ibid.

8. Patrick D. Healy, "Clinton Seeking Shared Ground Over Abortions," *New York Times*, January 25, 2005.

9. Ibid.

10. Ibid.

11. Ibid.

12. Ibid.

13. Tom Strode, "Hillary Clinton Softens Abortion Stance; FDA Delays Pill Decision; Dutch Doctors Widen Euthanasia," *Baptist Press News*, January 27, 2005.

14. Joseph Curl, "Hillary in the Middle on Values Issues," *Washington Times*, January 26, 2005.

15. Ibid.

16. Marc Humbert, "Hillary Clinton Says Bush Shortchanging Family Planning Efforts," Associated Press, January 25, 2005.

17. Ronald Powers, "Moynihan, in Break With Clinton, Condemns Abortion Procedure," May 14, 1996.

18. William Goldschlag, "Pat Voted to Ban Late Aborts," *New York Daily News*, September 28, 1996.

19. "Congressional Record—Senate," Wednesday, March 12, 2003, 108th Congress, 1st Session, 149 Congressional Record S 3460, Vol. 149, No. 40.

20. Ibid.

21. Ibid.

22. Ibid.

23. Ibid.

24. Ibid.

25. Ibid.

26. John Distaso, "Cuomo to Announce Monday, Poll: Bush Beats Cuomo in N.Y., Clinton Claims GOP Inflamed Divisive Issues," *Manchester Union Leader*, December 11, 1991.

27. Congressional Record—Senate, Loc. Cit.

28. Ibid.

29. Ibid.

30. NARAL Pro-Choice America, "Congressional Record on Choice 2006"; NARAL Pro-Choice America, "Congressional Record on Choice 2005."

31. "New York Senate: To March or Not to March?" The Hotline, December 10, 1999.

32. "Parade Group Allowed to Ban Gays," Facts on File, *World News Digest*, June 22, 1995.

33. Adam Nagourney, "Hillary Clinton Faults Policy of 'Don't Ask,'" *New York Times*, December 9, 1999.

34. Karen Matthews, "Hillary Clinton Says She Hopes to March St. Patrick's Day," Associated Press, December 9, 1999.

35. Robert Hardt Jr., "Gay It Ain't So! Hil Eyes St. Pat's March," *New York Post*, December 10, 1999.

36. Ibid.

37. Larry McShane, "Irish Gay Group Calls for Meeting with Mrs. Clinton," Associated Press, December 10, 1999.

38. Randal C. Archibald, "To March or Not: Irish Parade Is First Lady's Latest Issue," *New York Times*, December 10, 1999.

39. CBS News Transcripts, "Harold Ickes, Adviser, Discusses Hillary Clinton," *Face the Nation*, December 12, 1999.

40. Garry O'Sullivan, "Hillary Says She Wants to March: Gay Groups Angry Over First Lady's Parade Stance," *Irish Voice*, December 21, 1999.

41. Ibid.

42. Ibid.

43. Ibid.

44. Debbie McGoldrick, "Hillary Will March in NYC Parade: Still Undecided About Woodside Event," *Irish Voice*, February 1, 2000.

45. Ibid.

46. Joel Siegel with Bob Liff, "Hil to Join Irish Gay in March," *New York Daily News*, March 1, 2000.

47. Marc Humbert, "Hillary Clinton Takes Center Stage," Associated Press, August 14, 2000.

48. Beth J. Harpaz, "Hillary Clinton Gets Gay Group Endorsement," Associated Press, July 27, 2000.

49. Human Rights Campaign, "Congressional Scorecard 107th Congress"; Human Rights Campaign, "Congressional Scorecard 108th Congress"; Human Rights Campaign, "Congressional Scorecard 109th Congress."

50. Ed Koch, "Pols Were Cowardly in Passing Up Parade," *New York Newsday*, March 23, 2001.

51. Gregg Birnbaum, "Hillary Backs Gay Unions, Not Marriage," *New York Post*, January 11, 2000.

52. Nagourney, "Hillary Clinton Faults Policy of 'Don't Ask.'"

53. Congressional Record—Senate, "Federal Marriage Amendment—Motion to Proceed," Monday, July 12, 2004, 108th Congress, 2nd Session, 150 Congressional Record S 7903, Vol. 150, No. 95, Speech of Senator Orrin Hatch.

54. Larry Witham, "Ticket's Wives Seen Colliding on Issues; Feminist Hillary, Traditionalist Tipper," *Washington Times*, July 10, 1992.

55. Congressional Record—Senate, "Federal Marriage Amendment—Motion to Proceed," Tuesday, July 13, 2004, 108th Congress, 2nd Session, 150 Congressional Record S 1762, Vol. 150, No. 96, Speech of Senator Hillary Clinton.

56. Ibid.

57. Ibid.

58. Paul Schindler, "Absorbing Gay Pain and Praise, Clinton Says She's Evolved," *Gay City News*, October 26, 2006.

59. Ibid.

60. Hillary Clinton, *It Takes a Village* (New York: Simon & Schuster, 1996), 59.

61. Ibid.

62. Ibid., 70.

63. Ibid., 61.

64. Ibid.

65. Ibid.

66. Hillary Clinton, *Living History* (New York: Simon & Schuster, 2003), 375.

67. Clinton, *It Takes a Village*, 17–18.

68. Ibid., 20.

69. Ibid., 65.

70. Ibid., 69–70.

71. Ibid., 109.

72. Ibid., 260–61.

73. Ibid., 207.

74. Ibid., 177.

75. Ibid., 191.

76. Ibid., 195.

77. Hillary Clinton, "Keynote Address by Hillary Rodham Clinton to the Cairo Plus Five Forum," Netherlands Congress Center, the Hague, Netherlands, February 9, 1999. Http://www.un.org/popin/icpd/icpd5/hague/hillary.htm.

78. Clinton, *It Takes a Village*, 223.

79. Ibid., 249.

80. Clinton, *Living History*, 2.

81. Ibid., 252.

82. Ibid., 253.

83. Ibid., 271.

84. Ibid., 277.

85. Ibid., 424.

86. Ibid., 313.

87. Ibid., 339.

88. Ibid., 313.

89. Ibid., 410.

90. Ibid.

91. Ibid., 356.

92. "Hillary Clinton Urges Reproductive Freedom for All," Feminist Daily News Wire, February 9, 1999.

93. "Egypt; Address Hillary Clinton at American University in Cairo,"
United States Information Agency, *Africa News*, March 25, 1999.

94. Ibid.

95. Ibid.

Chapter Seven
FOR THE COMMON GOOD

1. Markos Moulitsas, "Hillary Clinton: Too Much of a Clinton Democrat?"
Washington Post, May 7, 2006.

2. Joshua Green, "Take Two," *The Atlantic*, November 2006.

3. Beth Fouhy, "Clinton Outlines Legislative Priorities," *Washington Post,*
November 13, 2006.

4. Hillary Clinton, "Hillary Rodham Clinton Delivers Remarks at
Democratic National," CNN.com, August 14, 2000. Http://www.cnn.com/
ELECTION/2000/conventions/democratic/transcripts/u020814.html.

5. Ben Shapiro, "There's Something About Hillary," Townhall.com. Http://
www.townhall.com/columnists/BenShapiro/2005/06/08/theres_something_
about_hillary.

6. Tony Snow, "Queen Tut?" *Jewish World Review*, July 8, 1999.

7. Ibid.

8. Ibid.

9. Ibid.

10. "Medicare Prescription Bill Drama; Interview With Hillary Clinton;
'Political Play of the Week' (transcript)," *Judy Woodruff's Inside Politics*,
CNN.com, June 27, 2003.

11. Hillary Clinton, "Remarks by First Lady Hillary Rodham Clinton," Liz
Carpenter Lecture Series, University of Texas, Austin, April 7, 1993.

12. Donna Hearne, "Goals 2000's New Life Agenda—There They Go
Again!" *Education Reporter*, November 1999.

13. Phyllis Schlafly, "NEA Agenda Is Frightening to Parents," July 26, 2006.
Http://www.eagleforum.org/column/2006/july06/06-07-26.html.

14. Ibid.

15. Hillary Rodham Clinton, *Living History* (New York: Simon & Schuster,
2003), 94.

16. Dick Morris, *Rewriting History* (New York: Regan, 2004), 109.

17. Clinton, *Living History*, 94.

18. David Horowitz, "Hillary's Solution: Screw the Children," FrontPage Magazine, June 23, 2000. Http://www.frontpagemag.com/Articles/ReadArticle.asp?ID=3208.

19. Morris, *Rewriting History*, 111.

20. Horowitz, "Hillary's Solution: Screw the Children."

21. Morris, *Rewriting History*, 111–112.

22. "Lazio vs. Clinton: NBC debate, Oct. 27, 2000," On the Issues, October 27, 2000. Http://www.ontheissues.org/NY_Senate_NBC.htm.

23. "Senator Clinton Offers 'Education Plan for All' Plan," Council on Foreign Relations, April 20, 2004. Http:// www.cfr.org/publication/6949/senator_clinton_offers_education_plan_for_all_plan.html.

24. Beth Fouhy, "San Francisco rolls out the red carpet for the Clintons," Associated Press, June 29, 2004.

25. Snow, "Queen Tut?"

26. Hillary Clinton, "Remarks by First Lady Hillary Rodham Clinton," Liz Carpenter Lecture Series.

27. R. Emmett Tyrrell and Mark Davis, *Madame Hillary* (Washington, DC: Regnery, 2004), 122–123.

28. Ibid., 136.

29. Ibid.

30. "Sen. Clinton blames tax cut for recession," Hearst News Service, December 22, 2001.

31. Hillary Clinton, "Remarks of Senator Hillary Rodham Clinton, John Jay College of Criminal Justice, New York City," January 24, 2003. Http://www.clinton.senate.gov/speeches/030124.html.

32. "Statement of Hillary Rodham Clinton on Estate Tax Vote," States News Service, June 8, 2006.

33. "The Week—Hillary Clinton's Spending of Taxpayer Money, Other News from around the World," *National Review*, April 22, 2002.

34. Amanda Carpenter, *The Vast Right-Wing Conspiracy's Dossier on Hillary Clinton* (Washington, D.C.: Regnery, 2006) 55–56.

35. Ibid., 70–71.

36. Hillary Clinton, "Remarks of Senator Hillary Rodham Clinton, Chicago Economic Club," April 11, 2006.

37. Lawrence Kudlow, "Waking Up to Hillary's Big-Government Nightmare," *Human Events*, April 20, 2006.

38. "Keep America Working: Restoring Jobs to Ensure American Prosperity," March 3, 2004. Http://clinton.senate.gov/news/statements/details.cfm?id=233755.

39. Clinton, "Remarks of Senator Hillary Rodham Clinton, Chicago Economic Club."

40. "Hillary Watch," *Human Events*, July 14, 2003.

41. Matthew Benjamin, "Americans Souring on Free Trade Amid Optimism About Economy," Bloomberg.com, January 18, 2007.

Chapter Eight
THE STEPFORD CANDIDATE

1. Maureen Dowd, "Obama's Big Screen Test," *New York Times*, February 21, 2007.

2. Markos Moulitsas, "Hillary Clinton: Too Much of a Clinton Democrat?" *Washington Post*, May 7, 2006.

3. Jacob Weisberg, "But Why Can't Hillary Win?" Slate.com, July 29, 2005.

4. Greg Pierce, "Inside Politics," *Washington Times*, March 9, 2007.

5. Anne Kornblut, "The Ascent of a Woman," *New York Times*, June 11, 2006.

6. WNBC/Marist Poll released February 19, 2007.

7. Bill Sammon, *Strategery* (Washington, D.C.: Regnery, 2006), 322; CBS News, "Hillary: Rove Obsesses about Me," February 27, 2006.

8. Harold Meyerson, "A New Hampshire Ghost," *Washington Post*, February 14, 2007.

9. Linda Feldman, "Hillary Clinton Targets Women," *Christian Science Monitor*, February 1, 2007.

10. Remarks from Clinton on ABC, *The View*, December 20, 2006.

11. Mark Leibovich, "Clinton Shaping Her Image for the Race," *New York Times*, March 6, 2007.

12. Beth Fouhy, "Bill Clinton Raising Funds for Hillary," *Washington Post*, February 17, 2007.

13. Dowd, "Obama's Big Screen Test."

14. WNBC/Marist Poll, released February 19, 2007.

15. Dowd, "Obama's Big Screen Test."

16. Jonathan Alter, "Is America Ready?" *Newsweek*, December 25, 2006.

17. Ibid.

18. Dowd, "Obama's Big Screen Test."

Chapter Ten
TWELVE QUESTIONS

1. Joshua Green, "Take Two," *The Atlantic*, November 2006.

2. Michael Goodwin, "Border Battler: Hillary Wants to Build a U.S.-Mexico Fence First—And She's Right," *Daily News*, April 23, 2006.

3. William Safire, "Blizzard of Lies," *New York Times*, January 8, 1996.

4. Maureen Dowd, "The Boy Can't Help It," *New York Times*, August 4, 1999, A19.

5. Maureen Dowd, "Obama's Big Screen Test," *New York Times*, February 21, 2007, A21.

6. Mike McIntire, "Rubbing Shoulders with Trouble, and Presidents," *New York Times*, May 7, 2006.

Index